DEC -- 2015

W9-BLR-737

AMERICAN SWEEPSTAKES

Kevin Flynn

AMERICAN SWEEPSTAKES

How One Small State Bucked the Church,

the Feds, and the Mob to Usher in the Lottery Age

ForeEdge

BELLEVILLE PUBLIC LIBRARY

ForeEdge

An imprint of

University Press of New England

www.upne.com

© 2015 Kevin Flynn

All rights reserved

Manufactured in the

United States of America

Designed by Mindy Basinger Hill

Typeset in Arno Pro

For permission to reproduce any of the
material in this book, contact Permissions,
University Press of New England,
One Court Street, Suite 250, Lebanon NH
03766; or visit www.upne.com

Library of Congress Cataloging-in-
Publication Data

Flynn, Kevin (Journalist)
American sweepstakes: how one small state
bucked the Church, the Feds, and the Mob
to usher in the lottery age / Kevin Flynn.
     pages   cm
Includes bibliographical
references and index.
ISBN 978-1-61168-702-6 (cloth: alk. paper)—
ISBN 978-1-61168-826-9 (ebook)
1. Lotteries—New Hampshire—History—
20th century.
2. Gambling—New Hampshire—History—
20th century. I. Title.
HG6133.N28F59 2015
795.3'809742—dc23   2015009836
5   4   3   2   1

To Molly, Sean, and Brendon
The best jackpot your uncle ever won

Contents

Photographs follow page 122

AS HIS HORSE ROUNDED the stretch turn, the fresh cigar in Frank Malkus's mouth dipped. He lit it when the race began, a mix of habit or superstition, as he did whenever he went to the track.

But today was different. For one thing, his wife, Eleanor, was with him. She was what the bettors would call a "pigeon." Malkus was mainly a chalk player — someone who liked to play the favorites — but he could read a racing form well and spot a "roughie" once in a while to lay a bet on. Also, he had a lot more riding on this race than a few skins.

The day was overcast, a gray New England afternoon in September 1964 with no hint of Indian summer in the air. There had been a light mist earlier, but the track was dry, hard. Malkus had never been to Rockingham Park in Salem, had never been to New Hampshire for that matter. He was from New Jersey, and his interest in this race was the result of happenstance.

Next to the Malkuses sat another unlikely spectator, a demure twenty-one-year-old coed in a heavy blue coat. Carol Ann Lee was surrounded by her girlfriends, her father, and her fourteen-year-old sister. She'd never been to a horse race before. The track was unfamiliar territory to her, mysterious. Today she was a VIP.

Lee began the race calmly fixed in her chair, peering through a set of binoculars. As the horses were on the backstretch of the mile and three-eighths, she moved to the edge of her seat. By the time the pack stomped around the home turn, Lee had exploded out of her chair and was screaming, "Come on! Come on!"

The leader was starting to lug out, couldn't keep a straight line. The jockey had let him run free and now his lead was gone. Around the final turn, a half-dozen horses ran shoulder to shoulder — a six-way tie — as they galloped their way like the cavalry toward an unseen enemy.

Despite the thousands of other spectators with two-dollar bets in the stands, these thoroughbreds were running just for these few people and a select group of about five dozen others. One hundred thousand dollars was on the line. These people were finalists in the first legal state lottery in modern times: the New Hampshire Sweepstakes.

As the horses bore down on the finish, someone's life was about to change forever. America was about to change forever, too.

IT'S A STORY LOST TO HISTORY. The first modern lottery in the United States was settled not by a numbers pull or a scratch ticket but by a horse race.

What has also faded from memory is that the New Hampshire Sweepstakes was both a national sensation and a national scandal. Lawmakers railed against it. The clergy predicted moral, perhaps sacramental disaster. Racketeers would invade the system. Politicians would be corrupted. Virtually every editorial writer in the nation opined on the sweepstakes, and most violently scratched their pens through the paper and into the pulp to condemn it. The federal government squeezed the state, unconvinced it could operate legally, hoping to see the effort wither on the vine. In 1964, people were actually arrested for being in possession of lottery tickets.

But during that spring and summer, tens of thousands of people flooded into New Hampshire to get their hands on one. Mail came from around the world stuffed with cash and requests for chances. Other states watched the proceedings with envious eyes. The nation's lottery dream was born.

Today, it's hard to image our national landscape without lotteries. Scratch tickets and Powerball terminals are ubiquitous at gas stations, convenience stores, supermarkets, and liquor stores from coast to coast. According to the North American Association of State and Provincial Lotteries, tickets are sold in more than 240,000 retail locations in the United States and Canada. More than $78 billion in lottery tickets was sold in the United States in 2012.

The days of legions of Americans playing the numbers racket, passing money back and forth with organized-crime bookies, faded soon after New

Hampshire's first sweepstakes. Instead of increasing the Mob's monopoly on wagering (another prediction from naysayers), state lotteries steadily cut into the underworld's market share for the sake of public financing.

According to a 1999 Gallup Poll, playing the lottery is the most popular form of gambling in the United States. Fifty-seven percent of Americans, about 179 million people, reported buying a lottery ticket within a twelve-month span. The poll also disputed long-held assumptions about who's been playing. The majority of players, 59 percent, are college graduates, and those earning $75,000 a year play the lottery at a rate three times higher than those earning less than $25,000. It seems there's no socioeconomic limit on those who are willing to pay a dollar for a dream.

Even 21 percent of those who say they strongly oppose gambling admit to having played the lottery.

OURS IS A CULTURE seemingly made for the lottery. Americans, born outside the boxy societal pigeonholes of our British roots, built a nation around the hope of ascending from one's inherited station. A Carnegie or a Rockefeller could come from humble beginnings, from any small prairie town or urban slum. Our culture of economic aspiration even has a slogan: the American dream.

In his book *Ponzi's Scheme,* author Mitchell Zuckoff begins with an anecdote about a door-to-door salesman who in 1920 peddled a tabletop machine that could take blank paper and "reproduce" hundred-dollar bills. The metal box featured flashing lights and other buttons, a wonder of modern technology. After he demonstrated its ability to spit out a "genuine" C-note, a little old lady from South Boston paid the princely sum of $540 for a machine of her own. But when she opened the brown paper package the salesman had handed her as he left, she discovered she'd bought a simple wooden box. After the con man's arrest, the newspaper report implied his crime was not duping the woman with a *fake* contraption but failing to sell her the *working model* of the marvelous dollar-duplicating machine. The dream of get-rich-quick, easy money has always been part of our national DNA.

As lottery jackpots have ballooned, so has our collective dream. A million-dollar prize was unthinkable in the 1960s. In the 1970s and 1980s, grand prizes grew into the tens, then hundreds of millions of dollars. At the time of this writing, the record jackpot of $656 million belongs to three Mega Millions winners who split a cash payout of $474 million. In just a few decades, the dream has grown from the prospect of living like a king to living like a Sultan.

The Massachusetts Lottery Commission once produced a TV commercial set in a stuffy boardroom. In the ad, serious-looking executives took turns asking each other who called the meeting. "I did!" proclaimed an elderly cleaning lady, mop in hand, who suddenly appeared in the room. "Have you all heard of Megabucks?" The camera cut from face to face as each executive mumbled in confusion, "Megabucks?"

"Gentlemen, I've enjoyed working for all of you," said the cleaning lady to the men, now holding mops of their own, "and I'm sure you'll all enjoy working for me."

The ad perfectly encapsulates the life-changing "take this job and shove it" reverie that lurks in the mind of every lottery-ticket buyer. In 1977, musician Lou Reed quipped in the Pasadena *Star Ledger,* "Money can't buy you love, but it can buy you a Cadillac so you can ride around and look for it."

We believe that many of the problems in our daily lives could be solved with huge sums of money, but time has proven again and again that the unholy accumulation of cash can be a problem unto itself. Elvis Costello posed the rhetorical musical question, "Was it a millionaire who said, 'Imagine no possessions'?"

Today the trope of an unsuspecting, ill-prepared lottery winner being cursed with a jackpot is common, and appears as a plot device in countless movies, books, and TV episodes. When we're watching these stories unfold in fiction, we wish these unsuspecting victims would be like Kino in Steinbeck's *The Pearl* and throw their treasure into the ocean for their own good. But cautionary tales do little to dampen our *own* fantasies of sudden riches, of the Good Life, of the seemingly cosmic confirmation that we are different, special, and worthy. Somehow, *our* American dream stays intact despite the warnings.

But what if New Hampshire's bold experiment in public financing had failed? What if any of the dire forecasts surrounding the sweepstakes had come to pass? What alternate history of modern America would be written?

We have state-run lotteries today because of a strange confluence of characters and events, a bizarre and serendipitous recipe for change. The Cuban Missile Crisis. A vaudevillian actor-turned-politician. The Brink's heist. A timely blizzard. The Irish Republican Army. A pistol-packing newspaper publisher. A little old lady. A bipolar Bible-thumper. A goodie-goodie racetrack owner. And a midcentury FBI agent reminiscent of Eliot Ness. These elements combined to make it possible today for any of us to take a dollar to buy a legal long-shot wager . . . not the American dream, but *the American daydream.*

Acknowledgments

HAVING UNEARTHED a newspaper-clipping book while working as an outside public-relations consultant to the New Hampshire Lottery, I instantly fell in love with the forgotten story of the sweepstakes and how it changed the world.

While 1964 is hardly ancient history, fifty years is just long enough to make eyewitness accounts few and far in between. I'd like to thank those who shared their memories and observations of that time and the personalities involved. They include Lou D'Allesandro, Ed Callahan, John Clayton, Brad Cook, Chuck Douglas, Robert Flynn, Sandy LeFleur, Michael Green, Tom Rath, and George Siegel.

For help in obtaining research material and photographs, my thanks to the New Hampshire Institute of Politics and Political Library, the New Hampshire Historical Society, the New Hampshire State Library, the University of New Hampshire, the Manchester (NH) Historical Society and Rockingham Park. I'd personally like to thank Jeffrey Barraclough, Thomas Bebbington, Malia Ebel, Neil Levesque, Benoît Shoja, Nancy Mason, George Naum, and Michael York from these organizations.

This book would not be possible without the stewardship of the New Hampshire Lottery. Among those I'd like to thank are Charlie McIntyre, Maura McCann, and Rose Longo-White.

I very much want to thank the staff at ForeEdge and University Press of New England for their guidance as I stumbled my way through my first attempt at historical nonfiction. They were very accommodating and put their considerable talent toward refining this book. I tip my cap to Stephen Hull, Lauren Seidman, and Bronwyn Becker.

Lastly, I'd like to thank my family and my wife, Rebecca, for their patience and encouragement as I spent many hours with my nose in a computer.

"Lotteries, a tax upon imbeciles."
Camillo Beson, Count of Cavour (1810–1861)

Part One

PLACE YOUR BETS

1

*The Song
and
Dance Man*

LAURENCE PICKETT RECLINED in one of the large leather chairs in the Elks Lodge off Concord's main street. The narrow clubhouse was only three blocks from the statehouse, and ducking out of the chamber was a common occurrence for all four hundred members. For Representative Pickett, Democrat from the city of Keene, the Elks Lodge was one of the many places he could hold court.

"I am certain," *Sports Illustrated* later recalled him saying, "we are on the threshold of a new economy which will make this state even more inviting than it has been to retired people, to industry" — Pickett tilted his rocks glass toward the frost-covered windows — "and to people who like our variety of climate."

In his late fifties, bald, portly, and serious, Pickett oozed charisma. And on this afternoon he oozed confidence. The March air signaled another New Hampshire winter was yet to cease, yet Pickett wore his light-colored suit with no care for the season's remoteness from Memorial Day. He was also fond of wearing a plantation tie, knotted in a bow like a Christmas gift.

The other Democrats in his caucus were trying to dress like Kennedy, but Pickett knew he was a character in a political theater and liked to play his part. He spoke with an old-time elocution some said was reminiscent of W. C. Fields, but perhaps Pickett heard himself as FDR on the radio. Twelve months later, reporters from across the country would interview him in this very spot about what he'd accomplished. Pickett's voice would vibrate with a pronounced tremolo, and he would say it all started with a little old lady.

AS A YOUNG MAN, Larry Pickett had been a performer in vaudeville. He'd traveled the country in the national tour of *No, No Nanette,* a musical that would forever live in infamy in New England. As legend has it, the show's producer (and Boston Red Sox team owner) Harry Frazee sold his star pitcher Babe Ruth to finance the production. Bambino curses aside, the touring experience would prove invaluable to Pickett as he graduated from song and dance and learned the craft of *working* an audience.

In 1952, Pickett began the first of two two-year terms as mayor of Keene, a tiny red-brick city in the southwest corner of New Hampshire, equidistant from the state lines of Vermont and Massachusetts. It was a ninety-minute commute on tortuous back roads to get to his part-time job in Concord: being one of a half-dozen representatives from Keene to the New Hampshire House of Representatives, although calling his service in the General Court a "job" might be too generous.[1] The state constitution in 1776 had locked in wages for state senators and representatives at one hundred dollars a year, and it had (and still has) never been adjusted for inflation.

The House comprised four hundred members, making it the largest legislative body in the country. Even the stingiest legislator could not live on fifty cents a week in the 1950s, so members generally fell into one of two categories: the retired and the independently wealthy. Pickett was neither, but since voting at the statehouse was by and large held only on Tuesdays or Wednesdays, he could make his schedule work.

Pickett recounted to the *SI* reporter a story he often told of how an elderly woman paid him a visit at the mayor's office. "She was," he would say in his sing-song voice, "a dear friend of my late mother's — and whose funeral I have, alas, also attended — to ascertain what I could do to assist her in a crisis brought about by the action of the assessors in raising the taxes on her property by a hundred dollars a year."

The city of Keene raised money like virtually every other community in the

---

1. In New Hampshire, the term "General Court" referred to the collective body of the state legislative branch. The term is analogous to the word "Congress" used to describe both the U.S. Senate and House of Representatives.

nation: through a local property tax. However, while neighboring states enacted income taxes and sales taxes, New Hampshire refused to issue any statewide, broad-based taxes. A prevailing thought was that it shouldn't cost too much to run a state like New Hampshire. It was, after all, a small state, with only about 533,000 residents in 1950. Slightly more than a dozen communities were technically "cities." Residents also took a certain cultural pride in their flintiness. There were cries — made mostly by Democrats and newspaper editorialists — that New Hampshire had to adopt new taxes to meet its growing financial demands, but these voices were drowned out by Republicans, who greatly outnumbered their foes and controlled the executive and legislative branches for decades.

Yet the cost of government continued to increase. There were calls for new roads and bridges, more state police troopers, a modern higher-education system. Elementary education remained strictly a local-control issue. The state legislature provided school aid to communities, but it was so paltry, it was hardly worth the effort to get the check from the mailbox. With the postwar baby boom, the cost of education was becoming one of the biggest drivers of property tax bills in the state.

Facing this political obstacle course, Pickett pondered what to do for his poor widow. There had to be a way to give this woman her daily bread.

Pickett, who didn't mind putting two dollars down on a pony, envisioned a five-dollar sweepstakes window at the track. The money would go into a state fund, perhaps to be distributed to pensioners and the disabled. The idea continued to evolve. He'd lay down a bet in Concord.

LARRY PICKETT wasn't the first politician in New Hampshire to propose a lottery. In March 1949, Republican Joseph Geisel of Manchester submitted House Bill 290, An Act Establishing a State Revenue-Raising Pool. Geisel, described by author Leon Anderson as a "laundryman and banker," proposed selling numbered tickets in a raffle-like drawing. Half the money raised during the sales period would go into prizes, with the grand prize not to exceed 10 percent of the total pot. The proceeds would go toward the general expense of government.

The hot potato bill was referred to the House Ways and Means Committee. Chairman Lane Dwinell sought an advisory opinion from the state attorney general's office on the legality of a state-run lottery. Several days later, a three-page typewritten response came from Assistant Attorney General William

Green. In it, Green apologized to Dwinell for inserting his own personal opinions along with his legal counsel, but wrote he felt he must do so in the interest of "the general preservation of wise public policy."

The rub was that several federal laws were on the books prohibiting lotteries and prohibiting players and bookies from crossing state lines with gambling paraphernalia. Most individual states also had laws against games of chance — lotteries specifically — dating back to before the Civil War. The attitude about why lotteries were so detrimental to public morals was summed up by Green quoting Supreme Court Justice Robert Cooper Grier in the 1850 decision in *James Phalen v. the Commonwealth of Virginia:*

> The suppression of nuisances injurious to public health or morality is among the most important duties of government. Experience has shown that the common forms of gambling are comparatively innocuous when placed in contrast with the wide-spread pestilence of lotteries. The former are confined to a few persons and places, but the latter infests the whole community; it enters every dwelling; it reaches every class; it preys upon the hard earnings of the poor; it plunders the ignorant and simple.

More case law and congressional actions piled on in the following decades. Examining the legal landscape in 1949, Green wrote in his memo that the greatest peril was that tickets to a New Hampshire lottery could not reasonably be expected to stay within the boundaries of the map: "The sources of conflict are so many that it is difficult to say how a state lottery may be conducted without having this state under constant and minute surveillance by federal officials."

Anticipating the committee's next question, *What if we move ahead anyway with a state law that invited people to break a federal law?*, Green wrote, "There is no case squarely dealing with this question, where a lottery is involved, since no state has had the effrontery to flout the federal statutes." A precedent had, however, been set in other cases where promoting conduct that leads to law-breaking had been considered illegal.

"In addition to the foregoing," Green continued, "it would seem appropriate for your Committee to consider the embarrassment and inconvenience which would be caused to neighboring states who might not share our approval of lotteries, and to further reflect upon the dangerous precedent we would establish which might ultimately lead to the general undermining of a long established policy for the protection of the public interest."

The message was received loud and clear, and Geisel's bill was killed in the House without a floor vote.

THE NEW HAMPSHIRE GENERAL COURT operated on a two-year calendar. Budgets were set in the first year, as were most of the major legislative initiatives. The second year of the biennium was often less eventful. It's believed the intention of the state founding fathers was that the citizen legislature could do its business in year one and go home in year two to farm and hunt and protect the homestead from black bears and wild Indians.

Whatever the intent, the parliamentary effect was that bills rejected in year one of the biennium could not be reintroduced in the second year. Thus the House did not have to deal with lotteries again in 1950.

Geisel won reelection in Manchester and was back in the capital in 1951 with another bill to create a state lottery. The measure would form a commission to carry out the law and sell tickets, and money raised was to be given to the state treasurer and placed in a special fund for the general expenses of government. Hearings on the bill drew dozens of letters in opposition, many from pastors and religious organizations.

"The women of the First Baptist Church, Salem Depot, N.H., as represented by the Missionary Society stand . . . in opposition to the state lottery bill," wrote Mabel Dickey, secretary of the Missionary Society.

A gentleman from Tilton wrote, "I should like to be counted as willing to pay a sales tax or almost any other kind of tax rather than see a state lottery established."

Geisel's bill lost on a roll call vote in the House, 169 for and 188 against. Larry Pickett was among those voting in the affirmative.

Geisel did not submit a lottery bill in 1953. Instead the Republican proposed a referendum question for voters to ponder. The ballot would ask, "If such revenue is to be raised by taxation, which of the following methods would you favor? (1) state lottery, (2) income tax, (3) sales tax, (4) head tax?" The measure passed the House, but the Senate voted the bill was "inexpedient to legislate," the procedural euphemism for "kill it."

In the following biennium, 1955, Geisel's lottery bill was refined to dedicate aid to schools. Many of the same opponents that lobbied against the previous lottery bills spoke out against this one as well.

The House Education Committee was clearly uncomfortable being dragged into the legalized gambling debate. One representative said it was a trap for schools and that education should be "dignified." Turning their backs on what they perceived to be dirty money, the committee recommendation was to reject the bill.

That year there were a half-dozen other bills addressing gambling — horse racing, greyhound racing, pari-mutuel pools — as a way to raise state revenue. All failed in the House. It seemed pretty clear where the General Court stood on this one.

Midway through the session, a representative from Moultonborough brought forth an otherwise nondescript bill on school building aid to provide grants of up to 50 percent of the cost to construct a new school. The measure would provide $350,000 in direct aid. It passed, but the state Senate had some changes, so it came back to the House.

That's when Larry Pickett finally made his move.

WHILE IN THE GENERAL COURT, Pickett had risen to the rank of House minority leader and had become a master of parliamentary procedure. When House Bill 136 came back to the lower chamber, it was August. The battle over the two-year state budget was finished. It was past the deadline for new legislation to come forward until 1956. In other words, everyone's guard was down.

During debate on the school-building-aid bill, Pickett offered a floor amendment to sections 4 and 5. "Sweepstakes," it was labeled, and it read: "The commission is hereby authorized and directed to conduct two sweepstake races a year with the enclosure of any racetrack licensed by the commission." It also laid out authorization to sell tickets, award prizes, and hire state employees to run the operation.

The sneak attack was a stroke of legislative genius, an end run around the obstacles that had tripped up Geisel's efforts. It being summer, nearly a hundred representatives — a quarter of the body — were absent, including the speaker of the House.

Unlike in Washington, nongermane riders could not be attached to pieces of state legislation in New Hampshire. This floor amendment was allowed because it simply added an additional financing method to the plan. The building-aid bill had already had public hearings in the House and Senate. It was too late for the usual opposition forces to mobilize their letter-writing campaigns or show up in great numbers at committee hearings and lobby against the amendment.

It was too late for the leadership of either party to caucus and decide positions for or against. House reps would just have to vote on the merits of motion.

In 1955 lotteries had a stink on them. They reminded people of mobsters running numbers and roughing a Jasper who couldn't pay. But a sweepstakes — that was a horse of a different color. In its novelty as a legislative proposal in New Hampshire, a sweepstakes was the promise of something greater — something more elegant — than just a raffle. A sweepstakes would be an *event*. It conjured images of the Irish Sweepstake and its popularity among gamblers in the United States. It couldn't have been more seductive in that moment if Pickett had proposed raising cash at a kissing booth with Kim Novak.

The bill's original sponsor rushed to the microphone and argued against Pickett's floor amendment. It was reprehensible, he argued, and not the intention of the building-aid measure. Another speaker moved the amendment be indefinitely postponed. A flurry of representatives, taken by surprise, paraded to the podium to speak in favor of postponement. House Majority Leader John Pillsbury of Manchester moved for a roll call vote to freeze Pickett's gambit. After each member had shouted their vote, only 121 were for indefinite postponement, with 165 against. The motion failed, and the amendment was still in play.

With debate now squarely on the merits of the amendment, the vaudevillian Pickett returned and unleashed an oratorical song and dance in favor of the move.

"This will improve and enhance the credit of the state," he intoned in echoes of FDR. "Not one cent" would go to the New Hampshire Jockey Club, the organization that ran the state's largest horse track. Pickett predicted a sweepstakes would raise $2 million for education aid.

The thrust of Pickett's argument was this: without a new source of revenue the state would be forced to enact a sales tax. One could virtually smell the brimstone and sulfur as the devilish prospect of a sales tax seeped through the chamber. It was the Pickett Doctrine: you're either in favor of the sweepstakes or you're in favor of a sales tax. Few lawmakers wanted either label on their political résumé.

Majority Leader Pillsbury soon followed to urge defeat of the amendment. The ills and evils of legalized gambling were listed one by one, among them: "It's nothing more or less than a lottery bill that will take money away from people who are least able to pay: the working people."

A pair of Republicans followed him and echoed the sentiment. They warned New Hampshire was on the "highway to hell" and that the state would become "the laughingstock of the nation." Floor whips scoured the hallways, bathrooms, and smoking parlors for any straggling legislators who had missed the previous ballot. The chair asked for a voice vote but Pillsbury insisted on a roll call. After twenty nervous minutes of the clerk calling for each member in the House, the chair moved to the microphone.

"The House will be attentive to the state of the vote," he said, "with 166 voting in the affirmative and 141 voting the negative, the amendment passes."

A cheer went up from the floor. The sweepstakes was now officially part of the aid bill. Moments later, the final amended bill was approved.

Pickett requested to be recognized and returned to the podium. "Having voted in the affirmative, I move for reconsideration on the previous vote." It was a play of parliamentary reverse psychology. Any one of the "yeas" who went home to angry phone calls and visits from neighbors might return to the House and request the body retake that vote. Pickett was slamming the door on any second thoughts by insuring a reconsideration motion would fail. By a voice vote, reconsideration was killed. The building aid/sweepstakes bill was now going back to the Senate.

THE AMENDED BILL intrigued Governor Lane Dwinell, despite the bitter taste the 1949 legal opinion had left in his mouth when he chaired the Ways and Means Committee. Reporters who had witnessed the dizzying debate ran from the House chamber and around the corner to the governor's office. Dwinell's legislative assistant said, to the surprise of all, if the Senate approved the measure, the governor would be inclined to sign it.

The state Senate scrambled the next day, Wednesday, to hold committee hearings ahead of a full floor vote twenty-four hours later, the final day of the legislative session. Senate President Raymond Perkins referred the bill to no fewer than three committees, an unprecedented parliamentary maneuver worthy of Larry Pickett himself. Perkins's hope was that public indignation would force at least one of the committees to stall the amended bill.

Few people made those hearings — having only learned about developments in the evening paper — but the script was the same as in past years. The strongest voice against the lottery belonged to the Reverend Harold MacFarland, the superintendent of the New Hampshire Christian Civic

League. He called it a "damnable bill" and warned Pickett's actions had only emboldened and unified the state's antigambling forces.

Despite the pressure, all of the committees advanced the bill for a floor vote the next day, Thursday, August 4, 1955. Feeling Governor Dwinell had clearly tipped his cards for their benefit, a bipartisan mixture of lawmakers approved the bill 13–10.

Dwinell promised to make his decision known by noon on Friday, but reporters anxious to make their midday deadlines learned his announcement would be pushed back several more hours. Despite having publicly declared his support for the sweepstakes, Dwinell sent a message to the General Court that he would be vetoing the bill — the only veto of his term.

In his message, Dwinell said closer examination of the measure revealed problems. There were no controls on ticket sales and no allocations for the operations of a sweepstakes, and the quandary of dealing with federal restrictions remained unresolved.

"It would seem that it is contrary to the best interests of this State to become reliant upon widespread sweepstakes sales as a major source of revenue to operate its state government," he wrote. "[The Sweepstakes would] place this State in the unenviable position of becoming an unwitting accessory to the violation of federal laws."

When buttonholed by the press, the governor explained his change of heart by citing "evidence of great public revulsion" and sheepishly admitting he had been on the wrong side of the argument. "I'm very frank to admit I made a mistake. I've made mistakes before, but they were in private. This was in public. I'm not ashamed of it. I'm sorry I made the mistake." He also conceded the issue could likely hurt the Republican Party in 1956.

Six years later, former Republican governor Wesley Powell told the Associated Press the real reason Lane Dwinell vetoed the sweeps bill was pressure from the Eisenhower administration. According to Powell, former New Hampshire governor Sherman Adams, then serving as assistant to the president (the forerunner of the position today known as chief of staff), had personally called Dwinell to make the case for veto.

Adams still cast a long shadow over New Hampshire politics. He told Dwinell a sweepstakes would expose the state to national embarrassment. The administration did not want to see a Republican sign a lottery bill, especially not before the president's reelection campaign could begin. At the time,

Dwinell denied there had been any Washington influence on his flip-flop, but many of his successors would retell Powell's version of the tale.

SITTING DEJECTED IN THE LOUNGE of the Elks Club, Larry Pickett contemplated his next move on the political chessboard. Time had run out for the 1955 session, and his pieces were in check. A good player knows when to retreat. He'd have to wait until the 1957 biennium to make his next move.

Pickett had now become the standard-bearer for a different kind of lottery: the New Hampshire Sweepstakes. He was referred to throughout the statehouse as "Mister Sweepstakes" (not always affectionately). Beginning to devour all the research he could about sweepstakes and legalized gambling from around the world, Pickett combined all of his skills — this new gambling expertise, his legislative prowess, and his flair for the theatrical.

To accomplish what no one in modern history had ever done, he would need to endanger the political lives of everyone who touched his proposal.

2

The Fates, the Founding Fathers, and the Golden Octopus

THE IDEA OF SETTING UP A LOTTERY to pay for public needs was not born in the Granite State, nor was the idea of a sweepstakes horse race to draw in the players. Lotteries, in their many forms, have been used for centuries by governments, colleges, and private enterprises as an alternative means of financing — a "painless" form of taxation.

The term "lottery" is derived from French, Dutch, and Italian words. Its English etymology can be traced to the word *loterij,* from the Middle Dutch noun for "lot." The word meant "fate." Translators ascribed the word "lot" to all sorts of games of chance played in ancient times. Stones, straw, dice, and other implements were used as part of an impartial method to settle conflicts. "To cast one's lot" meant to throw caution to the wind and let the fates determine the result. The word lot may only be a few centuries old, but the practice of assigning decisions to chance dates back to biblical times.

The ancient Hebrews used the drawing of lots in matters of grave importance. They believed the results to reflect the divine will of Yahweh. The Old Testament's Book of Numbers claims the Lord told Moses to destroy the inhabitants of Canaan, then divide the land among the tribes of Israel by drawing lots. God commanded Aaron to bring two goats to the Feast of Atonement. Upon drawing lots, one goat was to be sacrificed as a sin offering, and the scapegoat was to be returned to the wilderness. Lots were used to discern it was God's will Saul be king of the Israelites. Even the enemies of the Israelites used lots to guide their actions. Haman cast "the pur" to determine on which day he would attempt to destroy Mordecai and the rest of the Jews, but the Lord made it a date in the far future, which favored the Chosen People.

The early Christians also drew lots to make important decisions. In one of the first passages from the Acts of the Apostles, Jesus's followers picked beans from a basket to select between two men who would take Judas Iscariot's place among the other eleven disciples. Accepting that the Lord knew the hearts of all men, Matthias's lot was drawn, and he became the new twelfth apostle.

In secular narrative, Homer's *Iliad* describes how lots were drawn from the helm of Agamemnon to determine who would have the honor of fighting Hector in single-warrior combat (Ajax was the "winner"). King Menelaus won the hand of Helen of Troy the same way. Accounts of drawing lots are also found in ancient Celtic, Chinese, and Greek literature and oral history.

LOTTERIES, while also relying on fate, differ from the ancient casting of lots. A lottery is a contest in which the players must *pay* for a *chance* to win. In its broadest definition, it covers everything from church raffles to multi-million-dollar jackpots. Lotteries have often found favor because, from antiquity to the twenty-first century, they've been viewed as a fairly painless way to raise money for worthy projects.

Some of the earliest recorded lotteries come from the Western Han Dynasty, which spanned the period from 205 to 187 BCE. Historians believe an early version of Keno originated in the fractured Han kingdom at this time. It was called the "white pigeon game," as birds carried results from village to distant village. Proceeds from lotteries were used to repair and extend the Great Wall of China.

Western civilization also embraced the lottery. The Roman elite, the Patricians, would often hold raffles after their dinner parties. Guests received tickets and won gifts of fine goods such as cloth, art, or dinnerware. No money exchanged hands. The practice was a form of after-dinner etiquette and all guests went home with a valuable token befitting their station in the empire. Later, Emperor Augustus Caesar introduced a raffle-like public lottery in which citizens could purchase a chance to win. Prizes were often booty brought to Rome after military conquest. The proceeds of the games were put toward the upkeep of the city and the roads that led to it.

In the late Middle Ages, after the Crusades, the first lotteries involving prize money were recorded. They sprang up in the Low Countries (coastal regions in current-day France, Belgium, and the Netherlands). According to *The Lottery Encyclopedia* by Ron Shelley, games were organized by towns, which used the net profits to build walls and fortifications and other public-works projects. Often proceeds were given to help the poor. These lotteries, like the ones that came before them, enjoyed popular support from the people and with their leaders.

Lotteries returned to Italy in the fifteenth century. Milan used drawings to raise money for its war with Venice. In Genoa the first numbers lottery was invented. *Lo Giuoco del Lotto* was originally a random drawing of the names of politicians from the Great Council. Every six months people could wager on which five of the ninety council members would be selected, but demand for the *Lotto* was so great that organizers wanted to hold drawings more frequently. They replaced the names with numbered lots, creating the forerunner to the modern numbers game.

The French government created a lottery to raise revenue when the bond market collapsed in the 1700s. Investors were allowed to purchase a lottery ticket for 1/1000th the value of any bonds they had previously purchased. Two great thinkers of the Enlightenment, the famous philosopher Voltaire and mathematician Charles Marie de la Condamine, discovered a mathematical flaw with this lottery. By purchasing cheap bonds, they were able buy very cheap lottery tickets — thus flooding the drum with their own tickets. Though the government eventually caught on, both men made enough money to spend the rest of their lives comfortably engrossed in their academic pursuits (and academia is arguably the better for it).

According to Shelley, the first English government-sponsored lottery began in 1566, a three-year endeavor. Queen Elizabeth I herself drew the winners in 1569. Unusual for its day (or in any other lottery), this English lottery paid prizes to *all* of its players. While some received lucrative payouts — pieces of fine China or other objets d'art — the prize pool to players was equal to the total value of tickets sold. Everyone was a winner. No money was kept by the realm. Instead, the government benefited by a three-year interest-free loan to conduct initiatives of public good.

As was typical of all state-sponsored lotteries of the era, neither lawmakers nor civil servants ran the operations. Often a contract to establish ticket sales

and revenue collection was awarded by the government to a third-party prof-
iteer. These brokers hired runners and other salesmen to peddle the tickets.
Dozens of lotteries ran in competition with one another. The cost of tickets
was often steep, and few in the lower class could afford them. The brokers
often sold shares of tickets to poorer players, making them among the first
stockbrokers in history.

It wasn't only government interests that were financed via lottery. Private
industry — with the blessing of authorities — could hold chance drawings as
well. King James I granted the Virginia Company of London the right to hold
a lottery to raise money to establish the first permanent English colony in the
New World: Jamestown.

America itself is the offspring of a lottery.

THE TRADITION of using lotteries as means of financing without taxation
continued in the New World. The Dutch rulers of present-day New York
sanctioned one of the earliest lotteries in 1655. Players had to guess the total
number of Bibles sold in New Amsterdam over a certain period. One-third of
the receipts went to the poor.

Historians John Samuel Ezell (*Fortune's Merry Wheel*) and Richard
McGowan (*The Gambling Debate* and *State Lotteries and Legalized Gambling*)
have discovered more than two hundred lotteries that were sanctioned in the
colonies between 1744 and the War of Independence. The money was used to
build public infrastructure (bridges, roads, canals) as well as finance religious
and cultural institutions (churches, libraries, schools). The practice was even
put toward economic development, as private entrepreneurs (with the approval of lawmakers) ran lotteries to raise capital for new businesses, including
hemp-growing in New York and paper-manufacturing in Massachusetts.

American academia also owes a debt to lotteries. Using legalized gambling
to pay for education in America is older than the nation itself. Drawings were
held in Georgia and North Carolina to build "academies." These one-room
schoolhouses became the foundation for the public school system in numerous counties.

Many of the first universities in the Western Hemisphere got their financing through public or private lotteries. The first is believed to have been the
College of Pennsylvania, later known as the University of Pennsylvania. The
frontier college held a total of nine lotteries in the 1700s as its primary financing

method for the construction of new buildings. (Penn's motto: "Laws without morals are useless.")

Games of chance are twisted throughout all branches of the Ivy League. McGowan writes the first of King's College's five lotteries occurred in 1746. The school (later known as Columbia) petitioned the New York Legislature to raise £2,250 to build new classrooms. Not long after, Union College asked to run its own lottery that would compete with Columbia's. Looking to appease an aggravated Columbia and its powerful benefactors, the legislature conceded to the college a twenty-one-acre tract of land in Manhattan, including the land on which the now-famous Rockefeller Center stands. It was quite the consolation prize.

Samuel Hazard, one of the first trustees of the College of New Jersey (now Princeton), was instrumental in organizing a lottery to pay for the infant school. New Jersey legislators refused to allow a drawing in its colony, so the Connecticut legislature offered to sanction Princeton's lottery instead. Hazard's personal letters reveal though the governor of Pennsylvania fined a broker £100 for selling tickets in his colony, Hazard was able to prevail upon the governor to rescind the fine.

Rivals Yale and Harvard used this form of gambling to grow their campuses. The Connecticut legislature approved a £7,500 lottery in 1747 for the construction of new Yale dormitories. Harvard looked to conduct a £3,200 lottery in 1765, but organizers failed to sell enough tickets to realize the full amount because the lottery was competing against several others organized to raise cash to fight the French and Indian War. And Massachusetts wasn't alone in funding military operations with lotteries. Many colonies used them to finance British operations during the French and Indian War.

Our Founding Fathers organized lotteries too. McGowan writes Benjamin Franklin raised money to purchase cannons in defense of Philadelphia. Prizes were pieces of eight. John Hancock ran a lottery. An eighty-three-year-old Thomas Jefferson (who had supported lotteries as a tax "laid on the willing only") found himself $80,000 in debt near the end of his life. Unable to pay a $20,000 promissory note, he petitioned Virginia to allow him to run a personal lottery with his revered landholdings as prizes. Jefferson died before the lottery could take place, so those with designs on the late president's belongings were able to go instead to the estate sale. George Washington ran several lotteries with mixed results. In 1768, he was one of the investors in the Warm Springs

Mountain Road Lottery, which would build a path through the Allegheny Mountains to a proposed hot springs resort. Not all of the six thousand tickets were sold. The following year, Washington served as manager of a Virginia lottery that offered land and slaves as prizes.

In 1769, King George III banned lotteries in the colonies, reasoning they were diverting money away from Mother England, but lotteries would continue to play key roles in the New World. In fact, an argument can be made that the War of Independence would not have been won without lottery financing. The Continental Congress could not impose a tax to pay for its "no taxation without representation" war. To fund military operations, it borrowed heavily from European allies, issued Continental paper money that rapidly depreciated, and established a national lottery. General Washington purchased the first ticket. The goal of raising $10 million was not met, but virtually every colony held its own drawing in support of the war. Massachusetts raised $750,000 to fund bonuses for men who joined their regiments. Later, it would garner another $20,400 to feed, clothe, and supply its troops.

After the Revolution, the taste for lotteries did not subside among citizens of the new United States. Just the opposite. There was an explosion of public and private interest in lotteries during the first half-century of the nation. Drawings raised funds to build bridges in Connecticut, dig canals in Pennsylvania, rebuild Boston's fire-ravaged Faneuil Hall, develop water supplies in Kentucky, and purchase fire-fighting equipment in St. Louis and Detroit. A lottery was conducted to raise capital for the Capitol and to build Washington out of the swamps. This federal lottery was popular with the people, but states running their own public-works lotteries were resentful.

Over time, the growing strength of the federal government signaled a decreased reliance on legalized gambling. Governments (including those at the state, county, and town level) now had the power and means to raise money through taxation, and a stable financial system allowed for the issuance of bonds. Lotteries were deemed suitable only for funding smaller special-interest projects, like erecting monuments or hospitals. The operation of these lotteries was still outsourced to private brokers who claimed to run the contests cheaply and efficiently. In order to win these lucrative lottery franchises, brokers were not above bribing public officials. Some even told politicians in advance what the winning numbers were going to be.

The Grand National Lottery in 1823 was authorized by Congress to raise money for improvements to Washington, D.C. The jackpot was $100,000 —

more than $2.2 million in today's currency. The lottery was a success and hundreds of thousands of dollars in prizes were drawn. Before the winnings could be distributed, however, the organizers absconded with all the proceeds, never to be seen again. The grand prize winner sued the District of Columbia, and the U.S. Supreme Court ruled the government was responsible for making good on his winnings.

THE D.C. DEBACLE was hardly the first time scandal befell a lottery. In fact, deception, corruption, and suspicion have been woven into the cloth of lotteries for centuries. European lotteries, particularly the Italian games, were rife with cheating. Straw-man winners were common. Organizers or their patrons were often the miraculous winners of the lotteries they ran. Rambling brokers often pocketed their sales and destroyed the tickets. Agents found ways to skim for themselves between the prize pool and the profit.

The pious (and there have been many in the Western World in the past five hundred years) viewed gambling in all its forms to be a sin. Puritan attitudes toward hedonistic behaviors were reflected in early colonial law. Especially troubling to opponents was the observation that lottery players were mostly from the lower classes. Though gamblers come in all shapes and sizes, a large prize for a small cost was terribly enticing for a poor man, for a desperate man. American lotteries were sophisticated. Some even offered instant prizes. The bait was easy enough for any rube to take. More than one husband gambled away his family's meal money on lottery tickets. By the 1830s, this painless form of taxation, with odds of winning so long they were scandalous, had morphed into a regressive tax on those who could least afford it.

Unlike other forms of gambling such as horse racing, poker, or cock-fighting (most of which were deemed "gentlemanly" in their era), lotteries democratized gambling for the people. They were equal-opportunity exploiters and had the ability to draw in new players. Some historians estimate the majority of ticket buyers in this period were women. Towns were filled with roaming brokers for sanctioned and underground lotteries alike. They darkened doorways and preyed on the lubricated sensibilities of tavern-goers. To some, lotteries were public nuisances. Newspaper articles on fraudulent lotteries eroded public confidence in legalized gambling; papers that reported no such stories were maligned as being in the pockets of the crooked lotteries that advertised within them.

As the reform era in early America began, instigated by abolitionists and the temperance movement, anti-lottery forces persuaded state legislatures to ban lotteries, even change their constitutions to forever prohibit them. At the start of the Civil War only three states — Delaware, Missouri, and Kentucky — still had state-sponsored lotteries. Tickets to these drawings were sold through the mail and by smugglers across the land. Other lotteries simply moved underground.

After the War between the States, Northerners were loath to spend any money on Reconstruction, fueling a resurgence in lottery games in southern states looking for capital. None were more successful, more influential, or more corrupt than the Louisiana Lottery.

IN 1868, the Louisiana Lottery Company convinced the state legislature to grant the company a lottery to run on the state's behalf. The terms, as described in *Fortune's Merry Wheel*, were a twenty-five-year charter, with a $40,000 annual fee due to the state. The New Orleans Charity Hospital would receive $50,000 in yearly proceeds, and the rest would go into the state's general fund. This was the only legally sanctioned lottery in America at that time.

The Louisiana Lottery Company was primarily made up of carpetbaggers: a syndicate of obscure New York capitalists with a few front men in New Orleans. Their setup was a virtual machine. Through slick marketing and an army of traveling salesmen, the Louisiana Lottery extended throughout the country. Word of mouth increased its popularity from Maine to California. Its reach was so pernicious the lottery was called "the Golden Octopus."

It held two major drawings each month and $600,000 jackpots twice a year — worth more than 10 million in today's dollars. There were 180 retail shops that conducted daily drawings and dabbled in insurance on the side. Ticket prices ranged between fifty cents and twenty bucks. More than $28 million in gross tickets sales flowed in annually. Profits to this private business reached a tax-exempt $13 million a year. Stock prices in the company rose from $35 to $1,200 per share. Ninety percent of players resided outside of Louisiana, with the majority of tickets purchased by mail. More than half of the letters at the New Orleans post office were for the lottery.

The drawings were a show onto themselves. The second Tuesday of every month, an elaborate ceremony was held at the old St. Charles Theatre in New Orleans. The room contained two five-foot-wide glass wheels on elevated platforms. The draw was conducted by two heroes of the Confederacy: Lt.

General Jubal Early and "Little Napoleon" General Pierre Gustav Toutant Beauregard. Early would appear in his Confederate gray uniform. Beauregard, in a dark suit, would somberly survey the crowd, then make a boilerplate speech affirming that the draw was done honestly and in good faith. After consulting their pocket watches, the generals would declare the games open. The "number wheel" contained 100,000 slips of paper, individually encased in rubber tubes. The "prize wheel" contained 3,434 prizes of different values. Two blindfolded children would pull tubes from the wheels and pass them to the generals. Early announced a ticket number while Beauregard announced the corresponding prize amount. It became a must-see event in the city.

Accounts of life in New Orleans during the 1870s and 1880s were filled with tales of children selling lottery chances in the street and of paupers, the elderly, and men on crutches begging for coins to purchase more tickets. It was a lottery bowery. Efforts by reformers to clean up the Louisiana Lottery were blocked or shrugged off by the politically powerful company. Whether Republicans or Democrats, police or judges, governors or congressmen, the Lottery Company bribed whomever they needed to stay in business.

When allegations of illegal influence against State Treasurer Edward Burke surfaced, he ran off with $1.3 million in state funds. Two governors were also implicated. It was the largest case of political corruption in state history. The state legislature passed a bill in 1879 abolishing the lottery, but there were still fourteen years left on the charter. Before it could expire once and for all, enough new lawmakers were in the Louisiana Lottery Company's pockets that they obtained another twenty-five-year charter. The state was powerless to take down the Golden Octopus.

It fell to Washington to rein in the rogue gambling operation. In 1890 President Benjamin Harrison sent a special message to Congress: "It is not necessary, I am sure, for me to attempt to portray the robbery of the poor and the widespread corruption of public and private morals which are the necessary incidents of these lottery schemes." Writing that "the people of the States are debauched and defrauded," he reasoned it would be impossible for lotteries to reach their victims if the mails were closed to their advertisements and remittances. A month later, the Anti-Lottery Bill passed and was signed into law, making it illegal to use the mail to conduct lotteries — striking at the heart of the Louisiana operation. The company moved to Honduras, but its games of chance were never as popular again.

In just under a hundred years, lotteries had transformed from American institution to American disgrace. They were not tax alternatives. They were scams. They were hornswoggles run by hustlers and con men to enrich themselves and impoverish the general welfare. They preyed on pensioners and the poor. In this climate, closing the mails was all that it took to kill the legal lottery.

The 1890 federal mail law was still on the books when Larry Pickett proposed his vision of a New Hampshire Sweepstakes. But it was not the only legal obstacle his plan would have to circumvent.

3

The Federal Threat

IN THE 1957 New Hampshire biennium, Representative Larry Pickett submitted a new bill on "the conduct of sweepstakes races and the sale of tickets thereon." He told lawmakers he had addressed all of the concerns about sweepstakes operations that had forced Governor Lane Dwinell to veto the 1955 bill.

Sweepstakes tickets would be $5, and the top prize would be $25,000 (in today's dollars, roughly a $40 chance on winning $210,000). Money raised would go into the General Fund for later distribution to cities and towns. Thanks to Eisenhower's New Hampshire landslide, however, the 1957 state legislature was even more Republican than usual. The bill never made it out of the House.

Pickett resubmitted substantially the same bill in 1959, which passed the House. Newly elected Republican governor Wesley Powell was an outspoken opponent of the Sweeps. Powell was outspoken about virtually everything — often forcing fissures within his own party leadership. Senate president Raymond Perkins, still bruised from his inability to quash the sweepstakes measure four years earlier, assured the governor the sweepstakes would die in committee. Perkins made good on his promise.

During the 1961 biennium, Pickett's sweepstakes legislation won by a surprising 2–1 margin in the House: 240–101. The landslide was an absolute shocker, a virtual mandate, so Governor Powell again leaned on Perkins and Senate Republicans to stomp it out. On arrival in the Senate, Pickett's bill was postponed until the end of the session. Senator Perkins eventually recalled the measure only to kill it in late June.

NOW CAME THE DAYS of Camelot, even in conservative New Hampshire. The 1950s had been a decade of a particular zeitgeist, when martinis were made only with gin and vermouth, served by women awaiting the twilight arrival of bread-winning husbands with felt hats or metal lunch pails. We got our news from the movie theater, complete with a cinematic soundtrack. Children talked to strangers and braced for A-bombs beneath school desks. A television was a neighborhood amenity just like a backyard swimming pool. Or like a fallout shelter, to which everyone was welcomed to retreat and repopulate. Ike was liked, Lucy loved, and the Beaver was left to his devices.

Now it was the New Frontier. In the '60s there was a feeling something was coming, cannonballing down through the sky. "Let the word go forth . . . that the torch has been passed to a new generation of Americans," as it was said. The men who fought under Eisenhower were now coming into their own. John Kennedy was young, was earnest. He wasn't one of those white-haired politicians they had grown up with. He seemed like a leader with vigor, a war hero. He had a beautiful wife and a young family.

This period wasn't just a changing of the old guard. Kennedy ushered in a new self-image for Americans, filled with confidence and bravado. Historians and political science majors may forever debate the actual substance of the Kennedy administration, but in living rooms and kitchens around the nation the style *was* the substance.

Even in New Hampshire, which had been a red state long before that term came into use and which voted for Richard Nixon (though Kennedy lost by fewer than 20,000 votes), the optimism of Kennedy rubbed off. We were going to the moon. We were going to end poverty. We were going to unite the races. Like his campaign song said, we would be the ant that moved the rubber tree plant. We would do these things not because they were easy but because they were hard.

Kennedy was the sun that shone down upon all. JFK was part royalty, part celebrity, part deity. He was the patron saint of Irish-Americans, his photo hanging side by side in many homes next to Warner Sallman's ubiquitous religious portrait *The Head of Christ.*

In New Hampshire's New Frontier anything was possible. Even a sweepstakes. Not because it was easy, but because it was hard.

IN 1963, the fifth time Larry Pickett had submitted a sweepstakes bill in eight years, the stars were beginning to align. The financial pressures on the state had continued to grow. The mention of a sweepstakes, while not universally embraced, was not nearly as shocking a topic as it had been in the 1950s. The cry for a sales tax was getting louder and louder. Sitting in the Elks Lodge, working the plan in his head, nattily dressed Larry Pickett knew House support was high, though the Senate was the perpetual firewall. Also, the state had a new governor, John King. He was the first Democratic governor in New Hampshire since Prohibition, so Republicans would be poised to needle him for any political misstep.

Pickett's new legislation was filed on January 9, 1963, and was assigned House Bill number 47: "An act relating to the conduct of sweepstake races and the sale of tickets thereon." It was Pickett's most comprehensive sweepstakes plan yet. It would grant powers to the State Racing Commission to sell three-dollar tickets and run the race. There would be two sweepstakes races run each year, one in late spring and one in early autumn, but in the operation's inaugural year, 1964, only one race would be run. Prize amounts would be left for the commission to determine.

House committee hearings were lengthy and jam-packed with advocates on both sides. Supporters brought telegrams from businesses in favor of the lottery. Opponents brought petitions, many of them signed by parishioners and congregants at area churches. The Ways and Means and the Finance Committee hearings each lasted hours. Pickett was always first to speak in favor of his bill, followed by a few representatives and senators before the general public. Longtime legislators and veteran reporters had seen this movie before: a boisterous debate between state financing and state morality. The final reel was always the same.

This time, members of the Ways and Means Committee upped the ante. Pickett wanted to sell sweepstakes tickets only at the racetracks. They proposed an amendment to allow the sale of tickets at the forty-nine state-run liquor stores. City and town clerks were also empowered to sell tickets at town hall and keep 10 percent of the profits.

If this bill went through, it would bring the lottery to every corner of New Hampshire.

HOUSE SPEAKER STEWART LAMPREY knew that HB 47 would eat up most of the session on March 13, 1963, so he scheduled the bill as the first item of business. He called order at 11 a.m. The House chaplain began with a prayer delivered in somber, pious intonations: "Almighty God . . . inspire us as we strive to advance Thy kingdom in our daily choices. Watch over us as we endeavor to fulfill our sacred obligations." It probably seemed to Laurence Pickett that even the Lord was against him that day.

Lamprey began by calling on Pickett to plead his case. Speaking in his distinctive oratorical style, Pickett declared the sweepstakes would raise a fantastic $4 million for schools and provide property tax relief without a sales tax. The floor was then opened to a melee of verbal clashes. The pro-lottery army was largely Democratic, emboldened by a strong platoon of wayward Republicans.

The counterattack was launched by Republican Gilbert Upton, who moved HB 47 be postponed indefinitely, saying, "It's an unreliable source of revenue. After the novelty wears off, it will be a burden on those who can least afford it."

Majority Leader Walter Peterson of Peterborough, took to the microphone also to urge postponement. "I am not an expert in the legal aspects, nor am I a moralist. I buy a ticket once in a while," he said, referring to church raffles and the like. "This is little short of bringing legalized gambling to every community in the state. It proposes to make legalized bookmakers out of 233 city and town clerks."

In his seat from the gallery, Larry Pickett squeezed the arms of his chair, a rage building inside of him as Peterson began to eviscerate his bill.

"Are we so naïve," Peterson continued, "not to realize in the best intention and sincerity that what we're doing will strike at the very foundation of our social order and will hurt the youngsters? The time for action is now."

Pickett rocketed from his seat and urged Peterson to yield to a question. Pickett said that 281 people in Peterson's own hometown favored the sweepstakes and asked, "How would you like to read the names of the townspeople in several petitions?" Peterson brushed it off. He said that his neighbors are polite to a fault and hated to refuse the petitioners. The comment elicited a lame chuckle from the body.

The back-and-forth continued for two and a half hours. Every aspect of the measure was bickered over, including the possibility of federal entanglements. Finally the vote came. HB 47 passed, with the liquor store and town hall amendment, 196–166. As the 1961 bill had passed by 139 votes, this 30-vote margin was much smaller than supporters had predicted. It turned victory into confusion. Among those voting against the sweepstakes was Democratic Minority Leader George Pappagianis, considered to be Governor King's go-to man in the House. When questioned by the *Nashua Telegraph,* Pappagianis offered a brisk "no comment" and sulked away. The political tea leaves were indecipherable.

With his signature parliamentary move, Larry Pickett asked for reconsideration of the vote, and its designed failure to pass slammed the door on debate.

PICKETT TRIED to forestall the bill's referral to the state Senate, hoping that if debate didn't begin until the end of the legislative session the fiscal pressures of balancing the two-year state budget would force any undecideds to take the sweepstakes money. A quick head count of the twenty-four-member Senate found between eight and thirteen senators solidly against the sweepstakes, but several were publicly uncommitted. However, Pickett couldn't delay referral. The Senate wanted it, and they wanted it immediately.

Raymond Perkins was no longer in the Senate to strong-arm opposition, but he had left the team his playbook. The sweepstakes may be approved by the jubilant members of the lower chamber, but it would be dismissed after the sober, thoughtful examination of the Senate.

Senate President Phillip Dunlap assigned HB 47 to a joint committee of Finance and of Ways and Means. The hearing on the afternoon of March 27 was so large it was held in the four-hundred-seat chamber where the House deliberated, instead of one of the tiny committee rooms. Larry Pickett was followed by twenty-one other speakers in the marathon hearing. After three hours, the joint committee motioned to adjourn and continue the hearing the following week. Picking up where they had left off, at 7:30 p.m. on April 2 another thirty-eight citizens began parading to the microphone in a hearing that lasted long into the night.

The speakers brought with them letters and telegrams and petitions from neighbors, businesses, and churches. According to the audience sign-in sheet, 123 people identified themselves as favoring the Sweeps, and 225 wrote they were against it. A total of 1,295 names from various petitions were submitted in support; opposition forces' petitions showed only 80 signatures, all from local churches. Little of what was said at the hearings had not been heard years before.

The testimony that shook the General Court came, second-hand, from a minister from South Congregational Church in Newport. First Rev. William

Blair spoke against the evils of gambling: "Apathy and lethargic indifference are the most effective weapons the Devil wields. Society succumbs to satanic decay not because the forces of evil are sharp and strong but because the sword of righteousness remains sheathed in silence." Then Blair presented to the committee a letter he received from Assistant Attorney General Herbert Miller, head of the Criminal Division of the U.S. Justice Department. Blair said he had written to the DOJ to ask its opinion on the sweepstakes.

> It is unrealistic to assume that there will be no interstate traffic in these [New Hampshire] lottery tickets. Undoubtedly a score of federal violations will result . . . A lottery might also be used by racketeers who could siphon off a percentage of the proceeds as a cost of conducting the lottery. The history of this country indicates that each time a state used a lottery as a source of revenue, a large share went to the promoters, in spite of the controls enacted. Corruption of officials charged with the administration of the lottery seems to take place as a matter of course.

The hall was abuzz. It was official: Bobby Kennedy was going to come after the sweepstakes.

THE IDEA that federal authorities would come into New Hampshire and work to dismantle the sweepstakes, and throw organizers in jail, was a plausible worry in 1963. John Kennedy had shown he was not weak-kneed when it came to the fight between federal and states' rights. The president had sent U.S. Marshals to protect the Freedom Riders, mobilized the National Guard to restore the peace during the Montgomery riots, and sent federal troops to Mississippi to protect James Meredith as he attempted to enroll at Ole Miss. At the time the Miller letter was circulating in Concord, Robert Kennedy was actually in Montgomery meeting privately with Governor George Wallace in hopes of avoiding a segregation standoff at the University of Alabama. Some historians have devalued JFK's early civil rights interventions as halfhearted, more political calculation than moral stand. The hope was always these crises would blow over or be quelled by the states before the feds needed to step in. Historian Arthur M. Schlesinger Jr. wrote that Robert Kennedy, the U.S. attorney general, was often the one urging federal intrusion as a last resort. Any administration observer would know however that the president who had just gone toe to toe with Khrushchev in a game of nuclear brinksmanship in Cuba was unlikely to let any governor dictate terms to him.

It went without saying that Robert Kennedy was his brother's closest advisor in the White House. Some had questioned RFK's appointment as attorney general, labeling it a nepotistic move of historic measure. The younger Kennedy had no experience as a litigator in state or federal court. If he had been known for one thing before his brother's election, it was for his crusade against organized crime. In 1951, Kennedy had joined the Criminal Division at the Justice Department. After John Kennedy's election to the Senate in 1952 (and at the insistence of patriarch Joseph Kennedy), the chair of the Senate Permanent Subcommittee on Investigations, Joseph McCarthy, selected RFK as assistant counsel to the subcommittee. Previously a background figure, Kennedy became chief counsel and staff director to the subcommittee in 1955.

Robert Kennedy was thrust into the national spotlight in 1957 during the televised Select Committee on Improper Activities in the Labor or Management Field. Kennedy's investigation focused largely on racketeering among organized labor. Evidence of corruption, bribery, and blackmail was presented, much of it attributed to unions in bed with the Mob. Kennedy picked apart unions for bakers, meat cutters, retail workers and — most famously — the Brotherhood of Teamsters. The seminal moment of three years of hearings and fifteen hundred witness testimonies was the showdown between RFK and Teamster president Jimmy Hoffa. Kennedy grilled Hoffa as hard as he could, but Hoffa was evasive. He knew Kennedy was easily riled and baited him into arguments that undermined the interrogator's credibility.

In *Robert Kennedy and His Times,* Schlesinger wrote RFK was sincere in his belief that Hoffa was the most dangerous man in America, but that his handling of the committee hearings was ham-fisted and ineffectual. The Select Committee never took down Hoffa. Kennedy drew great criticism for the way he himself behaved, letting his impatience and temper get the best of him. He left the post in 1960 to run JFK's presidential bid. Whether he was successful or not as an interrogator, Robert Kennedy would forever be known as someone with a chip on his shoulder when it came to organized crime.

ASSISTANT ATTORNEY GENERAL HAROLD MILLER was no slouch when it came to confronting gangsters either. In his time at the Justice Department, Miller had testified before Congress on a number of anti-gambling measures designed to curb the influence of underworld forces. Miller was Robert Kennedy's man on Capitol Hill, and, like Kennedy had been, he was one of the DOJ's Young

Turks, brilliant and ambitious. He had been behind Justice Department–driven legislation to disrupt the way gangsters and bookies did business.

Among the laws passed at the behest of Kennedy's Justice Department included the Interstate Wire Act, which prohibited the use of wire communication (i.e., the telephone) in illegal sports betting. Bookmakers needed the phone to take wagers. Some even used the immediacy of the phone to get results of games and races before the bettors, allowing them to change the odds to their advantage at the last minute (think *The Sting*). Before the Wire Act, federal investigators had had little power to subpoena telephone records or tap lines of suspected bookies.

Another law championed by RFK, and germane to the sweepstakes discussion, was the Interstate Transportation of Wagering Paraphernalia Act. This made it a federal crime to move across state lines "any record, paraphernalia, ticket, certificate, bills, slip, token, paper, writing, or other device used, or to be used, adapted, devised or designed for use in" illegal gambling. The target was Mob-run sports books, numbers pools, policy and bolita games. Penalties for possession of slips and wagers by bookies varied from state to state and gave the feds very little leverage. Congress agreed that the act of bringing such paraphernalia across state lines fell into the jurisdiction of the FBI.

Kennedy and Miller also successfully lobbied Congress to pass the Travel Act in 1961. More expansive than either the Wagering Paraphernalia Act or the 1890 Anti-Lottery Act, it prohibited the use of the U.S. mail or the act of traveling across state lines to commit an unlawful activity. Again, its purpose was to hamper organized-crime activities. Miller explained to a Senate committee that the Travel Act would be a most effective tool in preventing corruption. Meant to be applied primarily to gambling, the law could also be used to fight prostitution and trafficking of liquor and narcotics. Miller said it was through these four specific activities that gangsters got their hooks into public officials. The power of these enterprises — and the money they reaped — allowed organized crime to influence police, judges, and politicians. As far as a potential sweepstakes was concerned, the Travel Act made it nearly impossible for ticket agents (sanctioned or otherwise) to roam the country and sell lottery chances.

Miller's and Kennedy's reputations as illegal-gambling and public-corruption watchdogs were well earned. By 1963, Kennedy's Justice Department made more gambling arrests than had occurred in the previous thirty years. If Miller's letter said a New Hampshire Sweepstakes was going to run afoul of federal law and promote graft, then you could bet it would.

DESPITE THE MILLER LETTER BOMBSHELL, the joint Senate committee voted 7–5 to recommend passage of Pickett's Sweeps bill to the full Senate. The bill came out of committee with three major changes. It dropped the authorization of city and town clerks to sell tickets. (This unpopular provision was likely responsible for the reduced number of yes votes in the House.) It also rejected the idea of letting the Racing Commission operate the lottery and proposed the creation of a separate Sweepstakes Commission.

The final amendment was the biggest. The law would mandate a town-by-town referendum vote on whether Sweeps tickets could be sold in each community. Any community could opt out but still receive its share of the lottery's proceeds. The first referendum would be held in March 1964 and would coincide with the presidential preference primary, a day when ballot boxes were already set up across the state. The measure also permitted referendum votes every two years in perpetuity. If towns had second thoughts about their participation in the Sweeps, they had a way to escape.

The effort seemed moot. Defeat of the bill by the Republican-controlled Senate was all but assured. The GOP outnumbered Democrats fifteen to nine in the twenty-four-member chamber. The majority whip said some senators were still wavering on fears that killing the sweepstakes would guarantee a sales tax to raise money, but it appeared HB 47 would receive only ten or eleven votes.

The weekend before the vote, three Republican senators who had been sitting on the fence said they'd vote in favor, tipping the bill toward passage. Senator Nelson Howard, who had previously said he'd vote against the sweepstakes, denied he had "bolted" from the party. He told reporters that neither the Senate Republican Policy Committee nor the Republican State Committee had ever taken a formal position on the sweepstakes.

On Tuesday, April 16, 1963, a displeased Senate president Dunlap called the body to order. Because the committees had amended the bill, any measure passed by the Senate would go back to the House for a formal vote on concurrence. Opponents' last chance was to tack on additional amendments to make the bill so unpalatable to the House that anti-Sweeps legislators there could close the thirty-vote margin.

The first move was to raise the proposed salaries of the new commissioners from $2,400 to $6,000 per year. Such a princely sum for a part-time job would be terribly unpopular. Unfortunately, it was so unpopular with both sides the amendment failed.

Another floor amendment, by Senator Robert Monahan, called for signs to be posted at every point of purchase that read "Warning — Any person transporting a New Hampshire Sweepstakes ticket across state lines by any means is liable for federal prosecution." It too failed to get majority support.

A final amendment, meant to stall the process, would send the bill to the New Hampshire Supreme Court for a legal opinion on whether the sweepstakes violated either state or federal laws. "If the proponents are so sure that it is not in violation, they should have no real objection to the advice and opinion of the Supreme Court," challenged Monahan. The measure was rejected, allowing debate on the actual bill to begin.

The first to rise was Senator Nelle Holmes, one of three women in the state Senate. "Legalized gambling is not good for the State of New Hampshire," she began. "This causes a general weakening of moral fiber as we all know, and I am not ashamed to want to avoid this . . . If anything is going to weaken our character as a nation and make us ripe for communism it is this attitude of being afraid to stand up for moral principle and being scornful of those who have the courage to stand up for one."

Holmes argued instead of balancing the state's books with lottery schemes they should do so with a sound tax policy. "If people can afford to spend millions on gambling," she said, "they can surely afford to pay taxes."

"We are about to set an awful example for our younger citizens," lamented Senator Paul Kerkavelas. Gesturing to his colleagues, he asked why the governor had not taken any leadership on this titanic issue and concluded, "This is a sorry day in the history of the Granite State."

Supporters were just as passionate. "Surely the urge to gamble cannot be all wrong," said Senator Nathan Battles. "Much of the greatness and power of America stems from the urgency of spirit which prompts man to back his hunches or judgment with a few dollars to make more dollars." Then, foretelling all lottery marketing plans ever to follow, Battles said, "Each purchaser of a sweepstakes ticket pays not for the mathematically slim chance at a prize, but rather for the privilege of dreaming. The hopes and dreams of people cannot be stifled." He said that, as had been proved with alcohol in the wake of Prohibition, the government could take back power from the underworld by controlling legalized gambling.

At the end, Senator Edith Gardner, offered a soliloquy that touched on every fear of the lottery. She did not repeat Holmes's premonition that the lottery would lead to communism, but she predicted it would lead to a rise in juvenile delinquency, foreclosures, racketeers, and — shockingly — people seeking to open charge accounts at local stores. She was certain Boston-based mobsters would come north and take over. "Let's not kid ourselves, those undesirables are only a few miles from our border. Should this bill pass . . . it wouldn't take long until we had visitors quite unlike the ones New Hampshire people are accustomed to."

A hush fell over the chamber now that every word had been exhausted. Dunlap called the roll. Thirteen said "aye"; only eleven said "nay."

A WEEK LATER the amended bill returned to the House. Opponents' floor amendments to run it off the tracks were floated and batted down. The House voted in concurrence, and House Bill 47 was on its way to the governor's desk.

Back at the Elks Lodge, Larry Pickett shook hands, greeted people in his W. C. Fields twang, and smiled as he peered out the window. The frost of March was gone, and the days were getting longer, brighter.

The sweepstakes was a dainty dish to set before Governor King. There were, however, no nods or winks from the corner office. King's staff said they had no idea whether he'd sign or veto. They weren't posturing. King was as silent on the bill in private as he was in public.

Pickett had no guarantee where the governor would come down, but the song-and-dance man had one thing going for him. While serving in the House of Representatives, John King had voted in favor of a sweepstakes bill twice.

4

A Dainty
Dish

AS THE CALENDAR FLIPPED to 1962, the Democratic leadership had approached John King about being their candidate for governor in the November election. King was a plain-looking man, average height; he looked good in a suit and had a winning smile. His hair was combed neatly over his thinning scalp and was held in place by a shiny smattering of Brylcreem. His browline eyeglasses were the only flashes of contemporary fashion he displayed. They made him look like the smartest man in the room, which he almost always was. He'd be a respectable candidate — if he could be convinced to run.

You need another sacrificial lamb? he quipped. Democrats had never fared well in the state. Larry Pickett himself had been led into the Republican abattoir in 1956 as his party's token candidate for U.S. Senate. Only one Dem had grabbed the governor's office that century: one-termer Fred Brown in 1922. The party was so weak that even the local media's staunchest right-winger, William Loeb III of the *Union Leader,* rarely gave the Democrats any poisoned ink (having more fun toying with the moderates in the GOP establishment). But they had to put *someone* on the ballot in '62.

King's career ambitions had never including running for governor. It was no secret the lawyer's long-term desire was to become a judge. But the Manchester representative thought the previous Republican governors had all made terrible mistakes in leadership and the Democratic candidates had unreservedly bungled their campaigns. King told friends there was no chance he could do worse than his predecessors, so hat entered ring.

BORN IN 1918, John King came of age in Depression-era Manchester, New Hampshire, the first-generation American son of an Irish immigrant father. Michael King, a humble shoemaker from Galway, now lived in the state's Queen City.

The Kings lived in "The Fields," a neighborhood filled with Irish immigrant mill workers. Everyone there worshiped at St. Anne Church, the "Irish" church in Manchester. The French and Polish immigrants had their own churches; theirs was a self-segregated Jim Crow Catholicism.

King was the only son in a household that included five sisters. In an Irish Catholic family, that made John the golden boy, the prince of the King family. He was quiet, thoughtful, and wonderfully studious. Even as a child, he was a voracious reader and collected books. As a young man, King worked for thirty dollars a month in the Depression-era relief program the Civilian Conservation Corps. Twenty-five dollars of his paycheck went back to his home in the Fields.

King started his higher education at St. Anselm College, a catholic school on the outskirts of Manchester. He won a scholarship to Harvard and then to Columbia Law School. After graduating, he practiced law for a time in New York City, but returned to Manchester in 1948 with his wife, Anna, to open his own practice. King's specialty was labor law, and the little office soon grew to one of the city's largest law firms.

Before John Kennedy made it fashionable to be an Irish Catholic politician, King demonstrated an avid interest in service. Irish Democrats from the Fields were not far-left liberals. He started with little interest in public office, but sought a seat on the 1952 state Constitutional Convention. Though the "ConCon" didn't result in great government changes, King so thoroughly enjoyed arguing the points of law he decided to run for state legislature.

King ran as a Democrat for the state House of Representatives in 1954 and won, carried on the back of the Manchester Celtic vote. Admired by colleagues in his caucus for his intelligence and even temperament, Representative King served as house minority leader (the post that Larry Pickett had previously held) for six years.

King threw himself into campaigning for governor and proved himself a fighter. He crisscrossed the state. He came off as an "everyman." King walked with the crowd and didn't lose the common touch. He had a strong ground game and glad-handed at every late summer and autumn fair, meeting as many tourists as he did voters. "No town is too small" in which to campaign, he told *This Week* magazine.

Democratic leaders, including Larry Pickett, said King was more than just their sacrificial lamb. They understood that King was formidable because few others in the General Court were as critical of incumbent Republican governor Wesley Powell. King's long, honed reproaches were so familiar he didn't need to write a stump speech. In the words of the *New York Times,* he elevated his criticism of Powell "to an art."

GOVERNOR WESLEY POWELL was a war hero. He had taken a leave while assistant to powerful U.S. Senator Styles Bridges — a post he'd held since earning a law degree in 1940 — to volunteer for combat service, and his left arm and hand were severely weakened from wounds he received over Munich as an aerial gunner in the Army Air Corps Bomber Command. Powell had spent a year in a military hospital recovering. Despite the disability, he often got in thirty-six holes of golf a week.

As governor, Powell had a reputation for self-aggrandizement and self-promotion. They called his style "rule or ruin," for special places in his hell were reserved for Grand Old Party members who crossed him. He was quick to cut down opponents, real or perceived, and for two terms as governor he had proven himself to be a poor loser.

Powell owed his political education to his mentor, the popular and powerful Senator Bridges, but he owed all of his political success to William Loeb III. The conservative editor of the only statewide newspapers, the *Manchester Morning Union* and *Manchester Evening Leader* (later known collectively as the *Union Leader*), Loeb was a bombastic publisher; his editorials, all printed on the front page, were as subtle as a jackhammer.

In today's political parlance Loeb might be classified as a Tea Party Republican. Moderates were the bane of his existence, as was GOP leadership. He called Harry Truman "the Maharaja of Washington" and called Eisenhower "Dopey Dwight," a "fake Republican" with "as much backbone and substance as a ribbon of toothpaste." For Republicans who read the *Union Leader,* Loeb was a political compass by which the common man could find his bearings. If Bill Loeb argued it was better to crack one's egg on the large end, then many readers would do so — and a grumbling minority would reflexively start cracking their eggs on the small end.

Loeb was the eight-hundred-pound gorilla, not just among the media, but in the very culture of the state of New Hampshire.

Despite Loeb's popularity, his papers were constantly hemorrhaging money. He wooed every captain of industry he could, but few wanted to get into bed with the prickly publisher. According to his biographer, Kevin Cash,[1] a young Loeb went one day into his private office at his Vermont paper and closed the door. A gunshot rang out, jolting the newsroom. Thinking they'd find the cash-strapped publisher with his head blown off, the staff instead found Loeb standing over the house cat that roamed the office. A smoke trail licked from his .38 as blood streamed from the animal's body. "I thought I told you," he said to no one in particular, "to get that goddamned cat out of here." The following day, his secretary went to each staffer to say Mr. Loeb had noticed the cat was very ill and had chosen to put it out of its misery.

In the late 1940s, Loeb was on the verge of being bought out by his partner when Styles Bridges intervened and convinced some deep pockets to invest in Loeb's own buy-out effort. Wesley Powell, then assistant to the U.S. senator, personally delivered a sack of money to Loeb save his stake in the *Union Leader,* and Loeb's gratitude to Bridges — and, by extension, Powell — manifested in the deepest of political loyalties. In print, Loeb revered Bridges like a saint and worked to get Powell elected governor.

All that crumbled when Bridges died suddenly in 1961, one year into his fifth term as U.S. senator. Knowing that Governor Powell had authority to appoint a temporary successor, Loeb's page-one editorials demanded Powell name the senator's widow, Doloris Bridges, to her late husband's seat. In a critical miscalculation, Powell ignored Loeb and appointed state Attorney General Maurice Murphy instead. What followed was a messy, public divorce. The publisher saw Powell's act as a betrayal of the Bridges's legacy and of himself personally. He vowed to see Doloris Bridges in Washington and Powell turned out of office.

---

1. Cash's book *Who the Hell IS William Loeb* was so radioactive that no New Hampshire printer would touch it. So explosive was the tome that when Cash died in 1985 — four years after Loeb's own death from cancer — the night-shift at the *Union Leader* got into a donnybrook over whether they'd get in trouble for printing Cash's obituary. Damned either way, the staff did not run the obit and was later reprimanded by upper management.

The custom for New Hampshire governors was to leave office after two terms. Powell had a heart attack in March 1962 and spent the following months recuperating. But tradition be damned, Powell was openly discussing running for an unprecedented third term. A summer of discontent settled over the GOP. Nobody wanted to work with the contemptible Powell anymore, and they knew the *Union Leader* wasn't going to back him.

Because of the heart attack, the governor's doctors urged Powell not to campaign as vigorously as he had before. Yet, despite his open distaste for the press, Powell's campaign strategy was to sit for as many newspaper profile pieces as he could. He did himself few favors, allowing scribes to tag along as he played rounds of golf or dined on grilled swordfish served by his dutiful wife, Beverly. Looking far beyond the imminent election, Powell unabashedly talked about his aspirations to run for U.S. Senate — or even the White House. The resulting image of an out-of-touch, overly ambitious politician hurt him in a way his campaign staff failed to understand.

Powell thought the stature of his office alone — and the bottomless respect of his fellow Republicans — would get him beyond the primary and through the general election. He thought he was impervious to Loeb's daily five-alarm editorials against him.

In September 1962, Doloris Bridges failed to win the Republican U.S. Senate nomination in a tight four-way race. Bill Loeb played the role of enfant terrible, declaring in print that "she was robbed," instigating recounts and court action. Loeb's advocacy split party loyalties and weakened nominee Perkins Bass heading into November.

Loeb did get one of his wishes. In a stunning upset, incumbent Wesley Powell failed to get his own party's nomination for a third term as governor.

POWELL'S MISFORTUNE wasn't all good news to Democratic candidate John King. His whole campaign had been built around the failures of Wesley Powell. Now he had to switch his game plan and find the soft underbelly of "Big John" Pillsbury.

Pillsbury, House majority leader, was now the GOP gubernatorial candidate. Pillsbury's deportment was stately. He roamed the capitol with a pipe clenched between his teeth. "Big John" — he stood six-foot-three and was 225 pounds — had the juice among lawmakers and sympathy from the party bosses.

In an odd reversal of typical partisan positions, Democrat King stood against a sales tax and pledged to veto one should it ever come to his desk. Republican Pillsbury had favored a sales tax in the late 1940s but now insisted he'd abandoned that belief years ago. King would have none of it, and he painted Pillsbury as ready to implement a sales tax the moment he got into office. Pillsbury's presumed tax sympathies turned off Bill Loeb, and the mighty conservative effectively stayed out of the governor's race (a tacit endorsement of John King).

Two strokes of political luck befell King. The first was an endorsement from an unlikely advocate: Wesley Powell. The incumbent, embittered by his primary defeat, promised to throw his weight behind the Democrat to snub Bill Loeb.

The other windfall for Democrats came far away from Concord. On October 22, 1962, President Kennedy addressed the nation about a looming crisis with the Soviet Union playing out in Cuba. Many Americans believed the United States was on the precipice of nuclear war with the Soviets.

Through a complex mixture of military bluster, a naval blockade of Cuba, traditional diplomatic negotiations, and back channel talks, the Cuban Missile Crisis ended on October 28 — a little more than a week before the election.

The palpable relief of pulling back from the edge of nuclear war was felt across America. Bipartisan reaction from Congress during and following the crisis was positive, with many leading lawmakers praising Kennedy for his handling of the situation.

Democrats ran into November with a full head of steam. Thomas McIntyre beat Perkins Bass for Bridges's seat, sending New Hampshire's first Democrat to the U.S. Senate in three decades.

At age forty-four, John King, the "sacrificial lamb," topped Big John Pillsbury in the governor's race, making him the first Democratic governor in New Hampshire in forty years.

IN EARLY 1963, as the sweepstakes bill was being debated by the state legislature, John King sincerely didn't know whether he'd sign the bill or veto it. He went into a type of monastic seclusion. King was famously contemplative already, but this was a deeper kind of conclave of one. "In many ways it was an agonizing period," he'd say decades later in a Bar Association interview. He knew the bill would affect not only the citizens of New Hampshire but likely the rest of the country. King closed the door to his office, read the latest round of letters and telegrams, and pondered the problem like a Talmudic rabbi.

These were the numbers: The Governor's office reported New Hampshire spent $2.4 million on state aid to education in 1962 and was ranked forty-fifth in the nation. At the time, they still had thirty-five one-room schoolhouses in the state. Increasing aid through a state sales tax would cost each family forty-three dollars a year — quite a bite when the average guy was bringing home sixty-five to seventy dollars a week. Although there was nothing objective to base it on, Pickett's $4 million prediction of annual Sweeps revenue seemed a truism and remained the ex-cathedra revenue target.

Even King's wife, Anna, didn't know his thoughts on the sweepstakes bill until he signed it. Anna was King's Jackie. She was in her mid-forties, polished, and put together like the perfect midcentury housewife. Though she admired the first lady and her style, Anna King was most like Jackie in that she had her own admirers and was comfortable in her own skin.

Anna woke each morning before her husband — even during the campaign when his days began at 4 a.m. The former nutrition teacher started King with a glass of milk before pouring him a cup of coffee from the percolator. A hearty plate of eggs or pancakes came next. Apron around her waist, Anna would buzz around the kitchen of their Manchester home until the governor's driver, a retired state trooper who lived down the street, would whisk King off to the statehouse. She'd look over the governor's schedule and send the driver with a picnic lunch or a thermos filled with soup if there were too many afternoon appointments for a proper lunch break. All her attention to King's stomach earned him the nickname "the Eating Man's Candidate."

King would not seek his wife's counsel on political matters, particularly when it came to something like the sweepstakes. Anna, who dutifully attended every women's tea and other pseudo-social obligation of a first lady, was the quintessential great woman behind the great man. King, however, was the quintessential 1960s traditionalist. Instead of a wedding band, King wore his class ring from Columbia Law. Could there be a more telling symbol of how John King ranked professional and marital obligation?

"He's governor in the state house," one of King's friends told the *Manchester Free Press*, "and he's governor in his own home."

King told people there were two reasons in 1962 he thought he had the ability to run for governor. One was that he and Anna did not have a mortgage on their Manchester home. The second was that they had no children.

King didn't linger long on the second point, lest his voice betray an emotion he'd rather not show.

JOHN KING, in his introspection, sat in the governor's office on the long couch that he and his wife paid for. Anna King had designed her husband's new office with relaxation in mind, removing the room's clerical trappings and adding leather side chairs and end tables. She was convinced some relaxation would keep him in the pink while holding his difficult post. There were several pieces by New Hampshire craftsmen, including several beautiful marble ashtrays strategically placed for guests (King himself didn't smoke). A collector of oil paintings, King owned more than a hundred, and he provided the artwork for the office. Behind his desk was a scene of New Hampshire's majestic White Mountains. At eye level on the opposite wall hung a painting of a sailboat being violently tossed on an indigo sea. It wasn't the serene landscape that Anna hoped he'd have selected, but the metaphor spoke to the Democrat. Despite all the assistance offered to him, it was he who felt alone at sea.

From the couch, King's view out the north window was of the state library. Built of linen-colored granite, the building was a tribute to New Hampshire. One-half of the Neoclassical Beaux-Arts building housed the state supreme court, an institution desperately in need of a space of its own. The library roof sported a square turret with semi-arched windows and a green, tiled roof, which balanced the asymmetrical design of the building. King *hated* the tower. He didn't mind the library, but the tower was his personal eyesore, rising to obstruct the view from his second-floor office.

Yes, he had twice voted as a House member for Pickett's sweepstake bills, but being governor of New Hampshire was no game. When lawmakers were publicly crying out for King to take a position and show them the way, he wasn't being coy in his silence. Not even his closest advisers knew where he would come down on the issue. It wasn't until he scheduled the joint address that he let a small circle of staffers know which way he was leaning.

The political consequences for King were not insignificant. The shelf life of a New Hampshire governor was dreadfully short: a two-year term and nobody had ever served more than two terms. It was Powell's hubris in seeking a third that had lost him the nomination in the most recent election. Moreover, King was a Democratic Daniel in the Republican lions' den, as no Democrat had ever served more than one term as governor in the history of New Hampshire. State GOP leadership was openly calling his election a fluke and predicting that the proper order of things would be restored in 1964. (Given the state's demographics, if King wanted that second term, every registered Democrat in the Granite State could vote for him, and he would *still* need a slice of the Grand Old Party.)

The smart play for King would be to veto the bill, find common ground with the Republicans who controlled the General Court, and do nothing objectionable for the remainder of his term. Do not give people a reason to vote against you. Two-year terms leave little time for political wounds to heal or reputations to revive. King was — ironically — not a gambler, but he understood he would be gambling his political career on the sweepstakes.

WHILE HB 47 was being debated, correspondence to the governor's office was vociferous. It ran right down the middle — half for it, half against it.

Protestant church groups led the veto movement with a series of group votes and petitions. Wrote Hartley Grandin, executive secretary of the New Hampshire Council of Churches, "We recognize the decision is yours and pray that God will guide you in His infinite wisdom and patience with our human foibles." Another preacher quoted Proverbs: "Righteousness exalted a nation, but sin is a reproach to any people."

Among the secular opponents included newspaper publishers, attorneys, insurance agents, and the secretary of Dartmouth College. Some were liberal, some conservative. They cited many of the same concerns about morality and public image, and they denounced the "something-for-nothing" philosophy Pickett's bill would invite.

One Sweeps opponent went so far as to send a check for three dollars — the proposed price of a Sweeps ticket — to the state treasurer. "I am in favor of good education," she wrote. "[This] represents my fair share of the cost of education for this year. Please allow me the privilege of voluntarily supporting that in which I believe." A man predicted in a letter that children would "go hungry and be cold and sick because their parents will buy lottery tickets with the money that is needed for food and clothing."

The enemies of the Sweeps had a counterproposal: enact a sales tax. They argued it would be the responsible way for the state to meet its financial obligations and wouldn't come with the crime and woe that legalized gambling would.

One woman wrote to Governor King that she was "stunned and sickened" that New Hampshire would resort to gambling to educate its children. She prayed King would "see the error of his ways." In the same pile of mail came a letter from this same woman's husband, praising the idea of holding a sweepstakes. The man added a postscript: "Governor, don't answer this letter."

GOVERNOR WES POWELL had left King with a holdover state attorney general, William Maynard, a diehard Republican openly opposed to the sweepstakes. King trusted Maynard for nothing, so he tapped a private-sector attorney to be his legal counsel. Joseph Millimet was a Manchester attorney, a contemporary of King's, and someone who had been an advocate of left-leaning causes during the 1950s. He was four inches shorter than King and looked up at the governor through eyeglass frames the size of saucers.

At King's request, Millimet wrote an analysis of HB 47, saying the obstacles opponents enumerated against a sweepstakes were legitimate and troublesome. As the day of the House vote approached, King read the report over and over again, unsatisfied. Later confessing to a pang of guilt for doing so, King literally placed Millimet's well-researched memo in the bottom drawer of his desk and ignored it.

Kennedy had used a back channel to get out of the Cuban Missile Crisis. King was going to use Millimet as his own back channel.

5
The Noble Experiment

JOSEPH MILLIMET PULLED UP to a Tudor-style home in Pride's Crossing, Massachusetts — a property on a hundred-acre estate so opulent an automotive company used its exterior as the backdrop for a luxury car advertisement. The home was surrounded by a tall fence and floodlights for security. The grounds were also patrolled by a Doberman pinscher and a German shepherd.

The oral history of Millimet's visit has been passed down from lottery official to lottery official. The lawyer waited on tenterhooks for the homeowner to answer the bell. William Loeb III greeted him with a warm smile and a mild demeanor, almost shy. He was the opposite of his pugnacious persona. He had a smooth bald head and dark eyebrows, a bow tie affixed to his collar. His wife, in the middle of a needlepoint design, also said hello. Nackey Loeb (née Scripps-Gallowhur), Bill Loeb's third wife, was the heiress to the Scripps newspaper fortune.

Bill Loeb raised his arm and gestured for his guest to come in. In doing so, the flap of his jacket opened, and Millimet saw the holstered gun concealed within. The newspaper publisher escorted him to his personal office. There was no typewriter on the desk. Loeb dictated his famous editorials to a secretary. As Loeb sat, he removed the revolver from the holster and placed it respectfully on the desk. It was a snub-nosed Charter Arms .38. The man never went anywhere without it.

Millimet was taken aback by Loeb's hospitality and meek deportment. He had turned his mighty verbal artillery at Governor King (never shy of name-calling, Loeb often derided the governor as "King John"; King, however, was quite pleased with the moniker because of his love of Shakespeare), but was a perfect gentleman. Given Loeb's meddling in the 1962 elections, one could say he had as much to do with King's election as Kennedy did.

The publisher prompted the Democratic emissary to get on with the business. Millimet asked whether, if King were to sign the sweepstakes bill, the *Union Leader* would support it.

Loeb smiled. Now comes the lamb to lie down with the lion. It was another affirmation that he was the kingmaker, the true power in the state of New Hampshire.

AFTER REPORTING BACK favorably from Prides's Crossing, Millimet hopped a train for Union Station in Washington, D.C., for the first of two meetings with top federal officials about the lottery proposal. Millimet had met Jack Kennedy in 1960 when the senator kicked off his primary campaign in front of Nashua City Hall. The state did not have many Democratic sherpas, so Millimet's counsel was appreciated by the campaign. Bobby Kennedy did not attend the event so the two had never met.

Millimet was greeted in Washington by a man nearly a foot taller than him. Deputy Attorney General Nicholas Katzenbach, in a rumpled wool suit, towered over his visitor. Yet his demeanor was warm, not intimidating. Katzenbach, who was unquestionably RFK's right-hand man at Justice, had the perfect disposition to handle the thorny, sometimes violent, conflicts between federal and state law.[1]

Katzenbach said the main sticking point for the DOJ was interstate trafficking of tickets under the Paraphernalia and Travel Acts. Both sides agreed there was nothing illegal about a visitor to New Hampshire buying a ticket,

1. In 1962, Nicholas Katzenbach walked alongside James Meredith as fifteen hours of race riots broke out at Ole Miss. Katzenbach had to use a campus payphone to call the White House and request twenty-five thousand federal troops to calm the situation. Three months after meeting with Millimet, the world would see Katzenbach stand eyeball to eyeball with Governor George Wallace in the doorway of Alabama's Foster Auditorium, cajoling the segregationist to let black students register for classes. The *New York Times* called him a "courageous egghead." Colleagues at the Department of Justice described him as having sang-froid, French for "cold blood."

but Katzenbach was doubtful that a sweepstakes operation could live wholly within the dotted lines of the Granite State. Tickets would cross the border, be scalped by mobsters. He said the Organized Crime Division within the DOJ was certain that syndicates would attempt to get large numbers of New Hampshire Sweepstakes tickets — by purchase, theft, or counterfeiting — and sell them across the country. Efforts to bribe or intimidate state officials and employees to gain access to the operation were a near certainty. The honey would be too sweet to keep thugs from trying to gain a foothold among the players, the bookies, or the politicians who ran the lottery.

Katzenbach eventually agreed with Millimet that the lottery was a state matter and that the DOJ would not actively try to block implementation of the New Hampshire Sweepstakes. The assurances only went that far. The inference was the FBI would be watching how the operation came together and whether it veered from the extremely narrow path laid for it within the gauntlet of federal regulations.

Millimet next met with the Internal Revenue Service. The tax implications for individual lottery winners were clear — as they were with all lucky gamblers. The IRS provided an informal opinion that the state of New Hampshire itself would have to pay a 10 percent excise tax on the gross proceeds of the Sweepstakes, just as did casinos in Nevada. There was an exemption in the law for nonprofit organizations that raised money for educational purposes — such as church bingo halls — but the IRS was not willing to extend that exemption to the state. That 10 percent hit would throw off the revenue estimates for the lottery. Also, every state employee who sold Sweeps tickets would have to pay fifty dollars for a federal gambling tax stamp in order to work.

Millimet returned to New England on an evening train. He prepared a new thirteen-page memo to King describing the meetings and listing the challenges. "I am satisfied," he wrote, "that the Sweepstakes Bill (HB 47) can be administered without putting the state in direct conflict with federal law."

When HB 47 passed the House and seemed doomed in the Senate, Bill Loeb made good on his promised to support the sweepstakes. Loeb wrote a series of powerful editorials in favor of passage, even printing the phone numbers of all twenty-four state senators on the front page. "No one *has* to go to the track and bet. No one *has* to smoke tobacco. No one *has* to drink," he wrote. "But how do those who oppose the sweepstakes propose to raise the money? Either a sales tax or a property tax or some other kind of levy that people will *have* to pay, even though it will hurt them dreadfully to do so."

Thanks to Loeb, support for the bill shifted from 14–10 opposed to 13–11 in favor virtually overnight. Though he loved to peeve the milquetoast Republican establishment, he was allied with King on the sweepstakes because it was an anti-sales-tax measure. The bonus for Loeb was that the Sweeps would be a thorn in the side of the man he hated the most: John F. Kennedy.

JOHN KING HAD BEEN an early supporter of John Kennedy. King had been friends with Kennedy's older brother, the late Joseph Kennedy Jr., when the two were at Harvard, so he felt a personal affinity for the Kennedy clan. In 1956, King wrote to the Massachusetts senator urging him to run for president. His was the political equivalent of a fan letter, but coming from the New Hampshire House minority leader, it wasn't completely meaningless. Kennedy thanked King, but turned down the invitation to run because, he wrote, "I've already pledged my support for Governor [Adlai] Stevenson."

If King's letter did not leave its mark on Kennedy's heart, it did leave its mark in his Rolodex. In the summer of 1959, he wrote to see if the minority leader was still interested in helping him launch a presidential run. King responded enthusiastically, going so far as to steer him away from "some of our lukewarm Democrats who would do you inestimable harm." The Manchester labor lawyer also promised help in getting Kennedy union support in the state. The correspondence, supplemented with Kennedy's parenthetical notations, continued. Mr. and Mrs. King were among those who received a Christmas card from the senator's family in December 1959. It was hand-signed "Jack."

On January 20, 1960, Kennedy asked King to attend his maiden presidential campaign appearances in Manchester and Nashua the following week. JFK drew huge crowds to both communities' city halls and met both mayors. King and several local Dems tagged along for Kennedy's photo op: shaking hands with unionized workers at a Manchester sweater factory.

The lesson John Kennedy taught the New Hampshire Democratic Party was how to better organize and campaign, knowledge the party used to get King and U.S. Senator Tom McIntyre elected. During the 1962 state election, JFK asked for near-daily updates from New Hampshire, curious about King's prospects — and likely his own for 1964. After King was elected, the president sent him two signed portraits: "To Gov. John King, With highest esteem and very warm regard. John F. Kennedy."

Kennedy was the gold standard for a politician, but John King fashioned himself — openly and unembarrassedly — as a skinny Frank Skeffington from

Edwin O'Connor's book *The Last Hurrah*. King said any politician worth his salt, "especially an Irish politician," had to get around the way O'Connor's character did. He had to be affable and shake hands, every hand he could. Not content with covering the state's southern cities, King campaigned in the towns and hamlets north of the Lakes Region and the White Mountains. "No town too small," he declared. There were a dozen major state and county fairs scheduled in New Hampshire before Election Day. King was at every one of them. He genuinely loved the interaction.

After he took office, this practice continued. King would go to wakes, weddings, graduations, funerals, and confirmations — even bar mitzvahs — just to meet people and press flesh. He'd go to a Rotary lunch or an Eagle Scout ceremony, or walk soberly through a social club, and shake hands. King would take a drink "now and then," but he never overdid it, so his wits would remain sharp. "John me boy," the old Irish buckos would call to him, slapping him on the back as if each has personally raised him from a babe. He visited churches that would have gotten a Catholic of lesser prestige excommunicated or beaten up (by his own Irish neighbors). He estimated he traveled nine hundred miles each week to get from this thing to that, Anna's picnic lunches somewhere in the car. King told *This Week* magazine he shook so many hands that for days later he'd complain to Anna about pain in the tender muscles of his palm and thumb.

His longstanding admiration for JFK was a driving motivator for John King. As the son of a shoemaker, he did not have Kennedy's pedigree. With his avuncular looks, King did not have Kennedy's sex appeal either. Pulitzer Prize–winner Red Smith of the *New York Herald Tribune* said, "[King] doesn't look like a bookie. He looks bookish . . . about medium tall and medium wide, with four eyes and enough hair. He is a long-vest man, possibly because New Hampshire has winters." King was, however, the biggest star New Hampshire Democrats had. He had to carry that torch. The reverie of the New Frontier bewitched him. The boldness of something like the sweepstakes seemed both visionary and achievable. With President Kennedy leading the country, anything could happen.

WHILE THE SWEEPS BILL sat on his desk awaiting either his signature or veto, King greeted a large contingent of Protestant ministers who called on his office. The governor was gracious and let every pastor who wanted to speak do so. He smiled, shook every hand, and then excused himself. The preachers told the newspaper scribes waiting in the hallway that King was polite but noncommittal. King sat at his desk knowing if he didn't veto the bill he'd lose the support of the traditional Protestants — but the Irish Catholic governor questioned whether he'd ever had their support to begin with.

The letters and telegrams to the statehouse were split evenly between passage and veto. Each one received was stamped with an office seal in blue ink and put on King's desk. A three-page missive from Edward DeCourcy, the editor of the *Argus-Champion* newspaper in Newport, went to the top of the pile. DeCourcy had been opining against the lottery for months. With the self-importance of any decent media mogul, DeCourcy wrote King because he felt he owed the governor an explanation of his position.

After doing his best Robert Frost describing the beauty of New Hampshire, DeCourcy lectured about the detriment to the state's children's morals and education by funding schools with gambling money. DeCourcy defended himself — from charges never actually made — as someone whose duty it was to frighten the people about communism, discrimination, inferior health care, and a whole host of evils that faced the nation.

"I don't know that the sweepstakes will fail in New Hampshire. I do know that the previous 1,371 recorded government lotteries in the United States failed," DeCourcy wrote. "I don't know that the sweepstakes will breed crime in New Hampshire. I do know that lotteries have always bred crime. I don't know that gangsters will muscle in on our lottery. I do know they always have."

Newport's *Argus-Champion* (circulation 2,926) was hardly the *Washington Post*, but it underscored another complication for the governor. Along with the churches, King knew he would lose much of the press if he okayed the lottery. The editorials would put the bull's-eye on him instead of Pickett. Campaign endorsements would be off the table.

Yet instead of the editorials, King's eyes scanned Joseph Millimet's final report from Washington. He did this repeatedly in the days leading up to his sweepstakes decision and speech. The report didn't tip the scales; it only added weight to both sides.

KING ANNOUNCED he would address the General Court on Tuesday, April 30, 1963, about the bill. Finally, the question of the sweepstakes in New Hampshire was raised at the White House on Friday, April 26, 1963. Responding to queries from reporters, Kennedy's press secretary, Pierre Salinger, simply stated, "I think that would be a matter for the State of New Hampshire."

The front-page headline in the *Nashua Telegraph* read, "President in Hands

Off Policy on Sweeps," with a subhead, "Salinger Says Lottery State Problem." The bold type was longer than the actual statement. Could anything remain in King's way?

In the Sunday newspapers, the pendulum swung back the other way. Forty-eight hours before the speech, someone finally claimed to get Attorney General Robert Kennedy's position on the New Hampshire Sweepstakes. Gwen Gibson of the *New York Daily News* got the scoop for her weekend column. She described RFK's position as "an emphatic 'no dice' policy stand" against a government sponsored lottery. Although no quotes were directly attributed to RFK (so the legitimacy of the reporting remains dubious), he allegedly said that "racketeers might infiltrate any government-backed lottery" no matter how stiff the local controls were. He said more than $50 billion was collected each year in underworld gambling, and a "lottery racket . . . is small potatoes" that wouldn't even be missed by the syndicate. Gibson's conclusion was that Justice intended a crackdown on any lottery and would "let the chips fall where they may."

Just when it looked like the Sweeps would get a pass from the feds, Washington contradicted itself again. The clouded crystal ball of politics had finally shattered.

TELEVISION CAMERAS from around the nation were wheeled into the House chamber for King's announcement. The back of the room was filled with cables that snaked through the representatives' cloakroom and out a window. An extra two dozen chairs were arranged in the front for the members of the state Senate.

Larry Pickett watched the pageantry and drank it in. Ten years of arm-twisting had brought the cause this far. All around him, the faces of sweepstakes opponents were twisted in anxiety.

The sergeant-at-arms announced the arrival of "His Excellency, the Governor," and the General Court rose to its feet. King entered the chamber from a door at the front of the room to the right of the speaker's rostrum.

"I come here this morning," King began, "to discuss with you in detail a serious piece of legislation recently approved by your membership and sent to my office for signature.

"A few minutes ago — in my office — I signed House Bill 47!"

The room exploded into cheers. Colleagues were slapping Pickett on the back and shoulders. He looked serene. He acknowledged a nod from the governor but otherwise made no sign of triumph. A good actor knows not to upstage the star of the show.

Seizing on the moment of legislative euphoria, King reminded the body that the sweepstakes belonged to both Democrats and Republicans, both the legislative and the executive branch. They all had a stake in seeing the lottery through and ensuring its success: "[We] must turn our minds and wills to the task of making the first state-operated sweepstakes in this country one that will be conducted honestly, efficiently, and in compliance with the laws of the United States Government."

King told lawmakers what Millimet had learned in Washington. The governor was open about the preliminary IRS opinion regarding the 10 percent excise tax, though he was confident a sweepstakes that raised money for education would fall within the exemption. He told the legislators he was convinced after Millimet's conversation with Katzenbach at the DOJ that it would be perfectly legal for residents and nonresidents to buy tickets and collect their prizes.

The details of selling tickets and operating the lottery would be left to the commission, King said, though he pledged the sweepstakes would not "reflect discredit" on the state: "We must make certain that the commissioners who will administer this law are men of unquestioned probity and rare judgment and courage. I am confident that such men are available."

King spoke for thirty minutes. Toward the end, he said he felt he owed the people an explanation for why he had signed the law. "I have not been unmoved," he said, "by the messages from many sincere people in our state who have deep convictions against this legislation. I have respect for those who have an honest, sincere concern about the morality of this action although I do not agree with them."

He said he believed the sweepstakes represented the will of the majority. The demands on schools were increasing while people were "already carrying a cross of taxation unequalled in American history." The people had asked for this voluntary method of raising revenue, this noble experiment, so he let it be so.

"I am unwilling to set myself up as a Solomon or a Caesar in the holy assumption that my views are more intelligent or discerning or moralistic than those of our people," King said. "Therefore, let the debate be ended. Let us assume the responsibility that has been thrust upon us and put forth our greatest effort to make this new venture a success."

The hall erupted again. King smiled and — having thoroughly disrupted the status quo — disappeared through the side door.

The New Hampshire Sweepstakes was off.

KING WOULD LATER SAY that though the Sweeps mail he received was 50/50 for and against passage of the bill, the people he met were overwhelmingly in favor of the plan. While gripping his cramped hand, they slapped him on the shoulder. "Sign it, me boy," they told him. He felt he'd heard what the people really wanted.

Before signing the bill, more than 1,000 letters flooded the governor's office. According to King, after it became law, another 506 letters, telegrams, and postcards came in. There were 460 messages of congratulations and encouragement. Only 46 letters were against.

"HALLELUJAH, HALLELUJAH, HALLELUJAH," began a letter written on the stationary from the U.S. post office in Whitefield. "There are ten of us here in this office and every one of them want me to express their thanks to you for the signing of the bill." The local postmaster crowed that she won a bet with her state representative over whether King would pass the sweepstakes. An employee at the New Hampshire Air Traffic Control Center wrote, "It is pleasing to know that we have a man in office with a realistic approach to our tax problems."

The majority of the letters of commendation came from out of state. Legislators from other states and Canada asked for copies of the bill and advice on passing their own lottery.

Despite the revelry, problems were immediately forming. From around the country, mail stuffed with money was delivered to the statehouse. King was like Midas at the end of the story. Dollar bills were falling into his lap, but he couldn't keep them. The state had no tickets to sell, no commissioners or staff, and attorney Joseph Millimet had already warned him that using the mail to promote a lottery would bring federal officials down on them. They weren't even sure if they could mail the money back without breaking the law. King had sworn the Sweeps would be run honestly and within the law, but no one had figured out exactly how they'd walk that tightrope. Yet more cash and checks kept coming every day.

"Here is $3 for a New Hampshire Sweepstakes ticket," wrote one advocate. "But please don't tell my husband I bought it. He wouldn't like it unless I won." Another letter said, "Anything's better than more taxes — here's $6."

Of all the fan mail he received, King had one favorite letter. It was sent by air mail from 9601 Wilshire Boulevard, Beverly Hills, and it praised him for the "courage and common sense" to sign the bill. "What this country needs is more governors like you. [signed] Groucho Marx."

"I have always wanted an Irish Sweepstakes ticket," said another writer, referring to the famous horserace-slash-lottery that was the blueprint for the New Hampshire Sweeps, "but have never been able to find anyone who could sell to me."

Curiously, a letter came to the governor by international post. All that was written on the paper was, "Please send me a sweepstakes ticket."

Attached to the letter was an Irish pound note.

6

The Greatest
Bleeding Hearts
Racket
in the World

THERE WERE FEW BETTER EXAMPLES than the Irish National Sweepstake for the casual American gambler to use as a reference point for the proposed New Hampshire Sweeps.[1] Even those who never purchased a ticket were familiar with the Gaelic operation. Tales of common folk on both sides of the Atlantic winning outrageous amounts of money had been celebrated in the press since the Depression.

Shortly after postal laws forced the Louisiana Lottery to Honduras, Congress passed supplemental legislation banning the importation of tickets into the country. Irish Sweep tickets were therefore illegal in the United States, but officials generally tolerated them. Governor King had been shrewd to cite the Irish Sweep as the template for New Hampshire's lottery. The major difference: the New Hampshire Sweeps would be legal.

The Irish Sweep's proscription rarely bothered the American press. Newspapers and movie reels relished the human-interest story of sweepstake winners who hit it big. What made a better photo than a middle-aged millionaire who was missing his front teeth? In a 1936 Fox Movietone newsreel, a group of newly minted winners from across the country was featured. They included several families assembled in their parlors, nervously twid-

1. In Ireland the event was generally referred to in the singular form of "Sweepstake" or "Sweep," although American players and journalists often used the plural forms of the words.

dling fingers or bouncing their legs. A group of ladies from the steno pool who had won told the camera the money meant wedding bells wouldn't be far off.

The highlight of the report was a New York family appearing in front of a bank of ancient microphones. George Curry's dog, Chicky, had won $150,000. Calculated for inflation, the prize would be worth $2.5 million today.

"Listen folks. Us winning this money isn't gonna give us a swell head," Curry said in a voice that sounded like Lou Costello's. "We are gonna be the same friends that we always was and we're going to speak to Joe the iceman and everybody on 87th street the same as we always did."

For thirty years, people in the English-speaking world looking to hit it big dreamed of their name coming up in the far-away Irish Sweepstake. Larry Pickett's masterstroke was to shift the legal gambling debate in New Hampshire away from a numbers-based lottery (associated in the United States with the Mob) to a similarly exciting horserace.

AS IN NEW HAMPSHIRE, the Irish Sweep's purpose was to help a charitable cause. Proceeds were to go to the Irish National Hospital and several other medical facilities.

Tickets for the Irish Hospitals' Sweepstake were ten shillings, or, $2.50. Many friends and office workers pooled their money to afford chances, and groups of connected winners were not uncommon. There were long lines to buy tickets at Irish banks and retail shops.

Chances came in books of twelve that looked like ordinary raffle tickets. Players would fill out their names and addresses on the top part, or counterfoil, of a ticket and tear off the bottom part. The counterfoil was sent to the private company running the lottery, Hospital Trust, LTD. Its head was the former Irish minister of labor Joseph McGrath, and the company kept 6 percent of the profits after expenses.

Outside of the Republic of Ireland, ticket agents roamed taverns, movie theaters, train stations, hotels, and dance halls in the United States, Great Britain, and Canada. They employed discretion, but it wasn't hard for anyone who wanted a chance to buy one. Although the sale of tickets of the Irish Sweep was banned in the United Kingdom (including the six counties in Northern Ireland), a huge number of chances were mailed in from the North. All told, the roguish Irish had the pluck to sneak tickets in and out of the fifty nations where lotteries were banned.

The first Irish Sweepstake was run in conjunction with the Manchester Handicap in November 1930. On the drawing day, a week before the horse-race, the Hospital Trust put on a show for the masses worthy of Louisiana's General P. G. T. Beauregard himself. A parade snaked its way through Dublin, white-starched hospital nurses waving to the crowd. Containers of hundreds of thousands of tickets received hearty cheers on their way to the Mansion House for selection. Sweep Day in Dublin was like St. Patrick's Day in New York.

To select winners, nurses dumped the counterfoils in a drum the size of a small submarine. Four blind children from St. Joseph's School in Drumcondra pulled the names of lucky players from one drum and matched them with names of horses drawn from another. The boys were rewarded with boxes of chocolate. The Garda (police) supervised the drawing, and the commissioner verified for the press that the children were — in fact — blind.

Sixty percent of winners of the first Irish Sweepstake resided outside of Ireland, with several from England, Scotland, Canada, and the United States. First prize of £202,764 (roughly $4.6 million today) went to a civil servant from Northern Ireland — a karmic slap in the face to the Crown — who split his winnings among the several people to whom he had sold ticket shares as a hedge.

The lottery raked in £666,000 in total sales. The six beneficiary hospitals received £135,000. £100,000 went as commission to the agents and bonuses to those who sold winning tickets. After paying related expenses, McGrath and the Hospital Trust promoters pocketed £46,000.

The Sweep's success was so amazing, the Hospital Trust held another four months later.

The ridiculous popularity of the Sweepstake continued to grow, both in Ireland and abroad. According to Marie Colman's *The Irish Sweep,* in its second year, 1931, more than £4 million in tickets were sold. During the 1930s (the height of the Depression), 142 million tickets were sold, bringing in £71 million.

The clamor from other hospitals to get in on the game was intense. The proceeds were soon reallocated by the Irish government to spread the wealth. New health facilities were built in remote areas of the country. Modern medicines and treatments for tuberculosis, fever, and psychiatric issues came to the Free State. The Sweep was such an audacious operation its reach dwarfed the Louisiana Golden Octopus by one-hundred fold. How in the world could a small group of capitalists in the impoverished nation of Ireland run such a profitable competition?

JOE MCGRATH, the head of the Hospital Trust, was a millionaire by 1935 thanks to the Sweep. He was the wealthiest, most powerful man in Ireland and purchased some of the most profitable businesses in the nation, including the Irish Glass Bottle Company, Donegal Carpet, and Waterford Crystal. He was the closest thing to a "godfather" on the Emerald Isle. It wasn't until the 1970s that the extent of the Irish Sweepstake's corruption became fully known.

Bookmaker Richard Duggan had started the Sweep in 1921 as a way to raise money for Irish sailors lost in the First World War. Encouraged by its modest success, he held another unofficial sweepstake in 1922 for Dublin's Mater Hospital, and the lottery's popularity grew each year. Duggan's organization never ran its own horserace, but rather wagered on major English or Irish races.

McGrath and Captain Spencer Freeman approached Duggan about expanding the lottery and making it legitimate. (Despite a long historical embrace of the game in Great Britain and Ireland, lotteries had been outlawed in 1823.) McGrath used his influence in the Oireachtas (the Irish legislature) to pass the Public Charitable Hospitals Act in 1930. This made the Sweep legal in Ireland — but *only* in Ireland. Meantime, the triumvirate formed the Irish Hospital Trust. They all knew that bringing the Sweep to the next level meant bringing the affair to the United Kingdom and United States. McGrath knew just how to do it.

A BIT OF IRISH HISTORY is important to this tale. Young Joseph McGrath had been working at an accounting firm with Michael Collins, the future George Washington of the Irish Free State movement. They were both nationalists, looking for Irish autonomy and separation from the British Empire. In 1916, they were both members of the Irish Citizens Army as the Easter Rising marked the beginnings of the rebellion. Collins and McGrath were captured, imprisoned, and later released.

The insurgents of the 1919 Irish War of Independence longed for a self-governing Irish Republic, an island free of British rule. As war gave rise to the Irish Republican Army, Michael Collins became the IRA's director of intelligence and then rose to the position of senior military commander. McGrath was part of his inner circle and funded the cause by sticking up banks across Ireland.

By 1921, the IRA had made little progress toward independence, was nearly out of ammunition, and had fought to a stalemate with the British. But English leaders in Parliament had grown weary of this war of attrition and pressured the prime minister to offer a truce. On behalf of the rebels, Collins was instructed to go to London to work out a treaty.

The proposal created the Irish Free State.[2] It gave dominion status to the nation (similar to Great Britain's relationship with Canada), but it partitioned the island. The six northern counties that were predominately Protestant and considered themselves loyalists to the Crown would remain part of the United Kingdom. The treaty deeply divided the insurgents. Some, including Collins and McGrath, pragmatically saw the treaty as the best the rebels were going to get. Others, the "Republicans," would settle for nothing less than a complete withdrawal of the British from island as a whole. This division led to a year-long civil war between the pro-treaty "Free Staters" and their former brothers in the IRA.

Collins, the face of the Irish Free State, was ambushed and assassinated on August 22, 1922. That very day Joe McGrath took over the position of director of intelligence for the new National Army and tortured captured Republicans in reprisal. The atrocities escalated on both sides. In 1923, after the capture of a valuable IRA leader, the antitreaty forces agreed to withdraw. The Free Staters had won. Dozens of IRA POWs were executed at McGrath's command.

McGrath took the position of labor minister with the Irish Free State, but he resigned in 1924. Although a Free Stater, McGrath was discouraged the new government was not pursuing the ultimate goal both sides had fought for: a completely independent Irish Republic. McGrath reestablished contact with his old IRA comrades, and by moving money and arms in and out of the country, he supported an ongoing guerilla war aimed at pushing the English out of Northern Ireland.

McGrath surrounded himself with "hard men" — a personal goon squad to do his bidding in business, politics, or otherwise. As uncovered in Paul McMahon's *British Spies and Irish Rebels*, MI5, the British Security Service, described McGrath's crew as "a private army of a number of the worst thugs and gunmen produced by the IRA in the troubled times." The agency's surveillance dossier said McGrath was prone to bouts of extremely heavy drinking, up to six weeks at a time, followed by periods of abstinence. When feeling religious, he would go to mass daily and do works for charity. He was self-made, confident, and shrewd. He was undeniably dangerous.

2. After the 1937 constitution, the country's name was changed to the Republic of Ireland.

WHEN IT CAME TO THE CHALLENGE of bootlegging Sweep tickets in and out of Ireland, McGrath already had a network in place. He would use the same methods and the same people he had used to move cash, arms, documents, and supplies to the IRA. It was a sophisticated web connecting Ireland with sympathizers in England and North America.

In the decades after the Irish Civil War, right up to the Good Friday Peace Accord in the mid-1990s, Irish-Americans surreptitiously sent millions of dollars to the Republicans to continue their fight with British forces in the North. Some of the cash was raised publicly as relief for the families of political prisoners. Some was given under the table from Catholic benefactors. What was hardly suspected over the years was how much overlap existed between the machinations of the IRA and the Irish Sweepstake.

The flow of Sweepstake tickets across the Atlantic, like IRA money and supplies, took various routes. Many tickets were smuggled via transport ship out of either Ireland or England. Montreal was the Northwest Passage of choice, but many tickets also found their way to piers in Boston and New York. Smugglers received £10 for every thousand tickets that made it to the United States or Canada. Agents got ten shillings for each book of twelve sold.

The tickets were smuggled the way IRA rifles and ammunition had been smuggled: packed inside coffins and laundry sacks on ships crossing the Irish Sea or the Atlantic Ocean. Sweep agents bribed sailors, police, customs agents, and longshoremen on both sides of the water.

A famous anecdote from this period involves a ticket agent who was arrested in New York at Pier 16 awaiting the Irish shipping vessel that would smuggle him home. The police found him with a fat stack of cash and a pile of counterfoils. The next day in court, he was hit with a heavy fine then released. The story went that the agent walked out of the courthouse whistling a merry tune. While he had been in lockup the night before, several Irish-American cops had copied the names on the counterfoils onto official police stationary and returned them to the agent. Due to the circumstances, the Sweepstake office in Dublin accepted them as bona fide entries.

For its part, the U.S. Post Office Department (as it was known before 1971) was aggressive about intercepting suspicious mail addressed to Ireland. In the early years, more than 1 million pieces of international mail was stamped "return to sender." Americans who were in the know could purchase tickets by mailing money to a number of dummy addresses in Ireland. Agents unable to ferry homeward also used these addresses to forward money and counterfoils to headquarters. This was another old IRA trick employed by McGrath. One of the fake addresses was an office in the Department of Taoiseach (the prime minister's department).

The post office in Dublin originally felt the need to police letters sent to the Hospital Trust that were illegally mailed abroad. This made the IRA drop points critical; however, many postal employees on the take would simply forward that mail directly to the Sweepstake headquarters anyway. Soon the Irish Post Office took the position that if Sweep mail was illegal in foreign countries, then it was the responsibility of those nations to screen their own mail. They left lottery correspondence alone.

After President Roosevelt appointed Irish-American Jim Farley to the position of Post Master General in 1933, sniffing out Sweep tickets ceased to be a priority. According to Coleman's book, Farley visited Dublin and openly had meetings with McGrath and associates. He even had his picture taken next to the ticket wheel at the 1936 Sweep. Years later, Ed Sullivan would say on his TV show that the best place to buy an Irish Sweepstake ticket was at the counter of the New York Central Post Office.

THE MAIN PLAYERS in the Sweepstake operation in the United States were all connected to the Irish resistance. Connie Neenan was the de facto leader of the IRA in America during the 1930s, and he was responsible for selling thousands of tickets in New York and Chicago. The tickets, proceeds, and IRA supplies all traveled through the same underground railroad Neenan conducted.

Sales in Philadelphia were handled by Joseph McGarrity, a failed industrialist saved financially by his role in the Irish Sweep. McGarrity claimed he gave the IRA £250,000 that he made from selling tickets. His favorite ploy was to occasionally tip off friends in law enforcement when a shipment of counterfoils was heading back to Ireland. If the feds snatched a few thousand tickets, it was no big loss. The players never held it against sellers if their chances got pinched, but in fact all those missing counterfoils, never documented by the Dublin office, were 100 percent profit for McGarrity, McGrath, and company.

Captain Spenser Freeman's brother, Sidney, was a bookie who had emigrated from London to the United States. He set up a Sweep office in New York's Ritz Carlton. There, he ran a scam as old as the Italian lotteries. Freeman would get early word by telegram of stateside Sweep winners, then he'd call them, posing as a broker who offered to buy a share of the player's ticket as a hedge. These winning shares stayed off the books and went right into the coffers of the Hospital Trust.

The only real competition the Irish Sweep had for the lottery dollar was, in essence, itself. The Sweep was popular but underground. Tickets were easy to counterfeit, as few people had seen enough of them to know the real thing. Any piece of parchment with a portrait of a lass would do. In America, Mob bookies sold "Sweep" tickets that had never spent a day in Dublin. Reselling losing tickets from old races was also a common ploy. What few complaints there were about the Sweep tickets had not to do with illegal gambling but with the prospect of being suckered by someone selling phony chances or tickets to a previous race. Even this sleight of hand benefited the Fenians. Nervous American gamblers just wanted to know the brokers were really with the Irish Sweepstake and not local racketeers. Suspicious of stateside con men, players never worried the Irish were ripping them off too.

BY THE END OF THE 1930S, the Hospital Trust employed four thousand people. The Trust building was the largest single office in the world, covering four acres. Someone walking from end to end of the office complex would cover an eighth of a mile. About a thousand employees, mostly women, spent their days handling tickets. Returned counterfoils from ticket books distributed to 190 counties were placed in a compressed air tank to be mixed and scrambled for three days.

Eventually the Hospital Trust's political power grew to match the size of its financial operation. As a revolving number of parties took control of the government, calls inevitably came to reduce the Trust's 6 percent fee. McGrath, however, had stacked the company's board of directors with captains of industry, government ministers, and influential citizens who always quelled the cry by making the case that McGrath's secret international trafficking network was expensive to maintain.

This claim was not true. Cash was king, but most bribes were given in the form of free Sweepstake tickets. Free tickets were not counted against sales figures, so keeping an army of smugglers, agents, and disinterested law enforcers was an invisible expense. When actual money was handed out, these co-conspirators were listed as "underwriters" in the Trust's accounting journals. And — predictably — the Hospital Trust had two sets of books. What its illegal take over the decades was can never be accurately calculated.

While they undoubtedly benefited from the Sweepstake, Irish hospitals were the biggest victims of the perpetual fraud. Once hospitals received their slice of the pie, the government took 25 percent of their windfall as a stamp tax (the for-profit Hospital Trust was exempt from taxation). It's estimated that only about 10 percent of the proceeds raised in the Irish Sweep went to the National Hospital and associated health-care facilities. Decades before the Irish press would shine light on the twisted inner workings of the scheme, *Readers Digest* called the Irish Sweepstake "the greatest bleeding hearts racket in the world."

HAD THE SINS of the Irish Sweepstake been known to the world, it's unlikely that Larry Pickett's idea would have found support. Surely it would have taken away the pro-lottery advocates' best talking point. While the Hospital Trust pulled its shenanigans, the press and the gaming community saw it as the best legally run gambling operation on the planet.

There were the two lessons Governor John King learned from the Irish Sweep.

First, between 1930 and 1963, the U.S. federal government had successfully prosecuted only one person in connection with the Sweep. He was charged with not purchasing the required fifty-dollar gambling tax stamp (the same stamp Uncle Sam now wanted each New Hampshire Sweeps ticket seller to purchase). This meant the feds had historically gone after ticket *sellers*, not ticket *buyers*. As the sellers, the state of New Hampshire already knew what it was in for, but the specter of buyer arrests would potentially have had much greater effect, scaring away many out-of-state players.

Second, 1961 ticket sales of the Irish Sweepstake reached a record £6.1 million, the majority of which came from outside the tiny island. There was a market for this kind of lottery even in regions where ticket sales were prohibited, and New Hampshire could tap that market.

What King could not have known was that it wasn't pluck that got all those slips in and out of Ireland. In that way, he was as blind as those four little boys from Drumcondra. It took a Joseph McGrath to build and maintain a matrix of shady channels to turn the wheels, skimming off the top as he went. And New Hampshire did not have a Joseph McGrath.

The New Hampshire lottery would need its own godfather to guide it through the electrified maze of federal regulations if the state was going to fulfill the promise to run the sweepstakes openly and honestly. It needed the exact opposite, ethically, of Joe McGrath, but the same results.

"No legislature can bargain away the public health or the public morals. [L]otteries . . . are a species of gambling, and wrong in their influences. They disturb the checks and balances of a well-ordered community. Society built on such a foundation would almost of necessity bring forth a population of speculators and gamblers, living on the expectation of what, 'by the casting of lots, or by lot, chance, or otherwise,' might be 'awarded' to them from the accumulations of others."

Chief Justice Morrison Waite, *Stone v. Mississippi*, 1879

Part Two
SEE HOW THEY RUN

7
This Shabby Dodge

ON THE MORNING OF MAY 5, 1963, the Sunday following the governor's signing of the sweepstakes bill, church bells tolled mournfully, calling the faithful to services. The day was warmer than usual. At the Congregational Church of Laconia, the peals melded with those from the Catholic Church up the street and echoed across Lake Winnisquam. The Congregationalists filed in and selected a seat among the mahogany pews the way Yankees do: searching for one with considerable room so as not to sit too close to a person on either side.

The Reverend Eric Bascom led the group through the usual hymns and scripture readings until he got to the Gospel. Bascom read from Mathew 27 — the story of how Judas hanged himself. Being just two weeks past Easter and the end of Lent, the passage may have seemed slightly dated.

"I want to tell you about the thirty pieces of silver that Judas got for betraying Jesus," Bascom said from the indigo-colored pulpit, an American flag perched over his right shoulder. He said that historians had pondered for centuries what became of the many artifacts of the Crucifixion — the cross, the burial robes, the Last Supper chalice, and the bowl in which Pontius Pilate washed his hands of the whole thing. Others have wondered what happened to those silver coins. The Bible said Judas threw them back at the feet of the high priests who recruited him in Christ's capture. When they refused to take the money back, Judas hanged himself from a tree in a potter's field. The coins were now considered "blood money" and could not be allowed into the Temple treasury. The priests then bought the field to create a cemetery, and the thirty pieces of silver changed hands once again.

"But these same pieces of silver have entered into legend," Bascom said, adding that some believed these same coins in the Old Testament had been given to Joseph's brothers to sell the boy into Egyptian slavery. After Judas's suicide, they were used to pay for the execution of Paul the apostle in Rome. The silver was then said to have traveled westward and rewarded the men who burned Joan of Arc at the stake, then turned up again and again at times of dark sin and betrayal. Bascom was describing a handful of coins that spanned history, saying "pleased to meet you; hope you guessed my name."

"Evidently these thirty pieces of silver possess an amazing staying power, and an astonishing ability to adapt themselves to the particular circumstances of any historical situation," he continued. "Sometimes they appear to be merely thirty in number, but in recent weeks in New Hampshire we have watched them multiply in the public mind until we have come to see them look more like four million pieces of silver." The minister said the price of betrayal this time was the promise of a better education for the state's children, and again the governor washed his hands clean of the deed. "One begins to wonder," he said, "whether there is anything which these thirty pieces of silver cannot do or any moral principle they cannot destroy."

Rev. Bascom's voice became louder and louder as he preached. The silver pieces bought the silence of good men, the "neck-preservers." It persuaded clear-visioned men to keep still. Victory for the Sweeps bill was not just a defeat for the Protestant work ethic, but a call to arms for Christians: "Gone are the days when we can assume that the Church has no role in political affairs, if such days ever existed. Gone the way of the dinosaur and the dodo bird is the cloistered life of the Christian congregation, which was based on the premise that as long as the Church could have its stained glass windows and beautiful music, its well-filled sanctuaries and up-to-date buildings, it could consider itself successful and effective in the modern world." The faces gazing back at him came alive as he spoke. "Coming too are the days when Christians must see much more clearly than they have up until now, their special responsibility in getting the right people to run for public office and in working directly to elect them."

Throughout New Hampshire, in homilies and sermons and *derashot*, priests and preachers and rabbis were offering variations on the same theme. They'd been had. The sweepstakes was either the fault of Satan or the men who didn't oppose it. They'd been brought to their knees, but now they rose in unison. The Christian soldiers were being mobilized as they rarely were outside of the Bible Belt. It was a baptism by fire.

"I don't really know what happened to the thirty pieces of silver that once belonged to Judas," Bascom mournfully intoned, "but I do know what happened to Judas."

Onward . . .

"In the name of God, Amen."

"IN NOMINE PATRIS, *et Filii, et Spiritus Sancti. Amen.*"

Sitting in St. Anne Church, awash in a Latin mix of Catholic *Kýrie eléisons* and *Dominus vobiscum*s, Governor John King never heard Bascom's sermon (though it later arrived in a letter). His parish priest was too polite to draw undue attention to the Kings during a homily. After mass, King could read the Sunday papers though, and the preachers on the editorial papers were calling him the "biggest bookie in the country."

Meanwhile interest in New Hampshire's "noble experiment" continued to grow at an exponential rate. Letters and checks and dollar bills were piling up at the statehouse, and King needed to get a sweepstakes commission created and have them open an office. They had to harness and direct the surge before they either drowned in it or it evaporated.

A major oversight in Pickett's bill was that, while empowering a sweepstakes commission to fund itself through proceeds of the lottery, it did not include any sort of appropriation to start up the operation. King feared it would mean the commissioners would personally incur all the expenses — hundreds of thousands of dollars in liability at the minimum — before a single ticket was ever sold. In his speech to the General Court, King instructed lawmakers to include a line item in the budget for the sweepstakes and stated that he would not appoint a commission until this was done. They complied. King nominated two Republicans and one Democrat in late June, and on July 1, 1963, the state's new two-year $97 million state budget went into effect.

The governor had promised the three men (and he did say "men") selected to run the sweepstakes would be "of unquestioned probity and rare judgment and courage." He nominated to the Sweepstakes Commission Henry Turcotte and Edward Sanel. Turcotte was the general manager of the Associated Grocers of New Hampshire. Sanel ran a highly successful business selling auto parts and industrial equipment. He was a benefactor to many causes, including having established a Boys Club in the state capital. Both men had strong ties and good reputations among the business community and were ubiquitous figures at chamber of commerce and industry gatherings in Southern New Hampshire.

King selected Howell Shepard to be chairman of the three-man panel. Shepard had been a House representative in the General Court and was a longtime member of the state Racing Commission and a retired chemical manufacturer. Pickett's five sweepstakes bills had all granted authority for running the lottery to Shepard's Racing Commission, including the 1963 measure that passed the House, but the state Senate proposed creating a new entity dedicated exclusively to overseeing a sweepstakes. Ironically, Representative Shepard had opposed the earlier sweeps bills until Pickett made some "house-keeping changes" to it. When the new commission was created, Shepard was happy to move over. It seemed he had always been destined to guide the sweepstakes.

Shepard was a tall man, bespectacled, and had a shock of healthy white hair that underscored his sixty-seven years. He had a grandfather's smile and was well liked by those in Concord. The governor may have felt he was installing a stately figurehead, but Shepard hustled behind the scenes to a degree not generally remembered by those who know the New Hampshire lottery's origins.

The standard term of a state commissioner was three years, but King was wary of seeing the entire panel retire at the same time. The governor staggered their terms, appointing Sanel for one year, Turcotte for two, and Shepard for three, ensuring some level of continuity as the lottery moved forward.

While the commission was the political overseer of the fledgling operation, the sweepstakes still did not have an executive director or a staff of any kind. There was no dedicated office until someone finagled an empty room for them in the statehouse. More importantly, no one was clearly responsible for working out the details of running the sweepstakes free and clear of federal complications.

Major problems faced the sweepstakes that needed to be solved. The short list of questions that needed to be answered immediately was as follows:

By what mechanism would players purchase tickets?

How could players legally take their tickets across state lines?

How much would the grand prize and runner-up prizes be?

How would prizes be paid to winners from out of state?

With restrictions on the mail, how would the sweepstakes notify winners?

What venues of advertisement were legally open to the Sweeps?

How could scalping of tickets by third parties be quashed?

What measures were needed to ensure proper handling, storing, and accounting for hundreds of thousands of tickets?

Would the threat of a federal 10 percent excise tax bump ticket prices to $3.30, or would the state absorb the cost, resulting in lower profits?

Could the state make the case to the IRS that it should be exempt from the 10 percent excise tax and the $50-per-employee tax stamp?

What would be done to prevent criminal infiltration in sweepstakes operations?

Who would be their Joe McGrath, the one who would solve these problems and run the lottery in the manner Governor King promised?

Of course, all of these questions would become moot if local voters rejected the Sweeps in the local referendum only nine months away.

JOHN KING HAD SIGNED the sweepstakes bill saying, "Let the debate be ended." But for those still opposed to the idea of a government-run gambling operation, the debate was just under way. Editorial writers had sharpened their pencils, some still in disbelief that such a questionable piece of legislation was expected to become law. The governor had done little to curb their fear that New Hampshire would rue its plan. For months, news clippings came in from all corners bemoaning the effort.

The majority of New Hampshire newspapers stood against the Sweeps, even as it slowly rolled forward. "We expect [the sweepstakes] will be proven at some future time to have been a tragic mistake," said the *Union and Rockingham County Gazette*.

The *Enfield Advocate* lamented, "New Hampshire is sure to get a bad name out of the Sweeps."

"The state asked for trouble," claimed the *Concord Daily Monitor*.

"We wonder about the long range effects on public morality," wrote *Granite State News*.

"[The sweepstakes] has a single passion — entice all the out of state suckers possible," opined the *Claremont Eagle.*

Said the *Derry News:* "The Devil himself would find audience here, if he had cash in hand, and a gimmick to exploit."

"Lottery schemes such as this have always failed," bemoaned the *Keene Sentinel.* "It would hold up the state of New Hampshire to national ridicule."

"Born of necessity and nurtured on the promise of 'get rich quick,' the fledgling lottery is already a juvenile delinquent which threatens to live its entire life outside the law," *NH Profiles* magazine said.

"By passing the sweepstakes we are binding together in a deadly union the greatest revenue challenge we have ever faced with a plan of state sponsored gambling," the *Manchester Free Press* explained. "How can we lull ourselves into the belief we can have the benefits of state sponsored gambling, yet are immune from the corruption and grief?"

Many echoed the fear that legalized gambling would change both the reputation and the character of New Hampshire. As stated in the *Somersworth Free Press,* "The work of a generation has gone into building an image for this state — of a place where families can enjoy the natural beauties of our outdoors, where industry can come and grow in a healthy economic climate, where young people can live and find opportunity for growth of their interests, where our aged citizens can retire and live in quiet and peace of mind. Now, almost overnight, all that is to be wiped out."

Another *Derry News* editorial professed, "A lottery that caters to the gambling, 'Get rich quick' crowd that lives like a parasite on the pocketbooks of hard working citizens, brings with it the kind of flowing that we fear will contaminate the countryside of our small, unprepared state."

Cried the *Lisbon Courier,* "What is happening to New Hampshire's image at the hands of politicians shouldn't happen to a dog."

Editor Edward DeCourcy from the *Argus-Champion* was not going to surrender quietly, not after his personal plea to Governor King went unheeded. "Regardless of the crime, corruption and economic degradation the sweepstakes would spawn," he wrote, "we would handcuff our children to inferior education for who knows how many years, because it is obvious that no New Hampshire legislature will attempt to provide adequate support for education as long as the sweepstakes is in operations."

Next to the *Argus-Champion,* one of the most colorful and prolific critics of the lottery was the *Franklin Journal Transcript*. This paper declared that the sweepstakes was "a cheap john way of raising revenues for a state that supposedly prides itself on its fiscal responsibility." Later it would proclaim, "The fact that many people like to gamble does not make it moral to deliberately and cold-bloodedly feed on their stupidity." They also wrote, "The poor sucker who's convinced that he can beat the odds through some mystic favor of Dame Fortune is neither moral nor immoral most times. What he is, is a jerk."

Both the *Argus-Champion* and the *Journal-Transcript* liked to raise the specter that other states, particularly Massachusetts, would ape any success and start their own sweepstakes. DeCourcy's paper published the opinion that "every other state will have its own lottery and New Hampshire will be left all by itself to freeze on the vine." The *Journal-Transcript* agreed: "It may well be that if other states, particularly others in New England, do follow New Hampshire's lead into the gambling business that we'll wish we'd never heard of the sweepstakes."

THE NATIONAL PRESS was mixed in its assessment of the New Hampshire experiment. The news and commentary magazines mostly viewed it with a jaundiced eye. The general-interest magazines were more intrigued. They were among the first to recognize the possibility of a nationwide impact should the Sweeps succeed.

Family Weekly magazine, a supplemental insert to scores of Sunday newspaper editions across the country, was far more interested in what the average Joe had to say than the politicians or legal scholars. "If you were voting [in the March 1964 local-option referendum], how would you vote?" it asked. "It is a question that may be raised in your state very soon." The magazine took a fairly even-handed approach to its story. It laid out the major questions about legality and morality and gave equal space to either side. It then asked its readers to send them mail declaring which side they were on. One month later, *Family Weekly* ran a follow-up article declaring readers favored a sweepstakes or lottery in their home states by two to one.

Sensing there were fewer opponents in the national press — and seeing a way to stay on message without having to face an antagonistic local press corps — King took *This Week* magazine up on its offer to let him write an op-ed. The title the governor came up with was "I am Not Ashamed of Our Lottery."

King admitted he wasn't a gambling man — never shot dice, played cards, or bet on horses — and no one had ever offered him a chance to buy an Irish Sweep ticket. He attributed any unease with the sweepstakes to the Puritanical heritage of the Northeast. Some called gambling sinful, just as they had drinking and smoking.

"Without getting into a full-length discussion of what is and what isn't a sin . . . in my mind a sweepstakes ticket, a cold bottle of beer on a hot afternoon, or a good pre-Castro cigar are all within the sensible limits of a non-sin," the Catholic governor declared. "You start sinning when you start indulging in excess."

King told a tale of an elderly man from St. Anne Church — a Boy Scout troop leader — who'd get full of vinegar talking about the evils of alcoholism. The man would take King ice fishing in the winter, and once the hole was cut through the bottom of the bobhouse, the fellow would pull a flask from his coat and take a swig. "Gets me started and makes the whole day better," he'd wink.

The governor said none of us should force our views of virtue on others. He grumbled that "the moralists" were focused on the lottery when other issues went unattended. "I worry about the incredibly rising divorce rate. I worry about the breakdown of respect in the home. I worry about the immorality of discrimination of all kinds," said King, soothsaying some of the central issues of what would become known as "The Sixties."

The positive reaction to King's *This Week* article, combined with the *Family Weekly* reader's poll, got the governor believing his state really was on to something. Despite all the posturing to the contrary, adults from across the nation seemed interested in taking the chance to dream. Perhaps they *could* count on the thousands of out-of-staters they'd need to buy tickets traveling to New England. Not all opinion-leaders were converted however. *Reader's Digest* asked rhetorically, "Is either New Hampshire or Uncle Sam so hard up that this shabby dodge is the only way out? . . . It will mean moral bankruptcy for New Hampshire."

GOVERNOR KING IGNORED most of the local op-eds, but those written in Boston worked him into a lather.

The *Boston Traveler* editorialized that the sweepstakes would be "a scandalous experiment in state financing which is not much more than a soak-the-poor tax." The *Boston Herald* wrote, "A legalized sweepstakes in New Hampshire is disturbing to the Department [of Justice] because it becomes a natural and most tempting new target for racketeers," while its Sunday edition said, "We hope [the lottery] will soon be returned to its grave as it has been each year for the last quarter century or so."

"The evidence that gambling is a major cause of political and government corruption is something for New Hampshire to ponder," penned the *Eagle-Tribune* in the northern Massachusetts city of Lawrence, only five miles from the proposed Sweeps racetrack in Salem, New Hampshire. In the western part of the Commonwealth, the *Berkshire Eagle* noted, "They raise a serious question whether all this work will be worth it."

Editorial writers from around the country found too much fodder in the gambling debate to resist weighing in. The editors of the *Lewiston Sun* of Maine wrote, "We still believe that New Hampshire will live to share our regret that it is leaning ever more heavily upon the profits from human weaknesses and vices to finance its operations."

The op-ed page of the *Milwaukee Journal* read, "It is an unhappy commentary of human nature that the citizens of New Hampshire, apparently unwilling to carry a normal tax load, are tapping one of man's less noble impulses to raise money for the education of their children."

"The outstanding danger in New Hampshire is posed by the undesirable elements that may attempt to muscle in," wrote Illinois's *Waukegan News-Sun.*

"In time, the Granite Staters may find they have made a poor gamble," claimed the *Miami Herald.* "It can lead to corruption and destroy an individual's sense of obligation . . . the ultimate deleterious effect upon society in general is left to your imagination."

More directly, the *New York Herald-Tribune* called the sweepstakes, "The shame of New Hampshire."

The national publications also got in on the act. "Gambling (legalized) attracts the worst in transients and frequently brings out the worst in people," wrote *Parade* magazine.

The *Saturday Evening Post* went so far as to say, "Many solid citizens are convinced that the horses in the inaugural running of the New Hampshire Sweepstakes will be officially trampling New Hampshire's very morality in the dust."

Not all the press was negative. Some editorial writers mused about how the windfall to New Hampshire pupils will have them riding to school in chauffeured limousines, writing with pearl-handled pencils, teachers motioning to blackboards with gold-tipped pointers, and water fountains that bubbled up soft drinks. The *Peterborough Transcript* defended the sweepstakes, saying, "Those who abhor the thought of using the profits of such a scheme to provide state aid for public schools can gain a measure of satisfaction by not buying a sweeps ticket."

The left-leaning *New York Times* failed to denounce the experiment: "In the history of the Granite State there is appropriately solid material for the conclusion that, once again, New Hampshire is demonstrating its congenial trait of independence."

Bad press about the sweepstakes, King knew, would not likely wreck the program. *Indifferent* press would be lethal, as the avenues for publicizing the operation were soon to be shut to them.

"It doesn't bother me that the moralists have attacked me," King said in *This Week*. "A little vilification is good for a politician's soul. It puts him in his place."

IN THE ABSENCE of any definitive rules or organizational structure, the idea of what a state lottery would look like was left to the imagination of journalists. The tale they spun was one filled with characters who had fallen from the pages of a Damon Runyon book: oily gangsters like Nathan Detroit, Sky Masterson, and Nicely-Nicely. The political cartoons painted the scenes. More than anywhere else in North America, New Hampshire was going to be *the* hot spot for gambling and the ilk it attracted. Like the song said, "It's better than even money" the guys and dolls would come. It would rain top cats and top dogs. A grotesquery of gangsters. Tourists who once stopped for directions to Lake Winnipesaukee or the Old Man of the Mountain would now have different questions. "Hey bub, where's the action?"

The narrative being spun was that the sweepstakes was not a one-day event, not limited to the moral barricades erected around four dozen liquor stores and a pair of racetracks. The whole state would be wired into a massive gambling machine, its currents running from the beach surf to the top of Mount Washington. The hundreds of thousands of dollars that the suckers won wasn't the prize, nor were the millions of dollars the other suckers lost. The true prize was control of the state, which would eventually be plundered by sinister forces salivating over an endless revenue stream — every nickel of which would be winked at as being "legal."

Few in the nation were old enough to remember the corrupted Louisiana

Lottery, but in the 1960s most had seen this game play out not long before. They had heard the claim made that if gambling were made legal it would end illegal gambling. That if it were regulated closely it would push out the underworld elements looking to score. That if it were dressed up, glamorous and glitzy, it would be respectable, temperate, and fair.

Few had heard of the Golden Octopus, but many knew about the Golden Nugget, the Pink Flamingo. And about the Sands, the Dunes, the Riviera, and the claim that lilywhite legal gambling would never be stained by the Black Hand. It had been sold to them before. They'd heard the line from respectable businessmen of unquestioned probity and rare judgment who had invested in the desert town of Las Vegas.

8

*Drive
an Honest
Racketeer
Crooked*

IF YOU LIVED in New Hampshire and wanted to gamble, you certainly didn't have to wait until a sweepstakes race to spin Fortune's wheel. The fact the lottery plan incorporated an established, regionally popular horse track within its borders might have been evidence enough for some that gambling already had a comfortable home in the Granite State. Players who could handicap the races — who knew what they were doing — could fare better than those who picked horses based on a colorful name. In New Hampshire the race season was limited by winter, and not everyone could drive to Salem's Rockingham Park to make post time. And weren't the grandstands filled with all sorts of degenerates in plaid coats smoking cigars and throwing away the mortgage? Winning at the horses was a skill, not Chance.

The casual gambler could find action closer to home. For a small ante, players could take a bet on Chance — pure Chance. They could play what looked suspiciously like today's lottery, only this game was illegal. They could play "the numbers."

NUMBERS GAMES, or, rackets, go back to the first American lotteries (and further back still) and were the seedy cousins of the raffle-type lottery. From these games comes the origin of the name "racketeer," made synonymous with any organized crime figure, and the modern definition of a "racket" as a dishonest scheme. The image of the rambling lottery broker selling tickets from village to hamlet for civic causes became conflated with the daily numbers games that openly functioned in the early United States. These rackets were run out of hundreds of tiny, semiprivate "policy banks" that would draw numbers and pay winners. It's believed the majority of these number games were fixed by the racketeers, and a resentful public soon caught on. There were riots in major cities, mobs of angry gamblers demanding justice (or at least their money back). The raffle-type lotteries (though hardly paragons of fairness) were caught in the public backlash and hastened the implementation of nineteenth-century anti-lottery legislation in virtually every state. While "lotteries" suffered, the "rackets" simply moved underground.

The underground policy banks of the twentieth century were similar to the performance — though not the pageantry — of the dauntless Louisiana Lottery. Just like getting hold of an Irish Sweepstake ticket, it was easy enough to find someone running a numbers game out of a bar, a social club, a newsstand, or a diner. Or even from a coworker in a factory, an office, or — believe it or not — the police force. These numbers runners were charged with collecting coins and cash from the diverse points of sale or going door to door to collect individual wagers from regulars. Gamblers could play on credit. Bets could be as small as a penny and usually paid 500:1 or 600:1 (on odds that any mathematician could calculate were 999:1 against). The policy banks would perform General Beauregard's kabuki theater with bookies selecting the three digits by drawing numbered balls from a sack (a game called *bolita,* Spanish for "little ball" and brought to the United States from Havana at the turn of the century) or by spinning a "policy wheel." If word spread that a certain policy bank had rigged its games (removing balls from the sack, palming balls with popular numbers, loading them with weights, or freezing them for easy selection), players would bring their business to a new bank — which probably cheated just as badly.

In a way, the policy banks had no choice but to cheat. The numbers racket was a "mutuel" that paid out at fixed odds, so players could potentially win more money than was actually in the pot. Depending on the wager and the amount of people playing a specific number, a racket could easily go bust on a big jackpot day. One Monday in Detroit, 8–0–3 bankrupted at least one shop. Hundreds of bettors had played that lucky number because they had sung hymn number 803 in church that Sunday. "It's things like that," *The American Weekly* reported, "that drive an 'honest' racketeer crooked."

As a whole, Detroit was one of the stronger rackets. The multi-million-dollar operation held its policy drawings in a style very similar to Louisiana's. Numbers were written on scraps of paper in rubber tubes and pulled from a hopper in front of a discerning crowd. The bookies, however, kept track of which daily numbers were "fancy" — that is, which had been heavily played and under no circumstances should come up. Those numbers went into marked tubes. The drawer held the tube in his left hand (palm away from the audience) and a pencil in his right. He'd remove the rolled-up paper by shoving it out of the tube with the pencil, but these pencils had secret hollow compartments. If a hot number came up, a tap on the lead tip of the pencil would push through a safe number and the tube would be casually tossed aside.[1]

With all this heat, the rackets had to come up with a different way to draw the number, one that all the operations could share. Because of the footwork required to sell tickets, most urban policy banks at the time were limited to neighborhoods. There were small rackets in Little Italy and the Irish Hell's Kitchen, Chinatown, and a slew of them existed in Harlem. The bookies figured correctly that pinning the game to a number that could be checked across a city or region would expand the racket from beyond the neighborhoods and create larger pools.

The bookies found their answer in the newspapers. The business and sports pages published balances and statistics and scores every day. This mutuel also gave the racket an air of impartiality, as the winning number was begot of something the organizers couldn't control. For some policy banks, the jackpot was the last three numbers of the day's U.S. Treasury balance. Others used the closing number on New York bond sales. Most often it was determined by "the handle," the amount of money wagered at a racetrack or a particular race on any given day. This figure was also carried in the newspapers and racing sheets, so all players could learn immediately if they had won.

Controlling these numbers was, however, something the racketeers would

---

1. The Detroit racket went on like this for decades — at least until one conman dumped his gal, who took it very hard. In 1939, police found Janet McDonald and her eleven-year-old daughter, her car running in the garage, dead by suicide from carbon monoxide. In her diary, investigators found a letter that outlined everything she knew about the city's racket, including the numerous judges, politicians, and police officers who'd taken bribes for protection. In the end, 131 people — including the mayor, county attorney, police superintendent, and 89 cops — were arrested. At trial, many of the racketeers didn't even bother to claim the games were on the level and bragged enough suckers would continue to play the numbers even knowing it was a swindle. (They were not wrong.)

learn how to do. As laid out in the *Encyclopedia of the Harlem Renaissance,* in the 1930s, a gangster named Arthur Flegenheimer, better known as "Dutch Schultz," made a killing rigging the numbers of the Harlem racket. The Mob had derisively called this penny-and-nickel operation the "nigger pool" — a name which stuck to this racket for decades regardless of who ran it — and had left Harlem alone. Schultz was the first to see the financial potential of consolidating small policy banks into one operation (which he did at gunpoint).

The Harlem racket used the handle from New York racetracks. Schultz's partner in the con was an easygoing, Rubenesque accountant named Carl Berman, nicknamed "Abba Dabba." He had a Rain Man–like gift of remembering the day's hot numbers, checking the track's tote board, and calculating how much Schultz should bet at the last minute to throw off the handle. It worked so well the racket pulled in $100 million a year. The scheme would have gone on forever if Dutch Shultz, Abba Dabba, and two of their soldiers had not been rubbed out in a New Jersey restaurant, Mario Puzo–style by rivals. On their table police found an adding machine and three strips of paper. Each had a total of $148 million, $236 million, and $314 million — the profits of their number racket.

In the 1970s, one of the biggest numbers rackets in Boston was run by infamous Irish mobster Whitey Bulger, head of the Winter Hill Gang. Instead of being derived from the complicated math of the handle, the number was chosen based on the silks from finishing horses at the Suffolk Downs racetrack. If the seven horse won, followed by the four and the three, then that day's number was 7–4-3. Luckily for Bulger, he not only ran the number, but he essentially ran the racetrack too. When the gang saw what combinations were hot, a Winter Hill soldier would go down to the stables and tell the jockeys who was coming in first, second, and so on; hundred dollar bills passed all around like cocktail napkins. Not content to pull the carpet from under his longtime customers, Bulger often played that prearranged number himself and took home the pot (he'd win the trifecta at the track too). The Italian lottery organizers of the Middle Ages surely would have admired his moxie.

IN THE OPINION of early Americans the only thing worse than a swindler was the professional card shark. Professional gamblers were especially hated, with some being lynched when they were discovered. The farther west they got from busybody Puritans, the more accepting the adventurous pioneers were of poker and dice players. Faster than you can "Deadwood," camp towns crept up from St. Louis to the Pacific — and along with them, saloons. Part tavern, part casino, part whorehouse, the batwing doors of cowboy fiction swung open for those with money to part with.

At the close of the nineteenth century, as the last of the Wild West territories became states subject to federal oversight, the golden age of the saloon ended. In the deserts of Nevada, however, one could still find gambling saloons of old.

The green-felt jungle of Las Vegas was built largely by mobster Bugsy Siegel, at least in American folklore. Siegel acquired the Flamingo in 1946 at the point of a gun with visions of turning the hotel into a Havana-inspired gambling resort and creating a tourist destination in the middle of nowhere. The business plan was to create a spectacular demimonde of entertainment and gambling to attract the whales and the guppies alike. Las Vegas would democratize gambling. Placing a bet wasn't just legal — it was glamorous.

Through the late 1940s, public relations were good. The widely held public suspicion was that, although the gambling was on the level, the Flamingo operation was run by the syndicate behind Siegel (and the casino owners who'd quickly follow). It didn't help that Siegel, who'd made enemies because of his caustic personality and costly construction overruns, was taken out in 1947 in an apparent hit. Nor did it help when police investigating a gangster assassination back east discovered slips documenting the Mob's skim from Vegas casinos — proving to the world that racketeers indeed had a foothold in Vegas. In 1951, Senator Estes Kefauver's riveting investigation into organized crime shone another spotlight on Sin City's open secret.

President Harry Truman said legalized gambling had made Nevada "the darkest spot on the continent."[2] Now editorial writers were quoting Truman and saying — with all sincerity — that the Sweepstakes race would put New Hampshire on par with freewheeling Las Vegas and it was only a matter of time before the next Bugsy Siegel moved in on the Granite State. Even the number-two man at the Justice Department told the state it would certainly come to pass.

Was there anyone with the muscle to keep the Mob out of the Sweeps?

---

2. In 1960, Nevada's population was about 284,000 — about half of New Hampshire's — but its revenue from gambling alone was $200 million, more than double New Hampshire's state budget.

9
Hoover's Favorite

WHO WOULD BLAME Governor King if he got nervous when he learned an FBI agent wanted an audience with him? It was spring 1963. The New Hampshire Sweepstakes existed only on paper, but the Sweeps's bacon was already dangling perilously over the fire. With hundreds of would-be gamblers from around the country calling and writing and sending money, there was already more bacon than their pan could handle.

As was later reported in a half-dozen regional newspapers, the agent met the governor at the statehouse. He was shown into King's corner office, where King likely apologized for the horrible view of the state library tower in his northern window. The governor's kitty-cornered desk was remarkably free of clutter: a blotter, an electric clock, a phone, and intercom. His framed portrait of Anna rested on the settee behind him. Standing next to his desk lamp was a small bronze statue of a young boy in fighter's trunks wearing boxing gloves too large for his tiny hands. The optimism of the figurine spoke to a man who punched above his weight.

The visitor introduced himself as Edward Powers, the special in charge of the FBI's Boston office. His territory covered four of the New England states and he insisted the visit was merely one of several courtesy calls he was making to all the governors.

Powers was affable, well dressed, and eager. He asked King if there were any federal-justice issues with which he could help. Talk naturally turned toward the sweepstakes. Powers was optimistic the state would make a good-faith effort at staying within the regulations. He gave the governor his phone number and offered to provide whatever guidance might be needed from the Bureau. King walked Powers to the door and watched the man stroll easily down the statehouse hall.

No one knew it yet, but that day marked a historical moment for the lottery — and a turning point in American culture.

PERHAPS THE LUCKIEST STROKE of the entire New Hampshire Sweepstakes was the selection of its executive director. Even more than being a man of "unquestioned probity and rare judgment," the leader of the Sweeps had to be someone who would instill public confidence in the operation. He had to be someone with the savvy to navigate the thickets of federal prohibitions. He had to be someone well spoken, with a deft touch for the public and the press alike. He had to be someone people would believe was above the influence of organized crime. He had to be an angelic version of General Pierre Beauregard, Joseph McGrath, and Bugsy Segal all rolled into one. He had to be King's John Kennedy.

In early summer of 1963, Edward Powers received a call from King's executive secretary, Tom Power. He asked the FBI agent if he'd be willing to visit with the governor again to talk about the New Hampshire Sweepstakes. Assuming he was seeking the Bureau's assistance in working out the unresolved enforcement issues, Powers offered to bring his staff's top people. The response was no. The governor wanted to talk to him about becoming executive director.

The idea of soliciting Powers for the post came from King, who had been greatly impressed by the agent's charm and quick intelligence. Tom Power had interviewed the FBI agent a few years earlier when he was anchorman for WMUR-TV in Manchester.[1] He agreed that Powers was a swell choice, perhaps uniquely qualified to handle the post. Howell Shepard and the rest of the Sweepstakes Commission were on board. They had a list of people to consider, but all fell short of what Powers could bring.

---

1. Tom Power was New Hampshire's first television anchor, manning the desk when WMUR signed on in 1954. The entire staff was let go during an ownership change in 1959, but Power was hired back. Three weeks later he suffered a heart attack and collapsed on the air. They fired him while he was home recuperating.

Within forty-eight hours, Powers was again welcomed to the statehouse, again ushered into the governor's private office, where King likely again made a disparaging comment about the ugly state library tower ruining the view. Instead of speaking from behind his desk, King insisted they move to the leather side chairs and talk more informally, more intimately.

Powers was clear that he was satisfied with his position at the FBI and hadn't been looking for a career change. King understood, but asked if the agent would hear him out. What King said about the importance of this "noble experiment," the public benefits that could result if its Gordian knots could be untied, resonated with Powers.

"Would I have the ability to pick my own staff?" Powers asked.

"With the approval of the Commission," replied King, "yes you would."

The agent said he'd consider the position only under one condition. "There can be no political influence in the operation of the sweepstakes. None what so ever. Not even by inference."

It was a bold demand to make face to face with a powerful politician. *You're not invited to this party,* he was saying. *You can look at these shiny things but you cannot touch.* As far as job interview strategies go, it was a pretty bad one. Powers was no stranger to interrogations. The governor's immediate response would be telling. Any hemming or hawing would mean that sooner or later, at the whim of the governor or legislature, the sweepstakes could be used to serve a partisan purpose. A straight-up rejection of the demand would be far more comforting than any white lie.

King did not hesitate. "Absolutely," he said. "Politics has no place in this arena. You have my word: no politicians, no hacks. You'll have a free hand in running the operation."

Powers asked for some time to think about it. King, who had spent two weeks secluded on that very couch weighing the same pros and cons, told him to take all the time he wanted.

Ed Powers was not an empty suit with a federal badge. He was not merely an FBI agent. The reason King wanted him was because Powers was an *extraordinary* FBI agent.

EDWARD J. POWERS was born on August 24, 1913. He grew up in Chicago, where his father was a police detective sergeant. The elder Powers was a twenty-six-year veteran of the city's bloody Mob wars during Al Capone's reign. In 1936, Ed Powers got a degree in accounting from Lawrence College in

Appleton, Wisconsin. He was Phi Beta Kappa and was a favorite student of future Harvard president Nathan Pusey. He managed an A&P grocery store before getting jobs in insurance and banking. It wasn't until 1941 that he followed his old man into the business of tossing racketeers when he joined the Federal Bureau of Investigation.

He started his career at the Bureau with assignments in New York City, then San Antonio. His cool intelligence and preternatural leadership ability won him a post as a supervisor in the Washington, D.C., office. While there, he put himself through Georgetown Law, taking classes five nights a week to earn his degree. He graduated second in his class.

With whatever free time he actually had, Powers began a polite courtship with a secretary at the Bureau. Melva Bearse, a beauty queen from Centerville, Massachusetts, she was a former Miss Cape Cod. She was no doubt a looker, but Powers was soft on the eyes as well. He was five-foot-ten, and when walking with shoulders back and chest out, he seemed even larger than he was. Powers was both brain and brawn; he had a lean frame but steely eyes that projected toughness. But he smiled easily, revealing perfect teeth and dimpled cheeks. He tanned easily.

Powers also had a natural agility and balance that helped him with any physical activity he did. He didn't ski or play ball, but he was a scratch golfer, regularly hitting in the high 70s and low 80s. Once, after giving a speech at a law enforcement academy, Powers was egged on to come to the firing range to give a demonstration. Using a pistol, he fired in front of the crowd from every distance and every position — standing, kneeling, laying prone — and scored 99 out of 100.

Needless to say, Edward and Melva made a beautiful couple. They were married in 1944, and two daughters, Jan Louise and Marcia, and a son, Thomas, followed.

A radiant force of nature in the Washington office, Powers immediately caught the eye of Director J. Edgar Hoover. He put Powers in charge of Internal Security, which in the mid-1940s focused nearly exclusively on socialist, Nazi, and communist activities. Hoover had been obsessed with the red threat since 1919, when fears of Bolshevism and anarchy would take hold in America, so making Powers supervisor of this office reveals how much confidence Hoover had in the young agent.

In July 1945, Hoover instructed Powers to open an investigation into the

Communist Party of the United States of America (CPUSA), with particular focus on the intentions of the national board of directors. Using informants, Powers's team was able to compile a dossier of nearly nineteen hundred pages on the board, its members, its beliefs, and its activities. Their work was the impetus for congressional hearings, including those of the "Hollywood Ten," a group of screenwriters who were blacklisted for refusing to cooperate with the House Un-American Activities Committee. Hoover ordered Justice Department prosecutors to indict the CPUSA for violations of the Smith Act — specifically, for organizing a group that advocated the violent overthrow of the government. Using the evidence gathered by Powers's team, the U.S. attorney general in 1948 charged twelve of the fifty-five members of the CPUSA national board (Hoover seethed that the entire group was not indicted). Eleven were convicted in 1949, creating the fertile soil for Joseph McCarthy and other anti-Communist crusaders.

Had he done nothing else, Ed Powers would be remembered as one of the Bureau's biggest commie crushers. Hoover rewarded him with a promotion by making him assistant bureau chief (assistant special agent-in-charge) of the Pittsburg office, and then Minneapolis.

Powers was now one of the Bureau's rising stars. Over the next twenty years, he was the special agent-in-charge of FBI offices in Miami, Boston, New York, Indianapolis, Baltimore, and then again in Boston.

At the time he was being wooed by Governor King, Powers had just finished testifying in the region's latest bank robbery case. He presented testimony on how John Dirring and Joseph Gleason had held up the Bristol County Trust Company in Taunton, Massachusetts, in April 1963. One of the reasons the Boston papers were enamored with the trial was that Dirring, objecting to entering the court in chains and manacles, had to be carried into the courtroom by the bailiffs. "What kind of a joint are you running here?" Dirring crowed, like Little Caesar.

Powers spent a solid two weeks mulling over Governor King's offer. Powers was not a gambler himself. He had only been to Suffolk Downs twice in his life, laying down two-dollar bets each time. While SAC in Miami, he had worked on a case of high-stakes race-fixing with some celebrated jockeys who'd been pressured by mobsters. Racketeering and all kinds of underground gambling touched the cases he'd worked on. He knew what the FBI was dealing with in Las Vegas and Atlantic City. As a student of history, he was familiar with the sordid history of American lotteries. He saw a common thread to all of these stories: in one way or another, all the games had been *fixed*.

Before accepting King's offer, Powers called the one man whose opinion on the subject he valued the most: J. Edgar Hoover. The director was pleased to hear from his protégé, and listened carefully to Powers's reasoning and plans. Hoover acknowledged Powers was the right man to run the New Hampshire Sweepstakes, gave his blessing, and expressed his disappointment to lose him. He had personally placed Powers in Boston (twice), and thinking of that reminded him of the previous success they had there. Powers had cracked one of Hoover's "favorite" cases. It was a triumph for Powers and for Hoover (any triumph for the FBI was a personal triumph for Hoover).

THE ANNOUNCEMENT of Powers's appointment was met with nearly universal praise. Previous speculation had been that the executive director position would be filled by some technocrat or political appointee, perhaps a retired police chief. Powers's "wow factor" was off the chart. Governor King and Commissioner Shepard were first to tout his qualifications. Powers was the *bel esprit* of the FBI, and worries that gangsters would infiltrate the sweepstakes virtually disappeared.

Even the Sweeps most persistent critics reluctantly admitted that Powers was an inspired choice. "We expressed regret" when the lottery passed, admitted editors at one local paper, "but we feel that credit should be given when due." Calling Powers's hiring "very commendable," the writers went on to declare that his appointment "should provide the closest thing there is to insurance against manipulation of the sweepstakes."

The *Concord Daily Monitor* called Powers's credentials "impeccable," a man who would get the lottery off "on the right foot." But they couldn't resist getting a zing in: "We hope Mr. Powers does his best and that he succeeds in holding corruption to a minimum, but we're (you should excuse the expression) betting that the sweepstakes will be a big disappointment to those who figure to have their cake and eat it."

None were more effusive than Bill Loeb. The *Union Leader* carried Powers's photo next to the front-page editorial. In a matter of fourteen column inches, Loeb anointed Powers to near-sainthood status. "Such a selection as Mr. Powers should meet with wide acclaim throughout the state and country," he proclaimed in a paragraph written entirely in capital letters. "The choice surely meets the oft-repeated criterion of this newspaper that experience and outstanding ability should be the only basis on which important government posts in New Hampshire should be filled."

Edward DeCourcy of the *Argus-Champion* remained among the few sourpusses. If supporters believed the lottery would not be a target for corruption, "why was it necessary to hire the former chief of the Boston Bureau of the FBI to administer the sweepstakes?"

Powers was unaffected by the publicity, good and bad, that came with his new position. He told the governor he would accept the offer, then he and his family immediately departed for an August vacation at a modest hotel on Rye Beach, New Hampshire. On the day John King announced who had filled the post, the cool-tempered Powers hit a seventy-four on the golf course — a personal best.

IF GOVERNOR KING WAS PLEASED to have Ed Powers take the job, then Melva Powers was downright elated. The couple was expert at packing up their house and moving. In the previous fourteen years, the family had moved nine times, following Powers to new FBI posts across the country. Their oldest daughter, Jan Louise, had attended four high schools.

"I'm as happy as a new bride," Melva told the *Union Leader*. "It will enable us to settle down . . . at last, we'll have a permanent home." She sighed as if *she* were the first big winner of the Sweeps. They had selected a house in Bedford, New Hampshire — a bedroom community known for its tony residents and colonial-era accoutrements.

While the couple wrapped dishes and other fragile keepsakes in crumpled newspaper for transport, the doorbell to the Powers family home in Norwood, Massachusetts, rang. It was a Friday afternoon in August. Powers was to be sworn in by the governor on Monday. He'd become accustomed by now to reporters showing up at the house unannounced to write profile pieces, so a distraction from stuffing boxes was welcomed.

The man on the front stoop peered through the screen door, his arms folded across his chest. He was about medium height, broad shoulders, early forties, dark hair. Though he wore a nice suit and a perfectly knotted tie, Powers immediately noticed the stranger didn't have a notebook or a press card at the ready.

"My name is Bill Witcomb. May I come in, Mister Powers?"

Powers recognized the name. Witcomb was a zealous opponent of the sweepstakes, the self-professed leader of a movement fixated on repeal. He pushed open the door and allowed Witcomb to pass. As they stood in the front hallway, Witcomb continued his cold stare. "I'm here to warn you and your family not to come to New Hampshire in connection with the sweepstakes. It can only lead to grief and disaster."

Normally affable, anger billowed in Powers's throat. The ex-G-man was used to hardened criminals making threats against him — but not in his own home. Knowing he'd later regret it, he found himself engaging in a debate with the visitor. He spoke plainly and forcefully, but never raised his voice.

Witcomb told Powers his opposition had moral grounds, that gambling was sinful and promoted coveting and avarice. Powers countered that the Sweeps were meant to aid education and were in many ways no different than church raffles or bingo games. Witcomb snorted at the example, saying, "I've left many churches when they've resorted to such tactics."

At some point during the discussion, Powers asked whether Witcomb opposed gambling at Rockingham Park, the track selected for the sweepstakes race.

"I do not oppose it," Witcomb said to Powers's initial surprise, "because the people have a better chance at winning there."

Powers had enough of the intrusion: "Mr. Witcomb, you have every right to your views as a citizen, and you have every right to come to my office and discuss them with me. But you have no right to invade the privacy of my family and issue such a warning."

Witcomb again stared down the lottery chief. As he turned to go, he threw out a Bible verse: "He that hastens to be rich has an evil eye, and considers not that poverty shall come on him."

Powers watched the well-dressed man walk across his lawn, climb into a shiny Plymouth, and drive away. His hand on the doorknob shook from the adrenalin. Was this warning the fantasy of a preacher or the threat of an extremist?

GOVERNOR KING swore in Edward Powers on Monday morning, August 26, 1963, at the statehouse, two days after his fiftieth birthday. King was several years younger, but Powers's vigor and vitality made him appear the more youthful. Commissioners Shepard, Sanel, and Turcotte looked on; Melva Powers, at her husband's right side, beamed as he took the state oath. After the brief ceremony, King and the entire Powers family posed for the press and fielded some questions.

"It will be my job to make sure the citizens of New Hampshire have complete faith in the honesty and efficiency of the sweepstakes," he said.

Afterward there was mingling, small talk about how Powers would run the Sweeps. He mostly shrugged, flashing a million-dollar smile, and said he had some ideas that he wanted to run by the commission at a later date. With little left of the future to discuss, the conversation quickly turned to the past. The scribes and the well-wishers wanted to hear the story that Powers had told again and again the past seven years.

They all wanted to know about how he solved the Brink's heist.

IT'S IMPOSSIBLE TO TELL the story of Edward Powers's life and how important his mere association with the lottery was without examining the Great Brink's Robbery. It would be like saying of John Glenn that before he was a U.S. senator, he had a job at NASA. Or that Paul McCartney was in another band before Wings.

Powers ran the Boston office from 1954 to 1957. The posting pleased Melva because they were finally close to her parents on Cape Cod, but Powers inherited the office's most frustrating unsolved case, one that six other agents had already investigated. It was the 1950 heist of the city's Brink's building by a gang of profession thieves. They got away with millions of dollars — and the statute of limitations on finding the offenders was quickly running out.

The Brink's heist was that decade's "crime of the century." When it was over, Powers was not only a legend within with law enforcement — he was arguably the biggest celebrity FBI agent since Eliot Ness.

10

*One of
Those
All-American
Guys*

AT 7:15 P.M. ON JANUARY 17, 1950, five workers at the Brink's Company building — three clerks and two guards — were in the counting room, sleeves on their dress shirts rolled to the elbow, sorting through the deposits from the day's armored car pick-ups. With hardly a peep, seven men entered the counting room. The intruders had passed through five locked doors to get there. Each wore a dark pea coat, gloves, and a chauffeur's cap — deceptively similar to an official Brink's uniform in the dark of night. Their faces were hidden behind rubber Halloween masks of Captain Marvel and other superheroes. Some were wearing galoshes to muffle their footsteps; one wore crepe-soled shoes instead.

The Brink's employees were dumbstruck. They had no time to reach for the four pistols on a wall rack, nor could they get to the button to set off the panic alarm. They were forced to the floor at gunpoint, wrists tied and mouths covered with tape. The robbers got into the vault and worked methodically, bagging the loot in laundry sacks, but froze when an entry buzzer unexpectedly sounded. One of the masked men ripped the tape from an employee's mouth and demanded to know what this unrehearsed hiccup in their plan was. A garage attendant was asking to get into the building. Two of the hold-up men went to the door, ready to snatch the interloper, but the attendant had wandered away, unaware of what was happening inside. Their plan nearly foiled, the group doubled their efforts to grab and run. With as much as they all could carry, they left eight smaller safes uncracked and more than $900,000 in cash scattered on the floor. As they slipped away, the gang left the five employees to wriggle out of their bondage. The first who got free ran to the phone.

"This is Brink's," he shouted. "We are cleaned out! We are cleaned out!"

At 7:27 p.m., the crew strolled out of the building and got into a waiting canvas-covered Ford truck and disappeared into the cold night with 350 pounds of loot. FBI documents showed in about fifteen minutes, they'd scooped up $1.2 million in cash and $1.6 million in checks and securities ($26 million in today's dollars). They had just pulled off the largest bank robbery in the history of the United States.

The papers loved the nerve of the heist. They declared it to be the perfect crime, and few investigators could disagree. J. Edgar Hoover inserted himself and the FBI into the investigation three days later, after Boston Police admitted they'd run into nothing by brick walls (the G-men could claim jurisdiction because some of checks and money orders had come from the Federal Reserve and the Veterans Association). City detectives conducted thousands of interviews and chased down hundreds of dead-end leads. The precision of the operation and the gang's effortless ability to circumvent the locks and alarms to get in and out of the vault meant either that it was an inside job or the detectives were searching for a crew of highly experienced professional robbers. Investigators questioned everyone who'd ever worked in the three-story building, but they suspected the heist was the work of pros.

The crew had left behind little evidence. There was the rope, a chauffeur's hat, and the adhesive tape. There were no fingerprints and no good descriptions. The knots in the rope suggested one of the men had nautical experience, and with the building's proximity to the Boston Inner Harbor, officials worked a theory the crooks could have sailed away.

A month after the job, some kids found a rusted revolver on the banks of the Mystic River. It was one of the four guns taken from the Brink's employees. A cop recovered another of the handguns the following day.

On the night of the crime, a neighbor had spotted a large green 1949 Ford stake-body truck idling near the Brink's front door. Given the number of people and amount of loot involved, investigators believed the truck was connected to the heist. In March, pieces of a large Ford truck turned up at a dump in Stoughton, Massachusetts. The vehicle had been cut apart with a blowtorch, the smaller pieces smashed with a sledgehammer and placed in bags. Cops traced it to a dealership near Fenway Park that had reported it stolen two months before the heist.

According to Stephanie Schorow's *The Crime of the Century*, the cops rounded up the "usual suspects," of which Boston had many in this line of work. The Boston mafia got roughed up. Tips suggested there were bands of Prohibition-era bootleggers who had the mettle to do the job. The feds even looked into the old members of "The Purple Gang," later immortalized as the rhythm section in Elvis Presley's *Jailhouse Rock.*

In addition to the city's organized crime figures, there were a number of loosely associated expert bank robbers and safe crackers who made a living off of small jobs. The cops tossed every numbers racket, brothel, and backroom card game they could. Any street-corner hood, anyone the authorities could get their hands on was questioned about whom they'd been with and what they'd been doing in the month leading up to January 17. FBI agents staked out casinos, racetracks, and vacation resorts for anyone dropping big chunks of cash, any marked bills from the case.

It seemed unlikely that a group as disciplined as the one that had carried off this caper would soon go on a spending spree. They wouldn't plan a robbery that far in advance and not consider what they'd do next. They knew all the serial numbers on the crisp, clean bills were recorded and that stops were sure to have been put on all the checks. The smart play was to lay low, let things cool off, and wait it out. The federal statute of limitations on the crime was three years; the state statute was six. Discipline, of course, would be key to getting away with it. There were just as many hoodlums as there were cops looking for their score, and a gang that large was bound to have its share of interpersonal drama. One Boston University psychology professor said, "The loot of the Brink's robbery will be one of the greatest sources of temptation since the apple in the Garden of Eden."

IN JUNE OF 1950, Joseph O'Keefe and his friend Stanley Gusciora left Boston on a road trip to St. Louis. The plan was to head west to visit the grave of Gusciora's brother who'd been killed in the war. Getting out of town seemed a smart move, as the heat on the two of them was getting high.

O'Keefe went by his nickname, "Specs" or "Specky," not because he wore glasses, but because he liked to eat ripe, speckled bananas. A forty-two-year-old hood, Specs O'Keefe had a long career of strong-arm antics working freelance with other Boston area hoods. He'd been arrested seventy times for robbery. He was bold. Rumor had it that O'Keefe initially kept his pockets fat by holding up gamblers stumbling from card houses. He soon graduated to sticking up bookies and cleaning them out. "Gus" Gusciora was O'Keefe's best friend. At age fifteen, Gusciora killed a guy while he was in reform school. They often worked jobs together, acting as the contracted muscle for a shakedown or a break-in.

The FBI had been keeping tabs on O'Keefe, Gusciora, and some of their associates since January — just a handful of the hundreds of likely perpetrators of the robbery. Neither guy had a terribly good alibi for January 17. O'Keefe told the cops he'd left his Boston hotel room at 7 p.m. and gone out drinking, but no one could verify his statement. Gusciora said he'd been drinking in a bar that night too.

One piece of circumstantial evidence that kept the pair under the microscope was that they both had family living in Stoughton, the town in which the vivisected getaway truck had been discovered. Police searched those homes, but nothing linking them to the Brink's heist was found. Later, acting on a tip, the FBI got a federal warrant to search another O'Keefe relative's home in Boston. The agents found a couple hundred bucks hidden in the house, but it wasn't connected to the investigation.

Taking the back roads, Specs and Gus rolled out west, making a few stops on their way to the Show-Me State. While passing through Coudersport, Pennsylvania, on U.S. Route 6, the two broke into Rosenbloom's Men's and Boy's Store, helping themselves to some fancy sports coats and clothes for the trip. They later broke into a store in Kane, Pennsylvania, and made off with a roll of cash. When they stopped to ask for directions from a cop in Towanda, Pennsylvania, he nabbed them for having a gun and 150 rounds of ammunition in the car, as well as burglary tools and the stolen clothes. They were able to identify the sports coats from Rosenbloom's by their designer labels.

The pair now faced charges in two Pennsylvania jurisdictions. Specs O'Keefe was convicted in Towanda and sentenced to three years in the Bradford County Jail. Gusciora was acquitted, but sent to McKean County to be tried on the other burglary charges. Found guilty, he got five-to-twenty in the state penitentiary.

According to United Press International, from jail O'Keefe called his wife back in Massachusetts to ask if she'd been questioned by any federal authorities. She said she had, but that she hadn't said anything. "Take good care of the baby," he told her — though they didn't have any children.

While O'Keefe cooled his heels behind bars, rumors around Boston were that Johnny Carlson, a racketeer friend of O'Keefe's, was putting pressure on certain people to send money for a legal appeal. There was some hemming and hawing, and the longer they stalled the angrier O'Keefe became.

One of the guys that Carlson was dogging was Anthony Pino. Born in Italy, never officially naturalized in the United States, "Fat Tony" Pino was another of those Boston hoods who floated from job to job. He was a natural comedian and amateur chef, a host most people liked to be around. Police liked him for the Brink's job because Pino was an A-1 "case man," someone who would have the patience and skill to case a joint and put together a major heist. In fact, the Brink's case had Pino's (figurative) fingerprints all over it.

Pino, unlike many of the other would-be suspects in Boston, had a pretty good alibi for the night of January 17. He had left his house around 7 p.m. and walked to a bar owned by Joseph "Big Joe" McGinnis. Inside, McGinnis was chatting with a police officer, who later confirmed the two men were there during the seven o'clock hour.

In his own right, McGinnis was a powerful criminal influence in Boston, someone who could bankroll Pino's grand scheme but not do any of the heavy lifting. A hit like Brink's would require a group of criminal specialists to carry off. There was high risk of detection, and a high risk of violence. They'd need someone who could handle a gun, and that's where Specs O'Keefe and Gus Gusciora came in.

Even though O'Keefe was growing impatient with Pino stonewalling him on money for his defense fund, and investigators were sure he was somehow central to the heist, O'Keefe did not crack. FBI agents visited him in his Pennsylvania cell and tried to exploit any animosity he felt toward Pino. Instead, O'Keefe retold his lines about having no knowledge of what went down at Brink's. Gusciora kept a buttoned lip too.

Much of Boston's underworld had been disrupted by the endless, intense search for the Brink's robbers. Under normal circumstances, there was an "understanding" between cops and robbers who lived and worked in the same town. Mostly, if the criminals took the drug dealing and prostitution off the streets — and kept things just discreet enough not to force legal intervention — police in most major cities could live with a little sin. This understanding was often sealed with more than a mere handshake. Boston gangsters of all stripes were becoming fed up with the police raids scaring off their regular customers, and things got to the point where dropping a dime was a good investment.

The scuttlebutt was several guys had been pressured to kick into O'Keefe's legal fund. Not all of them wanted to, some grumbled, but an important few caved. Pino, of course. Vincent Costa, Pino's brother-in-law and a numbers runner, got strong-armed. Adolph "Jazz" Maffie — a self-styled playboy — and Henry Baker were two others. Baker, who'd spent the last five years in jail for breaking and entering, had been released five months before the heist. His ride home from prison was Anthony Pino. Each one had an alibi that revolved around 7 p.m. sharp on January 17 (going to work, having dinner, walking around the block); O'Keefe and Gusciora mentioned 7 p.m. too. At ten minutes before the break-in, such a specific hour seemed like part of a scripted cover story.

In November 1952, days before the federal statute of limitations was up, a federal grand jury convened to determine whether to indict Pino, O'Keefe, and the rest of their crew. The grand jury investigated for two months. The alleged robbers would not talk. O'Keefe's wife, his parents, and his sister all appeared, all were found in contempt for refusing to answer the grand jury's questions. With no testimony, no physical evidence, and no one who could be identified underneath a Captain Marvel mask, the grand jury failed to indict. The clock had run out on the federal charges. Now the crew simply needed to wait another three years for the Massachusetts statute of limitation to pass before they'd be home free.

SPECS O'KEEFE was released from jail in Towanda, Pennsylvania, in January 1954, but he still faced charges for being an accomplice with Gusciora back in McKean County. In addition, Massachusetts wanted him because his arrest in Pennsylvania violated his parole. Before his McKean County trial, O'Keefe posted a $17,000 bond and returned to Boston to answer the parole violation charge.

O'Keefe's time back in New England was brief. He had less than two weeks to appear in Boston municipal court and then return to McKean County for his second trial. Though the federal statute of limitations had passed, this crime was a favorite of Hoover's, so he ordered his men to stay on the case. FBI agents tailed O'Keefe everywhere he went in Boston, and he spent most of his time calling on the other known suspects in the Brink's job. In all of these encounters, O'Keefe was visibly angry. He needed more money for his defense fund, and it appeared none of his compatriots was eager to open his wallet — or make a significant withdrawal from some other secret stash.

O'Keefe was convicted in Pennsylvania on the burglary charge but filed an appeal and was released on a $15,000 bond. The prosecutor put up little fight about the bond; the feds wanted to see what Specs would do if he got back to Boston.

O'Keefe wasn't the only member of the gang with legal troubles. During this time, Jazz Maffie got nine months for income-tax evasion. Gusciora was still in prison. But these cases were peanuts compared to what Anthony Pino was dealing with.

Technically an illegal alien since childhood, Pino had been at risk of deportation for more than ten years. As early at 1941, the Immigration and Naturalization Service had been trying to get Pino out while he was still a two-bit hood. His lawyer's plan was to get some of his early convictions expunged, taking away INS's legal justifications for deportation. After a complicated series of maneuvers, which included sentence revocations and gubernatorial pardons, Immigration finally thought they had the bad paper they needed to kick Pino out of the country.

After Pino testified before the Brink's grand jury in 1953, INS picked him up again. They claimed their justification came from a 1948 larceny charge against Pino in which his one-year sentence had been revoked and the case placed on file. Pino and his expensive legal team argued that a charge on file could not be the grounds for deportation, that there was no "finality" to the case. The argument worked its way up through the federal appeals courts, and the U.S. Supreme Court agreed to examine his case. The justices sided with Pino and let stand a lower court's decision to halt the deportation.

From afar, O'Keefe continued to simmer. There was "Fat Tony" Pino taking his case to the highest court in the land, while he couldn't even get the money to fight a lousy burglary charge.

SPECS O'KEEFE, out on bond while his second Pennsylvania conviction was being appealed, roamed the streets of Boston like a lion. Every crook in the city knew that O'Keefe was looking for the guys who had been with him on the "Big Job." In particular, he wanted to confront Jazz Maffie and Henry Baker. Rumors in the underworld were that the other robbers were dipping into O'Keefe's share of the loot. In particular, Maffie — whom O'Keefe had trusted with his cut of the cash — had been gambling it away. Right after O'Keefe reappeared in March 1954, Baker and his wife left town, telling neighbors they were going to slip away on vacation for a couple of weeks.

O'Keefe paired up again with Johnny Carlson, the racketeer who had tried to collect defense donations on his behalf. Now the two attempted to shake down old friends. Some guys were in jail, some were out of town, some were dodging them. Instead of chasing them all down, O'Keefe made them come to him.

On May 18, 1954, they grabbed Vincent Costa, dragged him to a motel room, and held him for ransom. O'Keefe told Pino if he wanted to see his brother-in-law again he had to come up with at least five figures. Pino hit up the rest of the gang and made some collections. The amount was far less than the figure O'Keefe wanted, but he agreed to let Costa go two days later — bruised and bloodied, but still breathing. When FBI agents questioned Costa and his wife about the kidnapping, they claimed it never happened.

Two weeks later, Specs O'Keefe was cruising in his car at night through Dorchester, when another vehicle pulled alongside at a light. O'Keefe, his head already on a swivel, ducked down in the front seat as a pistol sprayed his windshield before the shooter peeled rubber. O'Keefe was unhurt, but his temper was aflame. It was now an all-out war.

The duo of O'Keefe and Carlson rapped on Henry Baker's door. Baker had been the antsiest of all the players and answered the knock by pulling a handgun. O'Keefe had his weapon at the ready, and the pair exchanged gunfire right on the front stoop. With all the twitching and ducking, none of the bullets hit their mark, zipping instead harmlessly past one another. Baker fled, but O'Keefe had made his point.

Within days, a new goon was in Boston. Pino paid Elmer Burke, better known as "Trigger" Burke, $1,000 to get rid of Specs O'Keefe. Burke was a pure "kill-crazy psychopath" who had once shot a New York bartender in the face for breaking up a fistfight. He spotted O'Keefe walking through the Victory Road housing project in Dorchester (where his mistress lived) and that's where the ambush went down.

Burke jumped from behind a building firing an M-3 submachine gun. O'Keefe blindly returned fire, but it was Burke who had the upper hand. O'Keefe ducked into alleyways, only to be greeted by another salvo of bullets. He made dust running down sidewalks, jumping fences, ducking behind trash cans, and still Burke squeezed off more rounds. The shootout lasted nearly thirty minutes, Burke toying with O'Keefe like a cat would a mouse.

A shot finally hit its mark. A bullet struck O'Keefe in the wrist, shattering his watch. He kept running until he was hit in the leg and went down in a bloody heap. Burke calmly walked over to his prey. O'Keefe played opossum, hoping the hitman would think he was dead. Burke stood over him, pointing his "grease gun" down at the body, but distant police sirens were growing louder. He thought better of it and fled the scene.[1] O'Keefe opened his eyes and limped away to hide until Carlson could get to him. Patrolmen who arrived on the scene found a trail of blood leading to an alley, but the wounded man was already gone.

O'Keefe's anger had turned to outright paranoia. For protection he carried with him multiple firearms, including a machine gun. But packing all that heat was a violation of his parole, and police in Leicester, Massachusetts, arrested him on August 1, 1954, on a weapons violation. Convicted four days later for a twenty-seven-month hitch, O'Keefe was placed in Springfield's Hampden County jail — on the other side of the state — for his own protection.

Two days after O'Keefe was taken off the street, Johnny Carlson went missing. His car was parked near his home, but Carlson was nowhere to be found. Word on the street was the Brink's gang took him out for helping Specs.

SPECIAL AGENT JOHN LARKIN had worked the Brink's case from the very beginning. He'd been there the night of the holdup, walking through the mess of papers and cash flung across the floors. He was among hundreds of FBI agents across the country who had had a hand in the investigation, but he was better placed than most. Larkin grew up in the same Boston neighbor-

---

1. Elmer "Trigger" Burke, whose psychopathic tendencies and uncontrollable temper grew largely from the murder of his older brother while Burke was in Sing Sing, forged a legendary career as a mid-century hit man. Once released from prison, Burke shot the guy he suspected of killing his brother in the back of the head with a double barrel shotgun. He then went into business as a hired assassin, one who specialized in machine-gun killings. For whatever reason, he decided to spend another eight days in Boston after the O'Keefe shooting to do some sightseeing. A cop collared him, and he was charged for attempting to murder O'Keefe. While awaiting trial, Burke escaped from Boston's notoriously porous Charles Street Jail during an exercise break in the yard. Guards tried to intercept him as he ran to a steel exit door, but waiting there was an armed masked man, dressed in a fake guard's uniform, who helped him out and into a getaway car. Officials identified that car as being registered to Fat Tony Pino. A year later Burke was recaptured in Folly Beach, South Carolina, and extradited to New York to answer for the murder of the bartender Edward "Poochy" Walsh. He spent the night of his execution smoking cigars and reading his own press clippings. When the guards finally sat him in the electric chair, Trigger Burke gave a big wave and a smile to all those who gathered to watch him fry.

hoods the suspects did, so there was a natural rapport. He had spent most of his energy on Fat Tony Pino. Over five and a half years, he'd spent dozens of hours talking civilly with Pino, the agent waiting patiently for Pino to make a mistake that he never did.

Larkin tried to work on Specs O'Keefe while he was stuck in county jail. Carlson's disappearance weighed heavily on O'Keefe's mind. And Gus Gusciora, the friend who had been arrested with him in Pennsylvania, had died in prison of a brain aneurism. It wasn't clear who O'Keefe was protecting now, but he stuck to the code of silence.

Agent Larkin tried again in December of 1955, only a month before the state statute of limitation was set to expire, to get O'Keefe to talk. He was still uncooperative, but he said he'd like to talk with J. Edgar Hoover. Larkin said he couldn't make that happen, but would O'Keefe be willing to talk to his boss if he came out from Boston? O'Keefe agreed. That's when he first met Edward Powers.

Powers and Larkin returned just after Christmas, an emotional time for any inmate. By now, Ed Powers was the seventh special agent to lead the Brink's investigation and there were few grains of sand left in the hourglass. O'Keefe's impression of Powers was the same as everyone else's. He was a nice guy and had a magnetic personality that made it easy to talk to him. Powers saw something genuine in O'Keefe as well.

Powers reported their conversation was casual. By comparison to all the other interrogations, the talk with Powers was exceedingly short — one hour. When O'Keefe still refused to talk, Powers made a promise to come back and visit soon. He made it sound like it was to be a social call between friends, not a threat of a tougher grilling.

Powers and Larkin came back the following day. Instead of sitting with his arms crossed, O'Keefe's body language was more open. His tongue was none the looser, but Powers felt he was getting close.

The two men returned on January 6, 1956, days before the state statute of limitations on the Brink's heist would run out. Powers asked O'Keefe to consider giving up the other members of the gang. They'd shown no loyalty to *him* when he'd been jailed in Pennsylvania. They planted the dismantled truck near his home, likely to draw suspicion to him. They'd blown through his share of the score and weren't going to pay him back. They'd killed Carlson. They'd already tried to kill him three times. He was facing up to twenty more years in jail while the rest of the crew would be spending his cash. There was nothing to be gained from his silence.

Joseph "Specs" O'Keefe, broken from six years of bitterness and incarceration, looked over at Powers. He was surrounded in blackness, and Powers was pointing to a pinprick of light. "All right," he sighed. "What do you want to know?"

O'KEEFE FILLED IN ALL THE BLANKS to the greatest bank robbery in history. As he would later recount in his own book, *The Crime That Nearly Paid: The Inside Story of One of the Most Famous Hold-Ups in the History of Crime,* the heist was the work of eleven men. It was Pino's idea and been in the planning since 1947. He, O'Keefe, and several others spent months casing the Brink's building, planning to knock over armored cars in the garage, only to learn in 1948 that Brink's was moving its headquarters to a new location on Prince Street. The plan started anew. The Prince Street location was more ideal. The building itself was nondescript; few knew Brink's was inside. The rooftops from neighboring buildings provided excellent views for casing.

Each crew member took turns breaking into the building after hours. Each time they took with them the lock cylinder from one of the five doors they'd need to pass through to get to the vault. They'd quickly make a key for that lock, then replace it before anyone could suspect it had been tampered with. The team even visited the company that installed Brink's alarm to examine schematics. O'Keefe said that in the weeks before the heist, the men used their pass keys after dark to walk right up to the vault and kiss it, wondering what riches awaited inside. Honestly, the robbers were appalled at how weak the security at Brink's actually was.

The operation was planned for January. They had to strike while the building was empty but the vault was open, at approximately 7 p.m. They'd practiced the approach and getaway time and time again. The rendezvous point was in Roxbury, and on the ride over in the stolen Ford stake-truck, Pino passed around the pea coats, Halloween masks, galoshes, pairs of gloves, and pistols. Vincent Costa played lookout from an adjacent roof. By January 17, they'd done this run on six previous nights, only to be waved off by Costa because the conditions weren't right. On the night of the seventeenth, the lights on the Prince Street side of the building were off. Parking the truck on the back side of the building, seven robbers slunk through a playground and waited. Costa gave the "go" signal by flashlight, and the squad used their passkeys to move through the locked doors. O'Keefe, his handgun leveled, was first into the counting room.

Expert wheel-man Joseph Banfield and Pino — who didn't go into in the building — drove the truck down to the front exit as the robbers came out. Costa fled in a separate car, stolen days earlier. They drove to Jazz Maffie's parents' house in Roxbury. It was there that they unloaded the take and started counting it up. Pino and James "Jimmer" Faherty left immediately to establish early alibis; another robber, Michael Geagon, jumped the truck even before it got to Roxbury so he could do the same. Pino would later return with McGuiness, who collected the disguises and disposed of the Ford.

The remaining men spent the next ninety minutes sorting and calculating. Securities, payroll envelopes, and thousand-dollar bills — anything that could tie them to the robbery — were put in a coal hamper and destroyed. That still left $1.1 million in small, virtually untraceable cash to split. The gang inspected every individual bill, looking for pencil marks or other notations that could identify the money. Some worried that newly minted bills might be conspicuously crisp; McGinnis said he had an idea for quickly "aging" the money.

Every member of the Brink's gang got $100,000. O'Keefe had nowhere to hide the money other than his car trunk. Because he kept getting picked up by the Boston cops, he asked McGinnis to retrieve his money and stash it. When he later asked for the money back, McGinnis handed him a suitcase. McGinnis had shorted him by $2,000.

Before skipping town with Gusciora, O'Keefe asked Maffie to hold his cut. He took $5,000 for the road trip, but Specs O'Keefe said he never saw another cent from the heist again. Maffie gambled it away, and the other members refused to make him whole.

POWERS AND LARKIN MOVED immediately to get warrants for all the culprits. In one swoop, Fat Tony Pino, Big Joe McGinnis, Henry Baker, Jazz Maffie, Michael Geagon, and Vincent Costa were arrested on January 12, 1956. When an FBI agent tried to detain Maffie, his little son called the police to say someone was trying to handcuff his daddy.

J. Edgar Hoover announced the arrests from Washington. Gusciora and the driver, Banfield, had both passed away from natural causes, so the arrests left only two members of the eleven-man operation at large: Thomas "Sandy" Richardson and James Faherty. The men were boyhood friends and were surely on the lam together. They went on the FBI's Most Wanted List in April.

A longshoreman, William Cameron, tipped the feds that Richardson and Faherty were hiding out in a Coleman Street apartment in Dorchester. He knew the person acting as porter for the holed-up crooks, bringing them food, liquor, and other supplies. A month later, Cameron would be found slumped over the wheel his car, a bullet in the head — a mot juste from Pino and company.

The FBI staked out the tenement to see which unit the porter delivered to. Powers and his men drew an elaborate operation to secure the building before going in. With some agents dressed as custodians and tenants, they surround the apartment and had every door and window covered. A team of about dozen agents went to the door, pistols drawn, and battered their way in. Powers was first in the room.

The pair was sitting at the kitchen table rolling $5,000 in coins into paper packages, storing them in three beer boxes. Richardson's hair had been dyed blond. With the clattering of the splintering door, Richardson and Faherty were up from their chairs and reaching for the three pistols stashed underneath a towel in the bathroom. The agents tackled them both before any shots could be exchanged, and they were removed from the apartment so efficiently that the kids playing stickball in the yard never knew what had happened.

Powers had not only cracked the largest bank robbery of all time, but he became the first agent to capture two criminals on the Most Wanted List at the same time.

BASED ON HIS KNOWLEDGE of the case and his background as a lawyer, in August 1956, Special Agent Powers sat next to District Attorney Garrett Byrne during the two-month trial for the remaining eight Brink's robbers. It took two weeks and seventeen hundred potential jurors to finally empanel a fourteen-person jury.

Specs O'Keefe, who spent seven grueling days on the stand, didn't consider himself a stool pigeon. The deal was that if any of the gang "muffed," they'd be "taken care of." O'Keefe figured Pino and the others muffed when they tried to gyp him out of his share, so he took care of them. The money from the Brinks Heist was never recovered, but even without that critical evidence the jury took just three and a half hours to convict. In exchange for his cooperation, Specs was released into witness protection.

Before leaving in 1957 for his next posting as head of the New York FBI bureau, Powers met with O'Keefe in the East Cambridge jail to say goodbye and wish him luck. A strange bond had formed between the two men. Powers thanked him for helping him solve the case; O'Keefe thanked Powers for all he had done. It was an unusual parting. Perhaps they realized how they had changed the trajectory of each other's lives.

"O'Keefe is a strange mixture of human qualities," Powers wrote. "While he led a life of crime and was considered a most adept, skillful criminal, he was also a soft-spoken, well-mannered individual. He was alert, intelligent and well read."

Even with his deep admiration for the FBI agent, O'Keefe could never quite put into words why after nearly getting away with it, why it was *this* man he finally confessed to. Of everything written about Power, Specs may have summed it up best:

"He's one of those all-American guys," he said.

11

The
Crusader

ONE OF THE MOST MEMORABLE PHOTOGRAPHS of the sweepstakes news coverage was of an opponent urging repeal with the use of props. The still photo, taken during a television interview, showed a professionally dressed man holding both a chunk of granite and an equally large sponge. The point he was making was that the fine tradition of the Granite State was about to be usurped by moochers and leeches.

The props were not the most interesting part of the image. The man was also sporting a black eye. The caption writers were all compelled to note that the shiner was not the product of makeup, that it was the real thing.

Blossoming from the picture's thousand words was an assumed legend, that this anti-gambling Don Quixote — in some likely role as sidewalk evangelist — got socked in the face by someone who refused to be saved. Stoic and pious, the crusader declined to say how he got the black eye in the first place.

CHARLES W. H. WITCOMB had been in the news several times before the photo. Witcomb (the W stood for William, and everyone called him Bill) was the man who went to Ed Powers's house that August afternoon to convince the FBI agent to turn his back on the sweepstakes effort. Witcomb had begun his own one-man repeal campaign out of his home in the oceanfront town of Hampton, New Hampshire. After receiving some financial support from the Congregational Christian Conference of Concord, Witcomb printed a thousand bumper stickers reading "Repeal Sweepstakes." He said the colors were red, white, and blue because those were the colors of "the Christian flag."

"This is not a political movement," he told the Associated Press. "This is a spontaneous moral movement!" He also felt the legislature's vote passing the sweepstakes did not reflect the will of the people.

He tried selling the bumper stickers for a dime each, but resorted in the end to handing them out to like-minded residents. Witcomb mailed bumper stickers to Governor King, President Kennedy, and former President Eisenhower in hopes of getting their attention. Sweeps Commissioner Howell Shepard was flummoxed upon finding a repeal bumper sticker on his statehouse desk in the day's correspondence. Shepard later told a sympathetic reporter it "shook [him] up."

Witcomb made no secret about where the sticker idea came from. He said he was irked that Governor King had not responded to any of his letters on the subject, and he complained, "I thought I was at least entitled to an acknowledgment."

Before accosting Powers, Witcomb had organized a motorcade that would drive through Hampton protesting the impending lottery. His goal was to have motorcades roam across New Hampshire and enlist aid along the way. Witcomb wanted to get a sticker on every automobile in the state. On the Sunday afternoon of the demonstration, however, only about thirty people in a dozen cars showed up the rally point at Meeting House Green. Witcomb and his family passed out bumper stickers to everyone who came.[1]

Before the convoy could roll, its organizer gathered the protesters around for a speech. "The people of New Hampshire have been led down the garden path," he said. "The legislators of this state sold their honor and the honor of this state when they passed this gambling measure." Witcomb didn't want to wait until the local option vote in March. He wanted the legislature to reconvene now in special summer session to repeal the sweepstakes.

---

1. Ironically, no one can remember if Witcomb's own car had a bumper sticker. The man was obsessive about cleaning and polishing his Plymouth to the point that the hood literally had a wax build-up. Relatives say slapping a hard-to-remove sticker on his bumper would have been totally out of character for the man. But with lack of evidence to the contrary, let us assume Witcomb's commitment to the cause was deeper than to his car.

A reporter covering the rally asked Witcomb if was disappointed by the meager turnout. "No. Everything must start out small," he said. He repeated his complaint that King had not replied to his correspondence.

The motorcade story got carried in several anti-Sweeps-leaning newspapers. Some of the local broadsheets that had advocated *for* the lottery ignored the effort. It was a sign of things to come — coverage of the sweepstakes would eventually be unabashedly colored by each paper's editorial stand.

After the stories were printed, Witcomb received a letter from the statehouse inviting him to meet personally with the governor. He felt like his quixotic effort was gaining ground.

IN MANY WAYS Bill Witcomb had been tilting windmills all his adult life. The son of a British silversmith, he was conceived in England, born in Canada, and raised in the United States. When he was a boy, his father ran a little grocery store in Massachusetts. With young Bill at his side, he told customers that bread loaves were eight cents, "but we have a sale of three for a quarter." Those who were math deprived would leave with the bounty while father and son privately laughed about the extra penny they made on every deal. The mischievous ruse was light-hearted, but it was not a practice an older Bill Witcomb would have likely approved.

In high school, the class of 1938 voted Witcomb "most patriotic" student. "But Bill," protested his father, "you're not even American." The young man had never seen himself as a Canadian. On his own, he began the process of naturalization. With world war approaching, the twenty-year-old volunteered, proud of his citizen status and ready to serve.

According to biographer Paul Bagley, Witcomb worked his way up from cadet to bomber pilot in the 8th Army Air Corps and was in charge of a small crew of men. Their B-17 Flying Fortress was named *Lassie Come Home* after the popular film, but its double meaning was lost on no one. They trained in England and were soon flying over the English Channel, pushing farther and farther eastward into Europe.

Witcomb's younger brother, Ken, was in the infantry. There was an age difference between them, large enough to strain the usual fraternal bonds. The younger Witcomb visited his brother's airbase to see the bomber he piloted, and the men exchanged awkward hugs and made some small talk before 1st Lt. Witcomb said he had to get into the air. While taxiing, Bill saw Ken offering a crisp salute from the side of the runway. For brothers who weren't particularly close, it was a touching sign of respect. It was also the last time they saw each other.

Ken Witcomb was killed in June 1944 during a battle in the French town of Nancy. When Bill Witcomb flew home for the service, there was no body. Ken had been interred in a makeshift cemetery along with thousands of other U.S. soldiers on the European front. All that was left for his relatives back home was a medal and a folded flag.

Already a religious man, Bill Witcomb began attending church services several times a week on base. He didn't know how to reconcile his faith in Christ with his assignment of dropping bombs. Surely civilians were hurt or killed. He was also racked with guilt about his brother's death in the French countryside. Why should he survive, return to America, when his brother hadn't? He knew he was suffering from what was euphemistically referred to as "battle fatigue," what the doughboys had called "shell shock." Tens of thousands of GIs were given the same prescription: shove it down, shut up about it, and believe any pain you have is worthless compared to those killed in action.

Bill Witcomb pushed his combat crew farther into the combat theater, determined to end the war himself. As combat dragged on, supplies were scarce. With his unit low on fuel and bombs, Witcomb returned to the airstrip from an aborted mission with his B-17 still loaded with both. Standard procedure was to dump the fuel and drop the munitions so an aircraft would be light enough to safely land. Witcomb risked blowing out his landing gear — or blowing up his aircraft — just to save the supplies.

Lassie Come Home had a good string of luck. Witcomb's crew had made their thirty-five bombing runs relatively unscathed. The B-17 took flak from time to time, which chewed up wings and the fuselage. On one run they lost their engines and had to coast back to England like a 36,000-pound hang glider. According to Bagley's book, *Crosses in the Sky*, Witcomb attributed their good fortune to the fact that all the men in his crew prayed regularly. After completing that thirty-fifth mission, *Lassie Come Home* had met its quota, and the crew was free to leave the theater and return stateside. While the Flying Fortress had a few dings in its exterior, Witcomb's internal wounds would never heal.

BILL WITCOMB'S REPATRIATION STATESIDE was marked by two things: a deep, almost self-destructive sense of morality and justice, and fits of anger and depression. While still an army officer, Captain Witcomb had been assigned to lead an all-black unit, and he had given the men's race little consideration except when it came time to drill. The unit had a tight, rhythmic cohesion he'd rarely seen in white companies. After his tour of duty in Europe, Witcomb sometimes flew these soldiers home on military transports if he was heading to a certain part of the country. Often, if the tower spotted a black serviceman in the cockpit with Witcomb, his plane would be skipped over repeatedly for flight clearance. Once Witcomb caught on to the snub, he became enraged at the disrespect shown to his fellow soldiers because of race. That wasn't the kind of liberty he had fought for in the skies of Europe. One time Witcomb mutinied by rolling his plane forward to block the runway until the tower cleared them for takeoff. Once in a co's club on a southern army base, Witcomb smashed a soda bottle and brandished the jagged edge to stop a potential fight between a cluster of white soldiers and the captain's black companion. Witcomb would never be a civil rights activist in the traditional sense; he only cared about what he thought was right.

While in the army, Witcomb had taken a war bride. Ellie Atkinson lived in New England, and the couple had two baby girls. Upon his return state-side, Witcomb took a lucrative job at his father-in-law's lumber business. At a company meeting, his father-in-law announced they were going to merge with a crosstown competitor — a deal that, from Witcomb's point of view, could allow them to fix prices on unsuspecting customers. Witcomb stood up to his father-in-law, complaining bitterly about a decision he thought would lead them down an unethical road. None of the other employees expressed concern that the merger had nefarious overtones, and the boss insisted he had no intention of price gouging or using other unfair practices. But Witcomb would have none of it.

The accusations against her father did not sit well with Ellie, but her husband insisted he hadn't gone to war to fight against tyranny only to be a part of it at home. The war had only been over a short time. Ellie believed Witcomb didn't understand the lumber business yet, nor did he understand her father. Witcomb understood enough. He vowed not to return to the family business. In the postwar economy, jobs were still hard to come by, and Ellie implored her husband to think about their two children, the mortgage, and everything he was turning his back on. Nothing would satisfy him. He had taken a principled stand and would not back down.

Witcomb's mood swings were common now. His marriage was in free-fall. Ellie took the children and sought a divorce — a rarity in the late 1940s. Bill Witcomb was alone.

AFTER BEING SWORN IN to his new position as executive director of the New Hampshire Sweepstakes, Ed Powers was already sizing up the local press corps to see who was pro- and who was anti-lottery. Powers found all the men in question to be polite and personable, even those who were against the Sweeps for personal or professional reasons. It was through one of these initial contacts that Powers mentioned how Bill Witcomb had bull rushed him at home and warned him to stay away.

By Friday of that week, stories appeared in the *Boston Globe,* the *Manchester Union Leader,* and the United Press International wire service describing Witcomb's "warning" to Powers to stay out of the Granite State. The protestor found himself defending the visit to local radio and TV stations. Witcomb denied threatening Powers, saying, "I just wanted him to know that he and his family would have a tough row to hoe in New Hampshire."

Before the story broke, Witcomb had sent a letter to Powers thanking him for his time and said he found the discussion "revealing." He wrote, "We welcome you and your family to New Hampshire. However, please bear in mind there is an increasing number of solid New Hampshire people who are revolting at the principle of your family being dependent of its support on a mere game of chance."

Upon hearing of the incident in Norwood from Ed Powers and reading the news coverage, Governor King was furious. Witcomb was at that moment penciled in the governor's appointment book for the following week. King ordered Executive Secretary Tom Power to write Witcomb a letter canceling their meeting.

"The governor ordinarily extends the courtesy of an appointment to any New Hampshire citizen seeking one," the Associated Press wrote, quoting from Power's correspondence. "However, in light of your visit to the home of Edward J. Powers . . . the governor feels that no useful purpose would be served in any discussions with you."

Even this snub made front-page news in the anti-Sweeps press. The *Concord Daily Monitor* gave the rescinded invitation story twenty-eight column inches, including a sizable photo of Witcomb displaying his "Repeal Sweepstakes" bumper stickers. Later the paper ran an editorial entitled "Tough Row to Hoe." They described Witcomb as a "crusader," but said the substance of that afternoon argument wasn't important in itself. The *Monitor* said the incident was symptomatic of the kind of thing gambling breeds: "One would be naïve to believe that there won't be future headlines about efforts to smuggle New Hampshire lottery tickets across state lines." The editors questioned whether Powers could keep his finger in the dyke long enough to hold back the dark forces waiting to take advantage.

Such notoriety helped lift Witcomb's profile. He *did* feel like a crusader, one who was hell-bent on doing the right thing. But slowly, his euphoria morphed into a pensive melancholy.

No one knew Charles H. W. Witcomb was only a few months away from a mental breakdown.

AFTER HIS DISASTROUS FIRST MARRIAGE, Witcomb got a job working in logistics at American Airlines. He caught the eye of a pretty secretary named Frances Ackerman. They had similar religious and political beliefs. A second marriage and a second pair of daughters followed.

After leaving American Airlines, Witcomb tried a handful of new careers. He tried his hand at silversmithing, just as his father had. He worked in the basement trying to craft bits of art, but making money in this field was harder than it looked. Witcomb took a contract job with the George P. Pilling Medical Supply Company manufacturing silver stints for surgical procedures. He devised a method for making the component quickly and cheaply and was able to deliver his orders in record time. Impressed by Witcomb's output, executives at Pilling flew in from Philadelphia to tour his factory. Imagine their shock when Witcomb's "factory" was discovered to be nothing more than his basement, and his workforce to be no one but him. Witcomb explained to the executives his technique for improving the production of the stints. Quick as a flash, Pilling implemented the cost-saving, time-saving method at its own production facility, cutting Witcomb out of the process. His consolation prize was a job as a regional sales rep with the surgical-device manufacturer.

Hampton, New Hampshire, was a "dry" town, and efforts to bring alcohol sales back to their community already had Mr. and Mrs. Witcomb indignant and motivated. The arrival of the New Hampshire Sweepstakes was additionally troubling to them. Bill believed the lottery broke the commandment against coveting. He also thought it incited laziness, one of the seven deadly sins. His civic sensibilities were offended along with his religious ones. The vanity license plate on his Plymouth was "SERVE."

Dinners at the Witcomb house were accompanied by deep discussions, even with eight-year-old Sandy. Father would challenge daughter to give her opinion on topics from the news or around the neighborhood. They spent four days a week at their local church. Each day was a new lesson for the girls.

Frances could tell when her husband was about to go through one of his mood changes just by the way he walked and the songs he whistled. As their father's manic joy would overtake him, life for the children was a page from *Peter Pan*. Witcomb would ignore work and stay home to play, push the girls on swings, and embark on whatever adventures they could dream up. This period might last days or weeks, but eventually the energy would wane.

Witcomb would literally start whistling a different tune, and his body language would change. He'd yell out from night terrors and flop sweat. He was never violent with his family, never threatened them harm, but he filled the house with anxiety. Frances kept a close eye on him until it was time to announce to the children, "We're going to stay with friends for a few days." When the worst of the depression had passed, they'd return home until the next time.

It wouldn't be until 1965, when Sandy got off the school bus to see her father being pulled from their house in a straitjacket, that Witcomb began getting the mental-health treatment he needed. He was committed to the state psychiatric hospital for about a month. While in treatment, he did what very few veterans ever did: he talked about his war service and how it haunted him. Determined not to be relegated to a waiting room, Frances insisted on taking part in his therapy. She worked with the doctors to be an advocate and a nurse, a role she would play in his care for the rest of his life.

The psychiatrist determined Witcomb had more than combat fatigue; he had a bipolar disorder. It was one of the reasons why he couldn't discern between giants and windmills.

BACK IN THE AUTUMN OF 1963, as the sweepstakes operation began to take shape, Witcomb had the role of professional lottery opponent all to himself. Though other anti-Sweeps groups had been forming, Witcomb did not formally join them. He enjoyed his role as gadfly or crusader (depending on which paper got your eight cents). The press continually turned to Bill Witcomb to be the voice of dissent. To them he was "colorful." His detractors thought he was "crazy," by which they meant overly aggressive, overly indignant, and overly a pain in the ass. Everyone loves a Don Quixote, unless it's your windmill he's trying to tip.

Decades later, Sandy could still recall the time her father had been solicited to appear on a local television station to speak about the Sweeps. The whole family was on pins and needles to see him on the black-and-white box in their living room. None of them knew anyone who'd ever been on TV before.

Witcomb liked to use props to make his point, but he knew another bumper sticker wasn't going to have the same impact on television. He had some ideas and began rummaging through drawers and boxes. In his obsession he began throwing things on the floor, dumping out drawers, making a clanging mess. Frances went to him, hoping to calm him down or lend a hand. Amid the cacophony of scissors and spools and silverware, and his own manic murmurings, the room got louder and louder. Frances reached down to help him pick up a handful of jetsam. Witcomb didn't want her to touch it. They were both on their knees, trying to maintain their balance as their arms were busy entangling each other. Frances started to roll over and jerked her arms to break her fall. With that, her elbow smashed Witcomb square in the right eye.

The house fell silent. Frances covered the gasp escaping her mouth. Witcomb had landed on his back and slowly got to his feet. Like a slap across the face, the suddenness of the blow snapped Witcomb back to his senses.

Frances rushed to his side, her voice full of contrition. Her husband, calm as could be, told her to pay it no mind. "It was an accident," he said. "It wasn't done in anger."

The socket around Witcomb's eye grew darker. He put ice on it, but they all could see the skin growing dark purple.

"Oh, Daddy," Sandy cried. "How are you going to go on TV with a black eye?"

Witcomb just smiled at his daughter with the serenity of man who believed in a higher power, who believed everything would be all right.

Witcomb wore a dark suit and tie to the television station, and he was greeted by still photographers who wanted pictures for the following day's paper. Witcomb pulled out his props.

"This," he began, "is a piece of granite, symbolizing our Granite State." The gray chunk was the size of a basketball. "It's threatened to be replaced by this."

He held up a large round sponge nearly the same size as the granite. "Do we want to become New Hampshire, the 'Sponger State'?"

Someone asked about his shiner, clearly visible in any picture taken that evening. Witcomb said the sweepstakes would give New Hampshire "a black eye" unless it was repealed.

The bruise looked too real, too fresh to be a stunt. The reporters pressed further, and Witcomb shrugged it off as being genuine but "inadvertent." The sympathetic *Concord Daily Monitor* wrote that the black eye, "attests to the vigor of Witcomb's campaign."

The press lapped it up. Witcomb's face — like his B-17 — had damage that could be seen. But inside, he was barely holding it together.

12
The Charm Offensive

EXECUTIVE DIRECTOR ED POWERS estimated that in his twenty-two years at the FBI he had given a thousand speeches, so he was comfortable in front of a crowd. Possibly the only thing Powers was uncomfortable with was placing a wager at a real racetrack.

He didn't inherit a posh desk job where he could close his door and pretend to keep busy. The New Hampshire Sweepstakes was, six months after its passage, still more concept and less reality than Governor King or Representative Larry Pickett would have hoped. While it seemed a lifetime away, the March local referendum vote bought them the time to plan and the political cover to be unproductive.

Though New Hampshire was the first state to *pass* a modern lottery, it was hardly the first state to *propose* a lottery. Since 1934, Puerto Rico had been conducting a daily numbers draw lottery. In addition to the global reach of the Irish Sweepstake, many countries were running national lotteries during the 1960s. *This Week* reported West Germany ran the largest, grossing $320 million a year, followed by France, Spain, Australia, and Italy. Americans could get lottery tickets south of the border in Mexico, where sales topped $56 million annually. Most of these national lotteries however only contributed 1 percent or less to their country's revenue.

Upon his appointment, a very public letter of congratulations to Powers was printed in the *Worcester Sunday Telegram* from Francis Kelly and Robert

Donaldson of the Massachusetts Sweepstakes Committee. These neighbors to the south had a very active sweepstakes movement.

Kelly was the former Massachusetts lieutenant governor and attorney general and the effort's greatest advocate. His passion was so fierce that he often publicly berated those who took contrary positions. He appeared annually at the statehouse in Boston to push a lottery, but he was really ginned up in 1963.

"New Hampshire is making Massachusetts the laughingstock of the nation by getting the jump on us," he yelled. "New Hampshire will make so much money that instead of counting it, they'll weigh it on horse scales and bail it. That's how fast it's going to come in." Kelly estimated that $2 billion was illegally wagered in the Bay State each year, and they could recover between $150 million and $200 million with a sweepstakes to reduce real estate and property taxes.

Advocates like Kelly had been filing sweeps bills in Massachusetts since before World War II with little to show for it. A statewide referendum in 1950 on establishing a sweepstakes failed, but in 1958 voters passed a similar ballot question — by a 2.5–1 margin — urging the state legislature to enact an annual lottery drawing. Despite what appeared to be a clear mandate, lawmakers failed to pass any lottery bills. Kelly's ire grew.

"New Hampshire has recovered the ball that Massachusetts has deliberately fumbled and scored a touchdown," he wrote in his open letter, dismissing Sweeps critics as the same "do-gooders" who opposed repealing Prohibition or legalizing Sunday baseball.

Clearly his letter in the *Sunday Telegram* was less about applauding Powers and more about hitching his committee's wagon to New Hampshire's star. Kelly offered the committee's twenty-five years of experience to help the Sweepstakes Commission. The Massachusetts group, in an effort to instill confidence in public gaming, put up a $10,000 reward to anyone who could point to a Massachusetts state law that had more safeguards than the commission's proposal (the proposal was deftly named the "Sound Timely and Corrupt-proof Massachusetts Sweepstakes Bill").

If only to parade them before local voters, Kelly suggested Powers consider the many security measures Massachusetts would put in place if the state ever found itself in the enviable position of legalizing the lottery. They proposed mandatory one-year jail sentences for anyone caught tampering with sweeps operations, with increased compulsory sentences for further convictions. State-chartered banks, which sold U.S. savings bonds, could also sell tickets.

City and town clerks — who are trusted with collecting citizens' precious taxes — could be trusted to sell tickets too. The Massachusetts bill also required a detailed annual audit of the sweepstakes that would be published for public inspection.

Kelly declared he had no doubt that citizens could transport Sweeps tickets across state lines and said Larry Pickett's prediction of $4 million in revenue was far too conservative. "Good luck to you and to our progressive sister-state of New Hampshire for giving to the great majority of chance-taking American public an opportunity to lawfully and honestly spend American money on America — instead of patronizing and profiting other countries and bookies."

THE HONEYMOON for Executive Director Ed Powers began to wane once the press and the legislature got a look at his salary. While working as the FBI bureau chief in Boston, Powers made $19,000 a year. To attract him, King and Shepard made sure to top his federal salary. The offer was to pay him $20,000 annually, a modest 5.2 percent increase over his FBI paycheck. But giving him $20,000 (the rough equivalent of $150,000 in today's money) to run the sweepstakes made him the highest paid employee in state government.

The editorial writers, even those who had been moon-eyed over Powers's selection, were circumspect about such lavish compensation. *What does this say about our state's priorities?* they asked. The *Concord Daily Monitor* pointed out the commissioner of education's salary was $14,800. The highway commissioner made $13,770, and the attorney general was paid $13,064. Governor King himself made only $16,587 to run the state. It was clear Powers would have been unlikely to take a pay cut to change careers and tackle something as challenging as the New Hampshire Sweeps, but the idea his salary was influenced by his financial requirements and less by what the Sweepstakes Commission thought the job was actually worth did not sit well with frugal state lawmakers.

The executive director was doing his best to earn his keep within the first month. He did not want to kick the can down the road to March 1964. Powers was determined to put together as much of the program as he could immediately, to build local consensus, and then to draw the national publicity needed to make the Sweeps a success. While his hire seemed to put to bed overnight the fears that mobsters were going to infiltrate the state operation, there were still questions about how the sweepstakes could prevent ticket scalping.

Powers began by hosting meetings with the commission and representatives from Rockingham Park, the sweepstakes venue. There was, to Powers's surprise, a lot of infighting and disagreement between the groups. Representative Larry Pickett had never, in all of his years of filing sweepstakes legislation, conferred in detail with management at the track. Yes, they were naturally in favor of a sweepstakes. They didn't care so much for the color Pickett painted the New Hampshire Jockey Club in his fervor, unintentionally implying the Sweeps would be nothing but a payday for the track if it were not for the steady hand and altruistic objectives of state government.

Lou Smith, the long-time owner/operator of Rockingham Park, had his own opinions on how a first-class sweepstakes race ought to be run. While King and the commission had spent months agonizing about how to run a lottery, they had given very little consideration thus far to the horse race itself. The size of the purse had not be determined, nor was there agreement on how much the state would pony up and how much the track would throw in. They hadn't even determined a date for the race — which had to be on a weekend when no other major derbies were running in New England. The law allowed for tickets to be sold at Rockingham Park, but no deals had been made about how this would go or how the track would be compensated. Smith had some very strong opinions about how to sell the maximum number of tickets, and this was presently the biggest bone of contention.

Powers needed to broker a peace between the warring parties and fast. His coming-out party was just weeks away.

THOSE WHO STUDY the modern New Hampshire media landscape might be awestruck to see the size and breadth of the state's press corps in the 1960s. The Internet, broadcast deregulation, corporate consolidation, and changing demographic habits have forever altered what may have been the golden age for local news. Newspapers weren't closing; they were publishing both morning and afternoon editions. Virtually all AM radio stations had a news staff. There were two active news wire services. These organizations employed several hundred reporters, editors, and photographers — as well as salesmen, press operators, deliverymen, and clerical staff.

The one event that brought most of them together in the same room was the annual New Hampshire United Press International dinner. The soiree was held in Concord at the Highway Hotel. The hotel was so named for its proximity to the interstate, but it was kept in the black because of its proximity to the statehouse. It had a wicked reputation as the setting of lascivious behavior by lawmakers who would forgo a late-night commute in favor of roaming the bars and hopping beds. There were effectively no other banquet facilities in the capital city, so the Highway Hotel became the default location for any after-hours gatherings of note.

UPI's invitation to Powers was a no-brainer, but Powers's selection of this event for a maiden address was also shrewd. The executive director had been inundated with speaking requests throughout New Hampshire and across the country. With every reporter in the state in the room for the UPI dinner, he was guaranteed to get the maximum local press coverage. There were just six months before the March referendum.

Powers ate at the head table, seated between a Portsmouth radio news director and the UPI bureau chief, his meal cooling as eager reporters constantly interrupted to shake his hand. While dessert was brought around, Powers was introduced and walked confidently to the podium. His voice was crisp, in the mid-to-high range. If Representative Larry Pickett evoked memories of W. C. Fields with his speech pattern, then Powers sounded like Walter Winchell, the radio and print journalist who was the narrator for "The Untouchables." He wasn't as cartoony at Winchell, but his voice pushed the button that said "that's the way a G-man sounds." Was there *anything* about this guy that didn't ooze authority?

There was something in his manner, in the way he conjured a speech script from his coat pocket like a magician, the way he easily adjusted the microphone and made Mona Lisa eyes with everyone in the room, which made him look like Elvis, like Moses — like a leader.

A seasoned toastmaster, Powers knew what his crowd wanted. They wanted some of his law-enforcement mojo. Even as Sweepstakes executive director, the most interesting thing about Powers was still his FBI career. He began the speech by talking about one bank robber they caught. The guy had passed the teller a note that read, "Okay sucker. I've got a gun. Fill a bag with money and you won't get hurt." The teller read the note, then picked up his pen and scribbled something. He passed the note back to the robber. It said, "Straighten your tie, Stupid. They're taking your picture."

Riding the laughter, Powers told the crowd about the famously leaky Charles Street Jail in Boston, which thugs like Trigger Burke easily slipped out of. "Now when people show up to visit a prisoner," Powers said, "the warden says, 'Wait a minute. I'll see if he's in.'"

In the audience, forks and flatware were nudged aside so reporters could place notebooks on their banquet tables and begin taking notes. Even sweeter than dessert would be if the Sweeps boss "made some news." He didn't disappoint.

First, Powers announced that tickets would be $3 and not $3.30 — meaning the Sweeps were not going to pass the threatened 10 percent excise tax on to players. The commission firmly believed the state lottery for education fell within the federal exception and was going to fight the IRS on the matter.

He also noted "a number of important decisions were reached by the commission last week. It was voted unanimously that a name and address be required from each purchaser of a sweepstakes ticket." Scribes who were plugged into state government already knew about the behind-the-scenes struggle on this point. Lou Smith feared putting names and addresses on tickets would frighten off some players and put a damper on sales. Members of the Sweepstakes Commission agreed with him. If fears lingered that purchasing these tickets was illegal, who would want to sign their name on the blasted thing? Tickets could have a number — just like a raffle ticket — and whoever turned the winner in could get the money. Now Powers was saying there had been a "unanimous" reversal? How did this happen?

"This was a basic and most important decision," he continued, "because it has ramifications affecting all other phases of the program. I have felt strongly from the outset that a name and address should be required."

Powers openly admitted they would sell more Sweeps tickets if there were no names and only serial numbers. "But if this were done," he said, "our program could be sabotaged and thereafter fail because we would, in effect, be playing into the hands of thieves, racketeers, and bums who could set up operations in other states to sell tickets at a price above our charge of three dollars."

The idea that shady brokers who sold and resold tickets in smoky bars and gambling joints — as Irish Sweep brokers did — had been virtually snuffed out. No getting used tickets or counterfeit slips that looked bad in full light. Signing a New Hampshire Sweeps ticket would not be an admission you had committed a crime; signing a ticket would be a declaration you had purchased it legally. There you had it: the commission and the racetrack changed their minds because Powers said so.

Powers said he wanted this to be a long-range enterprise, one that would provide funds for the state for years to come: "I want to see the day, and I am sure that most of you do likewise, when New Hampshire citizens will speak proudly of their sweepstakes program — a program they have pioneered for the nation — as proudly as do citizens of other countries were some form of lottery is legalized."

The press corps applauded the executive director as he left the podium full of grace. Guests ducked out of the dinner to file stories on Powers's triumphant speech. Within twenty-four hours, details were on page one in all of the state's dailies; UPI's wire story appeared in papers nationwide. What didn't make any of versions was this: Powers was completely in charge of the sweepstakes, and he could bend the will of his bosses — maybe even the governor — to do what needed to be done. He was serious as a heart attack about every detail and keeping the sweepstakes clean. Powers wasn't hired because of his past. He was hired because he had a vision for the future.

POWERS WENT ON A CHARM OFFENSIVE. If he could get in front of people, he could win them over for the March vote and convince them to buy a couple tickets too. Over the next few months, he likely ate more meals at Rotary clubs and Chamber of Commerce meetings than he did at Melva Powers's kitchen table. While Anna King was packing the governor lunches every day, Powers went for long stretches in which he didn't even have to bring a sandwich to work. He was now on a revolving circuit of lunch and dinner, lunch and dinner, beef or chicken, beef or chicken, leather or feather?

Powers may have been taking a page from John King's "no town too small" playbook. Every appearance received news coverage in whatever local paper covered that community, almost always with an accompanying photo.

At each stop he would roll out an evolving version of the speech he had given at the UPI dinner. The same opening jokes. Something flattering about the hosts. Then he'd launch into a meticulous but entrancing talk about how the sweepstakes would operate and all that he would do to make it free from corruption.

"We are beaming this money-raising program toward honest, law-abiding citizens," quoted the *Peterborough Transcript*. "It's my job to ensure this policy."

It may have amused Sweeps detractors at how quickly Powers got religion when it came to legalized gambling and tax policy. He was the man who, after all, earned his new position by leading operations that broke up numbers running and racketeering. Now he'd become the most influential bookie in the United States.

"If [the Sweeps] can be proved in New Hampshire, it would spread to other states. If so, it could eventually become a national sweepstakes . . . operated by government and not by private interests for private profit."

At this point in his speeches, he'd spread his hands not unlike a revival minister, and say, "I don't want to sound like a dreamer, but here is a source of revenue that could be tapped for this country's tremendous programs. It is in accord with the American way of life: voluntary, without sleight of hand, without beguiling."

After a dinner speech at the Peterborough Rotary club, the president made a show of presenting Powers with a token of their gratitude. It was a small wooden placard, with rounded corners and beveled edges. It had a spring loaded clip. It looked like the kind of thing a freshman would make in Wood Shop. Etched into the pine, written in Olde English script, was "New Hampshire Sweepstakes Tickets;" glued above the clip was a plastic badge with Powers's name. They presented him with a second placard for Governor King, declaring that each gift was an official "sweepstakes ticket holder." They urged members to get one for themselves to mount on their walls and keep those paper tickets safe.

IT WAS AT A DINNER EVENT like this where Powers publicly addressed the thorny issue of tickets and ticket possession. Still hanging over everyone's head was the threat from the federal government that bringing Sweeps tickets across state lines would be a violation of the Travel Act and the Interstate Transportation of Wagering Paraphernalia Act. Powers unveiled his workaround.

Attorney Joseph Millimet, who arguably knew more about the legal machinations of the state lotteries than anyone on the planet, and Powers had come together to find a passage through the concertina wire strung around the state by the feds. And they did.

Powers said that after players paid, they would *not* get Sweeps tickets. Nor would they receive a counterfoil — which was basically half of a perforated ticket. Instead, they would receive a kind of carbon copy of their ticket that included their name and number.

Powers said these were not tickets, nor were they receipts. The slips players would be given were "acknowledgments" that they were in the sweepstakes.

Powers and the commission had worked closely with Millimet to craft this idea of "acknowledgments." As they interpreted the Paraphernalia Act, bringing a live ticket across state lines would likely be a violation. So they decided that their lottery tickets would *stay in New Hampshire.* If a player had signed the ticket, laid claim, and proven purchase of the ticket, there was no legal reason for that person to take the ticket out of state.

Yet, if only from a marketing standpoint, they had to give the player *something* — *some* documentation they purchased a ticket. No player would want to give the state three bucks and walk away with nothing, as if they just paid a parking ticket. Or worse: a numbers runner.

Retaining the acknowledgment would not be required to claim a sweepstakes prize. A winner would not have to turn it in. They could lose it or give it away. The player could take their acknowledgment and immediately tear it up. It wasn't part of the game play, part of the mechanism. The paper slip they'd be given would have no further purpose in the gambling operation. They had the same value as a betting slip from a race run the day before (an example the Justice Department itself used in defining what was and was not "paraphernalia"). The acknowledgment would be in the eyes of the feds — with any luck — worthless.

The use of "acknowledgments" was — pun unavoidable — a huge gamble. There is no evidence doubting the sincerity the Sweepstakes Commission. It made sense. What *didn't* make sense to them was the Justice Department's slavish adherence to the words of the laws and not to their spirits. Their lottery was not an underground, illegal gambling racket that benefited organized crime. It functioned out in the open under strict rules of operation. To Powers, King, and partners, the sweepstakes was as innocuous as a church Bingo game.

If you were a cynic, you could say the acknowledgment was a gentlemen's agreement. It was the brown paper bag around the bottle beer. The cop on the beat didn't care if you drank on the stoop so long as you put it in a bag. But if you flaunted the glass bottle in his face, you were just daring him to arrest you. The acknowledgment allowed the feds to walk on by, whistling past the stoop, and let New Hampshire have its fun.

The federal government, however, is not one beat cop. States cannot have gentlemen's agreements with federal executive, legislative, and judicial entities made up of individuals — individuals who have different interpretations of what a lottery ticket is. Powers and Millimet may have declared acknowledgments were legal to possess outside of New Hampshire, but it would eventually take the highest court in the land to decide whether that was true.

Representative Larry Pickett (center left) gathers with Governor John King (center right) and other Democrats to discuss political maneuvers. Pickett devoted ten years to getting a sweepstakes bill signed into law. John King Collection, New Hampshire Institute of Politics

King was an earlier supporter of John Kennedy for president, and JFK inspired King to run for higher office. Here President Kennedy meets with state governors in the family dining room at the White House on May 29, 1963. Abbie Rowe. White House Photographs. John F. Kennedy Presidential Library and Museum, Boston

Attorney General Robert Kennedy pushed for several tough laws against organized crime and illegal gambling operations. These new laws, combined with others from the nineteenth century, effectively boxed a state lottery within the boundaries of New Hampshire. Yoichi Okamoto. LBJ Library, Austin, TX

FBI Special Agent Ed Powers was famous for cracking the 1950 Brink's heist and being the first to capture two FBI Most Wanted fugitives at the same time. His selection to run the Sweeps was a masterstroke by King. John King Collection, New Hampshire Institute of Politics

Governor King shakes hands with Ed Powers after swearing him in as the first executive
director of the New Hampshire Sweepstakes. Seen are (left to right) Melva and Ed Powers,
King, Commissioner Henry Turcotte, Commissioner Howell Shepard, and Commissioner
Edward Sanel. John King Collection, New Hampshire Institute of Politics

The plans for running a state lottery without hitting any of the tripwires laid before them fell to Sweepstakes Commissioner Howell Shepard, Governor King, and Executive Director Ed Powers. Meanwhile, federal agencies were actively trying to derail the gambling operation. John King Collection, New Hampshire Institute of Politics

As the public and press look on, Governor King purchases America's first legal lottery ticket of the twentieth century. John King Collection, New Hampshire Institute of Politics

The New Hampshire Sweepstakes drew hundreds of thousands of players from across the country. Here, a player fills out his name and address on a specially made ticket machine while a sales clerk dials the number of tickets purchased. Still, the Justice Department warned that taking Sweeps tickets out of state violated federal laws. Union Leader collection, courtesy of Manchester (NH) Historical Association

Governor King makes a speech before the first sweepstakes drawing, July 1964. To his left is Lou Smith of Rockingham Park. This first drawing reveals several surprise winners. Union Leader collection, courtesy of Manchester (NH) Historical Association

From their VIP perch above the Rockingham Park racetrack, finalists in the New Hampshire Sweepstakes watch as their horses round the first turn in the one-and-three-eighteenths mile race. Union Leader collection, courtesy of Manchester (NH) Historical Association

On the final turn, the horses were six abreast, until three burst from the pack. Bolting for the finish line were Knightly Manor, Purser, and Roman Brother. Union Leader collection, courtesy of Manchester (NH) Historical Association

The media darling among the finalists, Carol Ann Lee is mobbed by reporters looking for her reaction to being a big prizewinner in the sweepstakes. Union Leader collection, courtesy of Manchester (NH) Historical Association

Mr. and Mrs. Paul Cadrone of Gloversville, New York, plant kisses on jockey Fernando Alvarez, whose winning ride in the New Hampshire Sweepstakes made them $100,000 richer. Union Leader collection, courtesy of Manchester (NH) Historical Association

Despite the national obsession with the New Hampshire Sweepstakes, it never regained the level of interest it garnered in 1964. Its popularity waned and other states began to offer their own lotteries. The last Sweeps was run in 1972. John King Collection, NH Institute of Politics

13
Last Full Measure

ON JULY 28, 1963, Governor King and a large delegation were invited by Red Sox owner Tom Yawkey to celebrate New Hampshire Day at Fenway Park. Each of the New England states had a ceremonial game and New Hampshire's was a Sunday doubleheader against the Los Angeles Angels. King sported a dapper white golf cap and jaunty light colored suit to the ballpark. Everyone around him wore dark suit jackets and ties like it was a business meeting. The governor threw out the first pitch to catcher Bob Tillman from the box seats (putting a dignitary on the actual pitcher's mound for this ceremony was unheard of at the time, and a surefire recipe for disaster). Though it was a short toss, King still made Executive Secretary Tom Power throw a ball around with him beforehand just to warm up.

In between the two games, King was ushered on to the field to address the crowd of 17,409 as part of New Hampshire Day. His goal was to urge them to visit the Granite State's tranquil lakes in the summer, its colorful byways in the autumn, and prodigious ski slopes in the winter. King, usually so sure-footed in public, stumbled and stammered during his speech. He may have been unprepared. He more likely was thrown off by the massive Fenway PA system. As any national anthem singer can attest, hearing a split-second echo of one's own voice can create a kind of cognitive dissidence; the brain thinks it's stuttering and overcorrects its speech patterns, compounding the problem. The ham-fisted address was widely panned back home, as New Hampshire editorial writers called it "embarrassing," and said King appeared unfit to be the spokesman for state tourism (read: selling sweepstakes tickets).

The seventh-place Red Sox lost both games of the doubleheader, 5–0 and 5–4.

THE BOSTON PAPERS had turned their attention away from baseball as the calendar flipped to August. Summer on Cape Cod meant the Kennedys were in town. Inside the Hyannis fortress, the clan did all the things that grainy 8mm film has now made familiar: sun bathing, football in the sand, children running free. Mrs. Kennedy, in her third trimester, was in a rented home on Squaw Island. She had been there most of the summer, unable to carry on official duties as First Lady.

On the night of August 7, Jacqueline Kennedy began having contractions just thirty-four weeks into her pregnancy. Mrs. Kennedy had a history of early labor. Her daughter, Arabella, had been stillborn in 1956, and John Jr. was born premature, just days after the 1960 election. The mother was rushed to the secure hospital at Otis Air Force Base and gave birth to a boy. Just four pounds, ten and a half ounces, he couldn't get any air into his chest. Doctors told the president the baby had a lung condition called Hyaline Membrane Disease, a respiratory disorder common with preemies. The decision was made to get the infant to the world's best facility, Boston Children's Hospital, but not before JFK summoned a chaplain to baptize the baby Patrick Bouvier Kennedy.

Over the next two days, Kennedy shuttled back and forth from Boston to Cape Cod (where Jackie Kennedy remained hospitalized) to bring news and check on mother and child. When he arrived at Logan Airport and darted for Boston Children's, emotionally tone-deaf admirers cheered the president.

The baby's struggle for life shocked the nation. They had followed Jackie's pregnancy from the first baby bump. The mystique of another toddler in the White House made surrogate grandparents out of the sentimental. It also made John and Jacqueline Kennedy appear much younger than they actually were.

"Wife of President Rushed to Hospital." "Baby Sped to Boston." "Whole World Taken by Littlest Kennedy." "Kennedy Baby's Doctors Hopeful." "4 Days will Decide Infant's Chances." The nation held its breath. But Kennedys had the luck of the Irish. And tragedy — *tragedy?* — could never befall the Kennedys.

"He's a Kennedy," a *Boston Globe* headline famously declared. "He'll make it."

Next to this historic headline, surrounded by photos and sidebars of the Kennedy drama, there was only one other *Globe* front-page story above the fold.

"Powers to Head N.H. Sweeps."

IN CONCORD, Governor John King glanced away from the coverage of his inspired lottery chief pick to read about Patrick Kennedy. He was heartbroken the following day to read the failing infant had been removed from his hyperbaric chamber and placed in the president's arms, where he soon died. King tried for a long time to compose a condolence letter to send to Kennedy.

King, of course, felt a genuine personal connection to the president, going back to his letter to the young senator in 1956. King had received a telephone call from Kennedy after his surprise gubernatorial victory, and they exchanged correspondence as a matter of their public duties. While he may not have been a close advisor, Kennedy appeared to have affection for King. No doubt he too harbored some nostalgic memories of beginning his campaign in Nashua with King in the crowd. Though no Pygmalion, Kennedy could take some of the credit for King's station.

Kennedy held a small luncheon for King and eight other governors in May 1963. They met in the Family Dining Room at the White House. Vice-president Lyndon Johnson was not invited but was literally penciled into the guest list. This necessitated a new seating arrangement that wedged Governor Otto Kerner of Illinois at the head of the oval-shaped table, awkwardly between King and Endicott Peabody of Massachusetts.

They started with a Flan Virginian, then had Sirloin Maître d'Hôtel and Potatoes Byron paired with an Almaden pinot noir. Over Pears Cardinal and demitasse, Kennedy talked about civil rights, mass-transit legislation, and other issues of interest to the states. As the luncheon broke up, Kennedy and King were seen chatting. The president's interest in New Hampshire's March 10, 1964, Republican primary was high. If the two talked about *that* vote, might the subject of the sweepstakes vote have come up?

John King had trouble putting his feelings about the loss of Patrick to paper. As jovial as he was, as cunningly smart as he was, King had one great sadness in his life. He and Anna had no children. He had come from a large family. His sisters were now all married and having children of their own. He loved to watch them rumble through his house, giving good-natured parenting advice to his brother-in-laws. He would give faux-reprimands to the mischievous, in the way only an uncle could get away with. And if something got out of hand, a stern look could restore order. But when visits were over, the house was quiet again, save for the chink of plates being put away and the scrape of chairs returned to their assigned positions. The ambivalence of childless couples: a peace that is both relief and melancholy.

As governor, King would greet field-trip classes with enthusiasm, paying more attention to the pupils than the teachers. When children were brought to his office, whether they were children of colleagues or a March of Dimes poster child, King would halt all business. The older kids would get to sit behind his desk and pose for a picture that King would sign and mail to them. He insisted on picking up the younger ones so he could talk to them. With babies and toddlers, King would sit in one of his leather chairs and place the child in his lap. He'd smile at them, all festooned in bonnets and lace. In that chair, he looked like an uncle. And he loved all the children that passed through his office, through his life, as a perpetual uncle.

He was an only son, and this line of Kings would likely end with him. With his father's health declining, all of these emotions brewed as he thought of the First Family's anguish. Finally, he called his secretary so he could dictate the letter.

"In this time of sorrow, words offer little comfort. However, Patrick has gone to a land far better than our own, and for that we must be thankful." King expressed further condolences and said, "May God give you strength to cope with this tragedy."

King's letter was among the thousands that poured into the White House. To a great many, the staff returned a printed card that read, "The President and Mrs. Kennedy deeply appreciate your thoughtfulness and expression of sympathy at this time." For others, there were personally signed letters from Kennedy. The president sent a note to King on August 16, 1963, thanking him for his letter of condolence after their "recent loss":

"Your personal expression was a source of strength and encouragement to us both."

NOT EVERY GOVERNOR had a sweepstakes to plan, but every one of them had a World's Fair exhibit to come up with. That event was to take place in New York's Flushing Meadows, beginning April 1964. (President Kennedy had helped break ground for the fair in December 1962.) The theme was "Peace through Understanding" — indicative of Kennedy's "High Hopes," New Frontier optimism. It was the first World's Fair of the Space Age. Writers said the New York World's Fair was symbolic of an exciting future, even if none of them could know what that future would be.

Seventy million people were expected between April 1964 and October 1965 (the fair would close for six months during the winter). The opportunities for public exposure were not lost on capitalist America, and although the event would eventually be overrun by corporations and manufacturers, making the World's Fair one of the largest consumer-goods conventions in history, prime real estate was set aside in this orgy of commercialism for all fifty states. Their invitation was to display their unique culture and character. The fair soon became a competition among dueling tourist campaigns to top one another.

Tourism efforts for New Hampshire were the province of the Department of Resources and Economic Development, an agency with the unfortunate acronym of DRED. Planning of a New Hampshire pavilion fell to this department, but King and other political leaders wanted great say in the final display.

It was the summer of 1963, shortly before Ed Powers made his triumphant debut at the UPI dinner, and the increasingly skeptical press corps believed the sweepstakes was going to tarnish New Hampshire's presence at the World's Fair. When quizzed by a columnist about how the sweepstakes might take advantage of the exposure, Commissioner Howell Shepard mused about selling tickets at the fair. "We could set up a model liquor store with all of our low prices listed," he said, "and right in the exhibit we could show them how the Sweeps tickets will be sold in the liquor stores."

Shepard's cogitations didn't fly with the papers (the *Concord Daily Monitor* put the statement in the "How-Far-Out-Can-You-Get-Department"). Every press card lawyer interpreted the federal laws to mean that nothing about the sweepstakes could leave New Hampshire. No tickets. No informational brochures. No paraphernalia. Some didn't even want the word sweepstakes on any lips outside the 603 area code.

Instead of creating their own individual pavilions, the six New England states pooled their money to build one building to house all of them. The $3.5 million pavilion was six hexagonal-shaped buildings arranged in a hexagon,

---

1. John King and the other five governors had an incredible affinity for one another. They were an unusual group of politicians for their time, all in their forties and most having succeeded stodgy old pols to win their posts. During regular regional meetings, despite partisan differences and geographic competition for resources, the group was always photographed smiling and laughing heartily. King often wrote to his colleagues and sent gifts, like the New Hampshire fishing license he sent Connecticut governor John Dempsey. In subsequent years King would send them and other governors around the country Sweeps tickets for good luck.

with an open air "village green" in its center. The pavilion sat right in the shadow of the fair's iconic Unisphere fountain, and the exhibit's motto was "Where our past began, our future begins." Governors from each of the six states attended the groundbreaking in late September 1963, and the first question from the New York press was aimed at King and whether Sweeps tickets would be available at the fair.[1] "Writers from all over the nation are doing the promotion for us, free of charge," he responded smoothly, "so we can devote our building to culture and our recreational and individual attractions." There would be recognition of the sweepstakes at the exhibit, but the governor promised it would be toned down and not be a distraction.

King, unused to anything but implicit hostility when talking about the lottery to New Hampshire reporters, did two broadcast interviews in New York that focused on the sweepstakes. Due to his packed schedule, he turned down requests for several others. Wherever he went, on the fairgrounds or in his hotel, people accosted him about the sweepstakes. He proudly told the *Concord Daily Monitor* on his return, "Everyone was complimentary about the sweepstakes and said they wished to buy tickets. No one spoke against it."

IN NOVEMBER, Commissioner Shepard reported to the governor there were issues arising with the sweepstakes ticket machines. As well as Ed Powers was doing on the rubber chicken circuit, King and Shepard were often in damage control back in Concord. When Powers announced that Sweeps tickets were going to be distributed by machines, there was a swift backlash from opponents who said these would be unmanned machines. Bulk purchases by bookies would go unpoliced. There would be no oversight to prevent the corruption of minors, as the devices would be as accessible as cigarette vending machines (concerns about minors and *actual* cigarette machines were slow in coming). The commission responded that ticket attendants would operate each machine and — although adults could purchase one in their name — minors were prohibited from buying tickets themselves.

Legal objections ran that such machines, if manufactured out of state, could not legally be transported into New Hampshire. The tickets themselves, if printed somewhere else, would be illegal coming *in* to the state as well as going out.

"It begins to appear that the only way to assure observance of federal laws against lotteries would be to repeal the New Hampshire law," wrote the *Concord*

Daily Monitor. "It could be held in abeyance if the cities and towns in which liquor stores are situated voted against lottery ticket sales [in March]."

King had come to expect this kind of antagonism from the *Monitor.* Normally a liberal-leaning publication in a sea of conservative newspapers, the *Monitor* was like a dog with a sweepstakes bone the governor could not wrestle from its mouth. To the paper, the Sweeps was a dodge from the real issue: an equitable realignment of tax policy in the state. The paper's editors believed a sales tax would raise just as much money without the shame.

The contract for fabricating the ticket machines went to the Adams Manufacturing Company in Chicago, which had just won a lucrative deal with the Publishers Association of New York for some high-end, internally heated, burglar alarm–wired, newspaper vending machines. The Sweeps machines would be tabletop devices similar to those at airports that sold do-it-yourself aviation life-insurance policies. They would be synched to a central mainframe that would use the latest in computer technology to track sales. The plan was to have one hundred machines on hand for March 10, then purchase up to a hundred more depending on the outcome of the vote.

However, Shepard said legal counsel for Adams Manufacturing was advising the company not to sell the machines to New Hampshire and under no circumstance ship them there. Justice Department officials in Illinois were telling the company that delivering the devices would break the Interstate Transportation of Wagering Paraphernalia Act.

King called Millimet and Powers together to find a solution PDQ. For as gregarious as he was, King was impatient with dithering and dismissive with those who slowed him down. He wanted solutions, not people finding new ways to restate the problem. "Get on with it," was a common directive when conversations were drifting off subject.

The secure machines were mission-critical to the sweepstakes. They had retained a security-paper printer in Nashua, but there were no companies inside of New Hampshire that could make a machine to the high standards that Powers had spent two months lauding. If they couldn't get the machines from Chicago, they were sunk. Even if they wiggled out of this one, as soon as the *Concord Daily Monitor* and the other anti-sweepstakes papers heard about it, they'd spin the change in plans as proof the scheme was fatally flawed. King wanted this solved.

Even with bipartisan support and growing confidence instilled by Ed

Powers, the sweepstakes still had plenty of enemies within the legislature. Trouble with a state contract was surely going to draw attention from people who were likely to pass that information on to the *Daily Monitor*. Sure enough, the newsroom put together an exposé about the delivery snafu and typeset it for the front page as the evening paper went to bed. Shortly after the Friday afternoon deadline, the presses stopped. All of the front-page stories and photos had interlocked the columns together like a jigsaw puzzle, so they scrapped everything above the masthead. Now, sitting on top of their Sweeps ticket story was the headline "President Assassinated."

JOHN KING HEARD of the shooting while out of the statehouse. By the time he got back to his office, Kennedy was already dead. Local reporters were waiting for him in the hallway asking for a comment. King opened his mouth, then pursed his lips to keep a sob from escaping. He brushed past them and through the door to his private office. Executive Secretary Tom Power, aware the journalists would chase King as he left the statehouse if he didn't make a statement, told the reporters to be patient. He would get them something as soon as he could.

From the outside, the door into the governor's private office seemed like a vault. Power had seen King holed up inside while contemplating the HB 47 vote. Now, there was an undeniable energy barricading the world out. Around the office, no one spoke. It was quiet, save for the hum of transistor radios. Everyone looked to Power for cues. Instead of knocking, Power turned back and sat at his desk while waiting for his boss to reemerge.

King sat in dark seclusion, in utter silence. He stared out one window, cursing both the tears and the state library tower for being in his eyes, then turned his briny stare to the other window. He sat alone in his office for several hours. Outside, in the pressroom and in the hallway, print and broadcast reporters waited.

King finally summoned Power by cracking open his door. They looked over some notes that Power had made, then the governor asked to be left alone with the text.

A Western Union telegram arrived for King from George Ball, acting secretary of state, officially informing the governor of the president's death in Dallas. Never had Samuel Morse's invention been so woefully unnecessary. The telegram instructed King all flags should be flown at half-staff until sundown on Sunday, December 22.

Power, trying to manage a restless press crew, said the governor had been "personally very shaken" by the assassination. So far the *Monitor* and the *Union Leader* had details about the governor's self-imposed solitude, but no actual statement from the state's highest-ranking official. Power promised a written statement from the governor as soon as it could be typed up. The half-dozen radio reporters who had been waiting asked if King would read it aloud for them. Power went back to ask King, who said he would not. For the first time in their long vigil, the radio reporters became agitated. They'd stayed, expecting to leave with some tape and were not going to leave without it. Power returned to King's office and insisted he reconsider reading the statement. King agreed on the condition that no one else could be in the room as he read it.

Power told the broadcasters it was a take-it-or-leave-it deal. Afterward they'd have to work out amongst themselves how to make copies of the audio, but only one recorder was going into the governor's office.

King stood with his back to the desk, as Power oversaw the radio reporter assembling the microphone and reel-to-reel tape recorder. The only thing the governor wanted to know was how to begin recording. The reporter demonstrated how to start and stop, then left.

King sat at his desk for a long time. Beside him was a book opened to the Gettysburg Address. He adjusted the mic's position so he could hold the paper while he read. When he thought he was ready, he hit the button. For a moment, the only sound captured was the slight squeak of the tape moving between the pinch roller and the capstan. King sucked in a final breath and spoke.

"In my tears and sorrow, it is hard to find words to express the shock and pain of our tragedy. It does not seem possible our President is dead. That our President, who in the short span of his life has given so much of himself to his country and to his world, is taken from us."

His voice was quivering. "There are no words of comfort that can be drawn from this sacrifice. In our grief we can only say that it is our people who must weep for themselves — and their children — for in the world today his loss is immeasurable. I ask people to pray for the repose of his soul and for strength and courage for his constitutional successor."

Emotionally exhausted, he forced himself across the finish line. "All people of all creeds must be reminded of the thoughts of another President who died for his country. And remembering him, I say that it is for us — the living — to be dedicated to his unfinished work. And from him we take increased devotion to the causes for which he gave his last full measure."

JOHN AND ANNA KING, Tom Power, and Senator Tom McIntyre's press secretary drove the next morning to Boston and flew to Washington to join other high-ranking officials to file past the presidential bier. King found the city's silence to be "impressive." They returned to Manchester Saturday night and attended the first of two masses that weekend to mark the death.

John and Anna King were escorted to the front pew at St. Joseph Cathedral — an unfamiliar seat for the St. Anne parishioners — for a special mass on Sunday. A Solemn High Mass of Requiem was planned for Monday, the same day as Kennedy's funeral in Washington. King had declared it a statewide day of mourning, closing schools and government offices. He urged businesses to shut down and asked those that couldn't to pause at noon while services in Washington took place.

Twenty-five priests participated in the special rites. The homily was short, but the vicar general urged the state's Catholics to "accept the will of God," and the monsignor prayed for the elimination of vengeful thoughts.

From the front of the cathedral, King could be seen reaching for his handkerchief over and over. The Ave Maria washed over him, the Latin incantations familiar and foreign at the same time. *Et in hora mortis nostrae, et in hora mortis nostrae* . . . (And in the hour of our death. And in the hour of our death . . .) So close to the altar, he could see the statues of saints, bleached and frozen, the martyrs and the angels weeping, the Virgin Mother mourning her son. He reached for the handkerchief again.

What had been this reverence he'd had for this man he didn't really know? King never wanted to be a politician; he wanted to be a judge. It wasn't the goading of Larry Pickett and the Democratic leadership that got him to run for governor. Would ego alone have driven him, the son of a shoemaker, to run for that high office? Or had he needed an inspiration to give him the strength, the audacity, to do it? What sent him to those county fairs and workmen's clubs to fawn over strangers as if they were friends, to sacrifice the tendons in his shaking hand again and again? It was more than a man. It was the *idea* of Kennedy. The New Frontier of which they dreamed. The world of rising tides and asking not, of coming to Berlin and going to the moon. King believed all of it, all of its saccharine, naiveté. King ran for governor not because it was his turn to be the sacrificial lamb. He'd swallowed the hook. He would move that rubber tree plant. Not because it was easy. Because it was hard.

He sat at the front of that cathedral and wept for those children, wept for that widow, wept for the nation. King was now the political orphan of an ethereal father.

Perhaps the Kennedy years, the New Frontier, weren't even part of that decade. In many of its black-and-white ways, they were the epilogue to the Cold War 1950s, not the prologue to the real 1960s that were about to explode. So much was already under way beneath the surface, like the needle on a barometer falling while winds spin distant weathervanes in new directions. The agents of change were hidden in plain sight.

Vietnam. The Second Vatican Council. The British Invasion. The counterculture. The civil rights movement. The sexual revolution. And thrown into that witch's brew of change was the seemingly inconsequential fad of the New Hampshire Sweepstakes.

"When will NH take the healthy step
of accepting its own economic responsibilities?"

The Christian Science Monitor, 1963

Part Three

ALL THE RAGE

14

The Committee of One Hundred

THE LOCAL-CONTROL VOTE wasn't a direct referendum on John King, in as much as any popular vote is or is not a referendum on the current leadership. The Sweeps *was* his major legislative accomplishment and had to be defended on all fronts. By now, King and his withered shaking hand were on a regular diet of meetings and luncheons on all points of the New Hampshire compass. Like a major league pitcher who could work on three days of rest, there were few politicians of his day who were suited for such a perpetual campaign.

For much of the time, the only high-profile opposition to the Sweeps had been self-styled crusader Bill Witcomb. Church leaders had been mobilizing the faithful, but their power and impact was fractured by the diversity of individual congregations, denominations, and loose coalition of church groups. The newspapers and magazines continued their guerrilla war, lobbing grenades when targets emerged. Yet although they had the biggest platform, media outlets were also competitors, and they lacked the coordination needed for an all-out assault. For all intents and purposes there was no effective opposition group to the sweepstakes.

In early November 1963, however, a coalition of more than a hundred citizens gathered at the University of New Hampshire to organize the "Committee of One Hundred." Members came from all ten counties of the state and were from a cross-section of businesses and professions. Their goal was to get as many communities as they could to reject the sweepstakes in the March referendum.

The committee was put together by two publishers from the area: John Ballentine was in charge of the *Somersworth Free Press*; Richard Plumer ran the *Alumnus* magazine at the University of New Hampshire. Their goal was to coordinate a letter-writing campaign and run political advertising against the Sweeps.

"We want as large a vote as possible March 10 as a critical expression of public opinion on the sweepstakes," said Plumer, who liked to be photographed with a pipe in his mouth. "Despite the governor's interpretations of the sweepstakes' narrow legislative victory as indicative of the 'will of the people,' there has been in fact no measure of public reaction to this evil."

One of their first salvos was fired at Ed Powers. It was clear he was winning the ground war with his speaking tour of the state. The committee charged that Powers was using public money to campaign in a public election. Although his advocacy was a presumed duty of the executive director, nonetheless the anti-Sweeps press perpetuated the claim there was something improper — something unseemly — about Powers lobbying on state time. Sweepstakes Commissioner Howell Shepard found himself on his heels refuting the claim in the papers, saying Powers only spoke at the invitation of private citizens. To counter Powers's Sherman-like cross-state march to the sea, the committee proposed creating a speakers bureau of its own to provide opposing viewpoints.

Ballentine and Plumer also believed their talents as writers could be put to good use. They offered to create broadsheets in the vein of Thomas Paine's *Common Sense* to enumerate the dangers of the lottery. They had teamed up before to try such a tactic when they created a pamphlet titled "Profile Papers: Citizenship and Wager" and attempted to get it into the hands of every legislator before the fateful sweepstakes votes the previous spring.

The pair quickly turned out *Consider,* a four-page bi-weekly mimeographed publication they described as a "fact and opinion sheet." *Consider* was mailed to about a thousand people who had been identified as anti-sweepstakes and who might promote action against the gambling initiative. Ballentine and Plumer were convinced the majority of New Hampshire citizens shared their views on the subject.

The press likened *Consider* to the abolitionist publications turned out by

William Lloyd Garrison and other antislavery journalists. "If New Hampshire people are expected to make an intelligent expression concerning the sweepstakes next spring, they are entitled to some hard facts and some blunt opinions to assist them in making their decision. They're entitled to more than a persuasive confidence game," they wrote in the first edition of *Consider*. "We do not think of ourselves as 'bleeding hearts,' 'do-gooders,' or spokesmen for any 'moral lobby'. . . We are convinced that sweepstakes government can have only unfortunate consequences and we stand on Edmund Burke's observation that 'All that is necessary for evil to triumph is for good men to do nothing.'"

The committee had representation from every sector — with members who included corporation CEOs and housewives — though it was heavily populated by academics and newspaper men. The executive committee consisted of the information director at the University of New Hampshire, a political science professor from Colby Junior College, the comptroller from the tony St. Paul prep school, and the headmaster of the equally tony New Hampton School. The ranks of the Committee of One Hundred included the publishers of several newspapers, including the *Derry News,* the *Hanover Gazette,* and the *Manchester Free Press.*

The committee had political muscle too. Chief among the current and former office holders was Raymond Perkins, the former Senate president who had out-maneuvered Larry Pickett throughout the 1950s. His know-how was welcomed and celebrated.

JOHN KING TOLD the Associated Press he was "not worried" about the formation of the Committee of One Hundred. "I saw a lot of familiar names on that list, most of them being people who want a sales tax."

Anyone espousing an income or a sales tax in Bill Loeb's New Hampshire got a political tarring and feathering in the *Union Leader.* Even those falsely accused found their skin smeared by steaming black tar salted with gossamer feathers. The pain would be swift and the sticky stain hard to remove.

When King said most of the leading figures of the Committee of One Hundred favored a sales tax, he was right. Many had said so, voted so, written editorials saying so. Among the ranks were surely those who opposed the Sweeps purely on moral grounds, or favored neither a sales tax nor a lottery. In fact, the committee's public positions remained tax-agnostic. But nuance doesn't succeed in politics. Larry Pickett got the sweepstakes passed in the

House by tarring its opponents as taxers, and King was prepared to use that winning argument again to poison the well with the specter of a sales tax.

King may have publicly said he wasn't worried by the formation of the Committee of One Hundred, but it must have been troubling. The priests and prophets were politically unsophisticated. An organized, well-reasoned group of prominent citizens would get plenty of ink from newspapers eager for their messages. He declared *his* committee of one hundred was the people of New Hampshire, and that for every member opposed to the sweepstakes, "there are 99 who favor it."

ALSO HINDERING THE STATE EFFORT to move the sweepstakes forward was continued opposition from the Justice Department to allow Adams Manufacturing to ship the ticket machines from Chicago to New Hampshire. The hold-up had made the local papers and provided new ammunition for anti-Sweeps editorials. King was growing impatient.

Ed Powers used his contacts at the FBI in Chicago to find out who in the regional office of the DOJ was giving Adams the warning. Joseph Millimet called the U.S. attorney for the Northern District of Illinois to plead New Hampshire's case. In return, Millimet got a recitation of the Wire Act and the Paraphernalia Act, as if he were third grader.

Millimet needed to go as high up the chain as he could go. He contacted Deputy Attorney General Nicholas Katzenbach, the official he'd met in Washington, and explained their conundrum. Millimet reminded Katzenbach of his pledge not to interfere with the implementation of the sweepstakes and argued again that the Paraphernalia Act only applied to the tools of *illegal* gambling operations. After some thought, Katzenbach said he'd call the U.S. attorney in Chicago and look into the matter further.

Days later, the *Concord Daily Monitor* announced the machines were on their way. Commissioner Shepard said the Justice Department had concurred with Millimet's interpretation of the Gambling Paraphernalia Act — namely, that "political subdivisions" could transport gambling equipment across state lines for legalized purposes. The $40,000 contract to purchase the machines was approved.

The Justice Department did not address the issue of whether private citizens could transport gambling paraphernalia for legalized purposes across state lines. The question about what would happen to ticketholders remained unresolved.

ED POWERS wasn't the only speaker in demand to give talks on the lottery. "Mr. Sweepstakes" himself, Larry Pickett, was fielding invitations from groups across the state. Pickett told the Exeter Jaycees that despite the efforts of the Committee of One Hundred popular sentiment for the Sweeps was too strong for repeal and the operation was here to stay. In addition to predicting a win in March, Pickett, in his singsong oratorical style, declared that the New Hampshire Sweepstakes would become the fourth jewel in horse racing's vaulted Triple Crown. The New Hampshire Sweepstakes would become a larger event than even the Kentucky Derby.

The lottery, Pickett told the *Union Leader,* was not an original sin and the sweepstakes was not the first lottery in New Hampshire. He reminded listeners that among the hundreds of early American lottery efforts — from funding colleges to financing wars — New Hampshire had also sanctioned lotteries. Like its Ivy League brothers, Dartmouth College had held lotteries when new buildings were needed.

Lottery financing had paid for important infrastructure projects since colonial days. Portsmouth Harbor, through which French supplies for Washington's Continental Army were delivered, was constructed with gambling proceeds. Eighteenth- and nineteenth-century bridges were paid for in the same manner. It was said there were more "lottery bridges" than covered bridges in New Hampshire. In 1811, the state legislature had approved a lottery to pay for a north-south road that became Route 16 — a major thoroughfare until the interstate highway system.

Private businesses had also petitioned the state to sanction lotteries to help economic development. In the late 1790s, entrepreneur Bob Hewes convinced the General Court to run a lottery to raise capital for a glassmaking business. He sold enough tickets to pay the winners and build a factory in Temple. He imported fifty-three master glass blowers from Germany, but as soon as production began, a fire razed the building. But, as Pickett quipped, that wasn't the lottery's fault.

After ten years of parrying the lunges of moralists and tax reformists himself, Pickett watched as that task shifted to King, Powers, and Shepard. In a way, he had become a minor figure in the effort. When questioned by the *New Hampshire Sunday News,* he said no one from King's office even *asked* if he would be interested in a position with the Sweepstakes Commission. This prompted the follow-up question of whether he would have liked a say in operating the lottery he'd birthed after a decade's labor. Pickett's manner turned thoughtful. He said if one had been offered, he would have taken a position, leaving the world to infer he was disappointed in how his role in creating the lottery had become marginalized.

NOTABLY ABSENT from the announced roster of professors and farmers and attorneys in the Committee of One Hundred were any clergymen. It seemed to be a calculated omission. Co-organizer John Ballentine declared the clergy's help would be needed to defeat the sweepstakes, but conceded that keeping the committee fully secular might help it avoid being painted as the "moral lobby," a smear that Bill Loeb had used effectively against the protesting Protestants in the past.

The head of the New Hampshire Christian Civic League was the Reverend Raymond MacFarland, the de facto leader of the religious assault against the Sweeps. It was MacFarland who as far back as the first bill in 1955 had organized petitions and the public hearing speakers to lobby the General Court. Going after a clergyman could backfire on a politician, but MacFarland's public indignation over the sweepstakes was so profound that he easily fell into John King's political jujitsu — using an opponent's own momentum to toss him aside. Although "extremist" was not a word used in 1960s New Hampshire politics, the governor was able to effectively frame MacFarland as a dangerous outlier.

Described as tall and saw-boned, MacFarland's voice would quiver with near rage when labeled a "professional do-gooder." He had been wagging his finger at the lottery since its inception. Although he had individual sympathizers and the ear of most local media outlets, MacFarland complained about slanted articles, loaded opinion polls, and suppression of the opposition viewpoint in publications.

The piece that had most troubled him was the national article Governor King wrote for *This Week* titled, "I Am Not Ashamed of Our Lottery." MacFarland declared, "I *am* ashamed of our lottery," and wrote to *This Week* editor Charles Sopkin demanding equal time for a rebuttal. Sopkin declined MacFarland's request. "For one point, we feel the arguments against lotteries have been made often and well. Secondly, we go to press seven weeks before publication, and we feel that by the time another article appeared in print most of our readers will have forgotten the governor's arguments."

MacFarland also bristled at the *Family Weekly* poll showing a 2–1 preference by readers to a lottery in their own states. He said the questions were biased and presumed that revenues from a sweepstakes would definitely lower taxes. Again, his protestations fell on deaf ears. "To my way of thinking," he wrote in a letter to Bill Loeb, "these are ominous signs of things to come."

MacFarland had found himself in the same boat as Larry Pickett: a figure of influence from the recent past who had seen the lottery debate move beyond their hypothetical framings. The torch had been passed — or snatched — by a new generation of advocates. Their place in the battle was uncertain.

LEADERS IN THE COMMITTEE OF ONE HUNDRED revved up their efforts as the calendar flipped to 1964 and the March vote approached. Ballentine, Plumer, and company distributed a twenty-thousand-piece mailer in communities with liquor stores laying out the ruin the sweepstakes would bring. They wrote that impartial economists determined every three-dollar ticket would provide only seventy-three cents to education. These same economists cautioned against relying on revenues from the "sin taxes" because 40 percent of those revenues were "unsound." Wryly, the committee pointed out that minors (the supposed beneficiaries of the lottery) were prohibited from entering Rockingham Park racetrack, but that the track was exactly where cash intended for minors was going to be raised.

One committee member, the business manager for Ballentine's *Somersworth Free Press,* printed a list of fifteen pointed questions to Commissioner Shepard asking him to defend the Sweeps. The writer, Robert Cullmane, enumerated a laundry list of operational weaknesses. He said the Sweeps's success relied on bulk purchases by problem gamblers and enticed citizen to break federal laws. In an op-ed response, Shepard refuted each of the claims, then charged Cullmane and the Committee of One Hundred to come up "with a better idea" to meet the needs of the state.

The committee tried to gin up more trouble by seizing on a comment made by Governor King in *This Week* magazine. As a rejoinder to claims the Sweeps would exploit compulsive gamblers, King had pointed to the fact the sweepstakes only happened once or twice a year.

"The odds are too long and the action isn't fast enough," he'd written, to entice the problem gambler to buy piles of tickets each week. As for worries that unsophisticated gamblers would be the ones purchasing more tickets than they could afford, King said the average person was "smart enough" to know the odds of any single ticket winning were such that their chances didn't greatly increase by purchasing more. Editorial writers jumped on the latter comment, claiming if King thought New Hampshire residents were too smart to buy multiple chances, he must therefore think out-of-staters were dumb enough to get suckered in and buy the millions of tickets the scheme required.

The newest talking point opponents made hay out of was the specter of criminal infiltration. The Committee of One Hundred said it was no coincidence that the state's highest paid employee was an FBI agent charged with keeping racketeers at bay.

Some of the loudest voices of this argument came from over the border. The Massachusetts Crime Commission, an anti-government corruption watchdog group, said that if the lottery were successful "the rackets would take [the sweepstakes] over." The group was led by Thomas McArdie, a former FBI agent.

Leaders from the New England Citizens' Crime Commission said the state was "wide open" to organized crime and attempted to get equal time at the many Rotary and Jaycees luncheons that Ed Powers had addressed. This action group had its origins in the nineteenth century, when it was formed as the New England Society for the Suppression of Vice. Its most notable accomplishments were banning several books deemed obscene from the Boston Library and local bookshops. Blacklisted titles included *Leaves of Grass, All's Quiet on the Western Front, God's Little Acre,* and *An American Tragedy.* The group even targeted lottery winner Voltaire and his work *Candide.* Their actions made the phrase "Banned in Boston" a badge of honor to the subversive and the profane. In the postwar years, the group changed its name and switched its focus to gambling.

"There is no power that can stop a crime syndicate from moving in on the New Hampshire Sweepstakes," Vice-President Charles Cataldo told the Rotary Club of Laconia. Cataldo had joined the organization while living in East Boston and expressing his concern to the police about teens using pinball machines falling into the wrong crowd. He told the audience the public "fails to comprehend" the reach and power of organized crime, that when mobsters see an opportunity they "move on in with force." Because the New Hampshire state police had no one investigating organized crime, Cataldo predicted racketeers would infiltrate the system within five to ten years, skimming from the pot and shaking down the forces of good. He claimed the syndicates had influence over legislators, the judiciary, and even the clergy.

Now it was Ed Powers's turn to play catch-up with the news cycle. The executive director said the hypotheticals floated by Cataldo made no sense and didn't jive with how real bookies operated. Racketeers couldn't steal hundreds of tickets not processed by the state's machines, nor could they anonymously buy hundreds of tickets to scalp. The safeguards he'd put in place, he believed, would be enough to keep the criminal element out.

As if to appeal to the pragmatists, Powers said no one setting up a business can guarantee against attempts to break the law. Opponents said Powers was parsing legal semantics and condoning the breaking of federal law.

Governor King took exception to the accusation that the lottery would draw mobsters into New Hampshire. "To try to frighten people into thinking that our sweepstakes will attract crime syndicates," the *Union Leader* quoted, "amounts to an insult to our Sweepstakes Commission" and the majority of lawmakers who worked endlessly to pass the law.

15

The Vote

UNLIKE THE PRESIDENTIAL PRIMARY, the sweepstakes vote was not a statewide contest. It was actually 234 referendums in 234 separate towns, each with its own political bent. In practicality, the vote only mattered in the 43 communities that had the state's forty-nine state liquor stores. Losing a couple of those communities wasn't just losing a point of sale. It would be a terrible affirmation of everything the Committee of One Hundred had been saying — that people in New Hampshire were afraid of the scourge that the sweepstakes would bring to their home towns.

The town of Salem was especially critical to the vote. Salem had the largest liquor store in terms of volume of sales and would be a major outlet for Sweeps tickets. It was also the home of Rockingham Park racetrack. If Salem voters rejected the referendum, then tickets could not be sold at the two biggest venues in the sweepstakes sales operation.

Even if Salem were a lock — even if the Sweeps passed in all forty-three municipalities — the measure of the victory was just as important. It could pass in all 234 towns, but a tight margin would be a political disaster. It needed to win decisively if King was going to claim to have a mandate. It had to win 2–1, and it had to do that with just Republicans.

PRESIDENT LYNDON JOHNSON would surely win the state primary with no effort, so motivating Democrats to come to the polls on March 10 was problematic for sweepstakes boosters. Was there enough support among GOP primary voters to give the Sweeps the mandate it needed?

With about two weeks before the Primary vote, a trial balloon was floated: a write-in campaign for Robert Kennedy for president. The idea was *not* to deny President Johnson the party's nomination, but to send a strong signal that Democrats should put RFK on the ballot as vice-president. The idea was electric — though based more on emotion and less on electoral strategy. John King, who previously said LBJ should be allowed to select his own running mate, reversed his previous position when Kennedy was mentioned. Other leading New Hampshire Democrats followed and suddenly a movement was born. Meanwhile, the White House was in a panic about the potential embarrassment if Kennedy outpolled Johnson in New Hampshire.

At first, neither Johnson nor Kennedy addressed the write-in movement. Even when RFK finally publicly discouraged the effort, enthusiasm did not dampen. Governor King's support of Bobby Kennedy was surely sincere, though the write-in campaign was serendipitous. Democrats now had a reason to go to the polls on March 10.

THE COMMITTEE OF ONE HUNDRED was not letting up on its effort to kill the sweepstakes at the ballot box. The newest argument was the sweepstakes was no longer a New Hampshire problem, that the "associated evils" of a lottery's easy money would spread throughout the country. They also warned if the sweepstakes failed to make enough money the state would then hold more drawings and more races, and move to other kinds of gambling for easy money.

The chairman of the state board of education, Franklin Hollis, said New Hampshire schools needed $20 *million,* not $4 million to improve quality. At the same time the legislature passed the sweepstakes, it rejected a $3 million pay increase to state employees. And the issue of the $4 million estimate itself, the one that had so easily tripped off Larry Pickett's tongue, was a bald-faced guess and unreliable.

The Committee of One Hundred raised $3,186 for a print and broadcast offensive. A second political action group, the Concord Committee Against the Sweepstakes, raised only $375.25 leading up to vote. The committee had forty contributors, including the editor of the *Concord Daily Monitor.* A win in the capital would be an embarrassment to the governor.

Finally a pro-sweepstakes action committee sprang up. It was formed and financed by William Walker, an auto dealer from Littleton who was active in

Democratic politics. He put $1,342 of his own money into the Committee for the New Hampshire Sweepstakes. The fund was controlled by Governor King, and payment for advertising was handled directly by Tom Power at the statehouse, a questionable activity for a state employee on state time.

ED POWERS and the Sweepstakes Commission had one last card to play before the referendum. One of the bits of information not yet revealed about the sweepstakes was the prize schedule. How much would the ticket holder of the winning horse and all the runner-ups win? Some of the previous Pickett proposals had a $25,000 prize figure, but he'd left the number up to the commission in his ultimate bill.

With less than a week before vote, Powers announced the grand prize would be $100,000. It was a staggering amount, twice what most reporters had been guessing.

The rest of the prize schedule was also impressive. The player holding the ticket on the second-place horse would get $50,000. There would be $25,000 for the third-place winner and $12,500 for fourth. Ticket holders on any of the also-rans would get to split a pool of $27,500. Though no one knew for certain how many horses would make the final cut and run, hundreds would be nominated. Players paired with horses that did not make it into the sweepstakes would split a pool of $120,000–$165,000. An additional hundred names would be drawn for consolation prizes of $150–$200.

What was more, each of these pay-out figures were part of a series of $1 million drawings. At three dollars a ticket, a drawing would be conducted once 333,333 tickets were sold. Once all the players' names had been assigned to horses, the commission would hold another drawing from the pool of the next 333,333 sold. So there would now be *two* $100,000 winners, two $50,000 winners and so on. The process would be repeated each time another million dollars in tickets were sold, so there was no limit on the number of jackpot winners the New Hampshire Sweepstakes might produce.

The details of the payouts put dollar signs in everybody's eyes. The news was carried in papers across the country. The timing of the announcement couldn't have been any better. Kennedy had had his October surprise in '62; King had his March surprise in '64.

The tide of good news did not sit well with *Argus-Champion* editor Edward DeCourcy. He fired off a lengthy letter to the governor to denigrate the sweepstakes operation. On the eve of the vote, King wrote back. "I respect your opinions and I feel that you do mine," he said. "The passage of time will determine which opinions are more correct."

THE COMMITTEE for the New Hampshire Sweepstakes purchased fifteen minutes of air time on fourteen radio stations and the state's television station for King and Powers to make a direct pitch on the Friday night before the vote.

Invoices show the cost of the combined airtime was $881. They used an additional $391 to buy newspaper space to advertise the broadcasts. The copy said simply: "WHY Sweepstakes in your community? Tune in." They placed front-page ads in thirteen state papers. The only papers that refused a page-one spot were the *Concord Daily Monitor* and the *Argus-Champion,* which begrudged them space deep inside the paper.

In the radio and TV spots King wasted no time going after the Committee of One Hundred. "Powerful forces, the majority of whom are sales taxers, are working feverishly to kill the sweepstakes in the referendum in Tuesday's primary. While I am confident that the majority of our New Hampshire citizens are favorable to the sweepstakes, it is possible that if they fail to get out and vote for it, the sweepstakes program could be adversely affected."

King underscored that sweepstakes proceeds would be used either to increase the resources available to community schools or could be added to existing education budgets, thereby lowering each town's property-tax burden.

The governor turned the microphone over to Ed Powers. He was good on the radio but was radiant on television. He did his own run-down of how and where people would be able to purchase Sweeps tickets and touched on all the safeguards put in place.

"One thing I want to make perfectly clear," Powers said. "This program will not violate any existing federal or state laws . . . To set up this program in any other way would be completely alien to me in light of my background as a law enforcement agent for over twenty-two years."

King made the closing argument. "If you believe in our sweepstakes program and the benefits it can bring to your community — let your voice be heard. Go to the polls next Tuesday and vote 'yes' for the sweepstakes."

Governor King felt the broadcasts had been persuasive. With 60 percent of New Hampshire Republicans undecided, and Democrats coming to write-in Robert Kennedy, turnout was going to be high, a good sign for the Sweeps.

It seemed the only thing that could derail a referendum victory would be if those people didn't get to the polls.

THE BLIZZARD THAT ARRIVED on Tuesday, March 10, 1964, started as rain Monday night, then the temperature plummeted. Those trying to get to a polling station Tuesday morning slogged through a mix of rain, snow, and sleet that threatened the cuffs of their pants. Early reports from city voting stations were that turnout was light.

Rain turned to all snow — four to six inches before lunch. Wind gusts between thirty and forty miles an hour made new snow drifts where paths had just been shoveled. City residents complained the plowing on busy streets was lousy, as some highway superintendents held crews back until the rain ended and then were never able to catch up with what followed. With the mercury flat-lined in the single digits, drivers found that what roads had been plowed had turned to ice. Power lines were snapped by falling branches, and ice jams on the Connecticut River made water levels crest the banks.

From the governor's office, John King shook his head at the terrible luck. Rain and snow discouraged the fair-weather voter. Who does that leave at the polls? The zealots. The die-hards. The ones who feel so passionately about an issue or candidate they'd crawl on their knees to get to a voting booth. People who would do anything to see the sweepstakes defeated.

There was an early bit of good news for the movement. The tiny northern hamlet of Dixville Notch (registered voters: nine) traditionally voted at midnight. This quirky, first-in-the-nation sideshow in the first-in-the-nation primary always drew national press coverage. The Sweeps had passed in Dixville Notch 9–0.

By the time the snow had stopped, fifteen inches had fallen on parts of the state. Despite the weather, nearly 32 percent of registered voters still made it to cast ballots, only slightly off from 1960. It took until 3 a.m. in most northern towns to finish counting. Those looking for a protest vote found it.

One-third of Republicans selected Henry Cabot Lodge, the ambassador to South Vietnam, as their presidential nominee. Lodge never campaigned, never even came to the United States, but those close to the Bostonian wrote in his name anyway. Goldwater trailed Lodge by ten thousand votes, with Rockefeller another three thousand votes behind him. The Republican deck had been reshuffled.

Despite White House anxiety, Johnson outpolled Robert Kennedy, 21,898 to 17,683. The incident did little to improve their strained relationship — or to endear the president to Governor John King.

The clear winner on March 10, 1964, was the sweepstakes. Of the 234 cities and towns, only 13 opposed the measure, none of them with liquor stores. The final statewide vote was 113,748 to 31,147. In the end, the Sweeps didn't get their 2–1 mandate. It was almost 4–1.

Wherever they went — King, Pickett, Powers, Shepard — they got handshakes and slaps on the back. The vote was an affirmation of what they'd done so far. Now they had to get the lottery mechanism running. A glance at the calendar said time was against them. They had fewer than six months before the race and millions of tickets still to sell.

16
Dreams
Are Born

THE MORNING AFTER the landslide victory, Ed Powers sat in his office surrounded by unopened boxes of ticket machines. After being moved two previous times, the Sweepstakes were in their final home on the third floor of the annex building next to the statehouse. Powers had a picture window with an unreal view of the statehouse golden dome. His was a view that would have turned John King green with envy.

A bank of machines was installed at Rockingham Park. Dozens more had been delivered to various high-volume liquor stores and one hundred more were being held in Chicago pending the outcome of the vote. The rest of the machines — each about the size of an electric typewriter — were taking up floor space.

The New Hampshire Sweepstakes Commission had a handful of paid employees. Powers's secretary spent every day opening mail that contained checks and cash from people around the country. (The Sweeps had inspired more letters than Santa Claus — and with the same amount of pleading). She typed a daily report of who had mailed what that went to both Powers and Governor King. Before the vote, $200 a day came in and went back to ticket seekers.

They came from every part of the country and from across the globe, from Mexico to Guam. Postmarks included Christchurch, New Zealand; Yamota, Japan; and Kilbeggan, County Westmeath, Ireland. They were written on fine parchment and faded paper, in fancy strokes and scribbled lines, in English both posh and pidgin.

No letter arrived without a note of justification or persuasion, and King was all too pleased to share their contents and gin up interest. "You may keep half my winnings," offered one writer. "Prize money to be divided between Philips Exeter Academy and Dartmouth College," said another. "I don't gamble on a large scale, but I do buy chances at church festivals," began one woman. "I can only afford one [ticket] as my husband died Easter Sunday." Another man wrote, "I am 63 and I know winning a substantial sweepstakes prize is the only way I can accumulate an estate."

"I am 70 years old and I can use a little cash right now. My doctor said go to a warm dry climate like Arizona."

"I disconnected my phone to spare you the $3."

Some admitted to knowing the postal regulations prevented them from getting tickets through the mail, but they wrote anyway. "Send 200 tickets . . . please use plain envelope." One sly fellow penned, "Can these be sent through the mail, or carrying pigeon, just put the tickets in a box and mark 'write-in vote'?"

"I don't want to break any laws," said one. "I am somewhat in politics and have to be careful. I can't afford any publicity for the same reason. I write to you because I do not know any person personally in the state . . . I might have misspelled a few words when I write fast I do that. Spelling was my weak subject anyway."

"I have been giving my money to the Irish Sweep for the past 20 years, but why should I give my money to another country? I want to leave money in the good USA."

"I resent losing my money to professional gamblers in Vegas (where there are financed many Communist Front organizations)."

"My stamp collection is incomplete without one of the first lottery tickets."

Everybody who could not drive, fly, or sail into New Hampshire and wanted to play begged for a ticket. Everybody had a daydream, and now New Hampshire was going to make it come true. The mass of men may lead lives of quiet desperation, but some could do it with such literary pizzazz.

"A couple of other glorified hobos besides the writer wish hopefully to participate in the slicing of the most sumptuous melon of green with big numbers."

POWERS'S RIGHT-HAND MAN was James Kennedy. Like Powers, Kennedy was a fifty-year-old retired FBI special agent. His position was executive officer of field operations, in charge of logistics and security. A *Union Leader* profile said Kennedy had received his law degree from Harvard, but had spent all of his professional life with the Bureau. Kennedy had worked in the Boston office since 1943 and worked under Powers during both his tours there. His salary was not as generous as Powers's however. The position paid between $8,764 and $10,284.

There was a second executive officer for the sweepstakes. Leo Hogan was in charge of systems control. Hogan was a former IBM employee who specialized in networks. He was a critical choice, as Powers envisioned ticket sales and retention as being highly secure, highly technical. They weren't going to just scoop up an armful of tickets and throw them in a drum like a church raffle. Hogan's system design would complement the other security measures Powers and Kennedy had promised.

Powers was given free hand to hire his staff (as Governor King had pledged). Beneath Kennedy and Hogan were four sweepstakes supervisors. Their backgrounds included a Manchester deputy police chief, a grocery-store owner, an innkeeper, and state civil defense worker. More than two hundred people were interviewed for these positions.

As a way of ensuring their probity, judgment, and courage, Bishop Primeau wrote to the governor demanding to know the religious denominations of the Sweepstakes Commission and staff. The commissioners were Protestant, Catholic, and Jewish. Powers, Kennedy, and Hogan were all Catholics. The supervisors were three Catholics and a Protestant. King conceded it wasn't a "balanced ticket" (it's unclear whether a glut of Catholics would have reassured or shamed the bishop), but he said each man was "the best qualified available for the job."

Not included among the staff — because there was no other staff — were the dozens and dozens of clerks who would be manning the ticket machines at the racetrack and the liquor stores. The liquor commissioners had ambivalent feelings about the sweepstakes. The extra foot traffic would surely drive up liquor sales, but at what cost to them? They were losing counter space to ticket machines, and their employees would be doing double duty. They would be commingling sales. Their workers would have to be trained on state time to use the equipment. There was worry the stores would have to hire new employees just to handle to the demand. Now the Liquor Commission was *losing* money on the deal. The papers got in on the act. Commissioners complained bitterly to the governor about the imposition the sweepstakes were to their operations. King, who didn't want to hear any griping from the ranks, told Howell Shepard to settle it. The Sweepstakes Commission announced it had reached a "mutually satisfactory arrangement" to reimburse Liquor for staffing. A similar arrangement would be made with Rockingham Park.

GIVEN HIS DECADES fighting illegal gambling, Ed Powers was determined to counter any perceived weakness in the sales operation with overwhelming strength. The Sweeps were a Serenity Prayer, and he would dive into the things he could control. Powers confessed to the *Patriot Ledger* the sweepstakes would only be successful if people believed it to be on the level. Yes, the odds might be long, but the game would be fair. The commission needed to stand by every ticket, have confidence in every ticket.

Bigger than a bread box, the gunmetal ticket machines featured a rotary dial like a telephone. The clerk would dial the number of tickets the buyer wanted to purchase. A panel in the machine's center would slide open to reveal the first in a continuous roll of tickets. "STATE OF NEW HAMPSHIRE, FIRST SWEEPSTAKES RACE, SEPTEMBER 1964." Players would be given a pen and asked to sign their name, their number and street, and their city and state. They did not have to show an ID and could write any name they chose — so long as the person named could show positive identification if he or she won.

Each slip was 3½ by 5½ inches and printed on red and blue security paper. It was bordered with twenty-three horse heads, horseshoes, and red and blue triangles. The sides were dotted with small circle holes where the ticket machine sprockets had guided the continuous-feed paper. A watermark of the state seal splashed across the ticket. Each slip had a seven-digit serial number. Embedded in the ticket were several anticounterfeiting measures. It bore the signatures of Governor King, Director Powers, and the three commissioners, and it notified its owner that it was merely an acknowledgment of purchase and did not need to be retained for payment. Each slip included a mild scolding that the acknowledgment was "non-saleable" and "non-transferable." It looked more like a small birth certificate than a lottery ticket, but such pieces of paper appear whenever a dream is born.

The purchasing process took less than a minute. When finished, buyers would push up a lever, and the carbon-copy acknowledgment would be dispensed below while their ticket stayed behind in the machine, part of one continuous strip of paper. The tickets and proceeds were to be placed in bank drop boxes each night, along with serial numbers of the first and last tickets sold that day, and funds were to be credited to the commission's account. Every couple of days, a sweepstakes supervisor would visit local banks and microfilm all of the tickets to ensure that no tickets were removed or added to the pile and to create a backup record in case some calamity befell the paper originals.

From there, the tickets were to be taken to a clearinghouse the commission had established at Merchant's National Bank in Manchester. The commission had leased a vault and additional space for accounting. Bank staff members would have access to the latest in computer and data-processing equipment, and they would provide daily updates on tickets and funds for each location. Serial numbers would be entered into a computer to credit each liquor store or racetrack for their sales.

The long strips of ticket originals would be filed in sequential order. They would stay in the Merchant's National vault until a drawing could be coordinated at Rockingham Park for public viewing. When a drawing was ready, the rolls of tickets would separate and 333,333 of them would be transported under armed guard to the racetrack and placed in a 2,400-pound, six-foot-high, four-foot-wide electronically rotating Plexiglas drum.

Powers and his staff felt the declaration that each person who paid had his or her ticket in the drum was unassailable. With the duplicate documentation and use of modern technology, the commission could identify every person who bought a sweepstakes chance and know where and when they did so. In all the ways imaginable, the commissioners safeguarded against every known trick to tamper with draw. The executive director instituted one further security measure: no one from the Sweeps was allowed to buy a ticket.

ON THURSDAY, MARCH 12, 1964, Rockingham Park opened its doors for the start of the trotting season. Eight inches of snow had to be removed from the track to allow the horses through. The secretary of state expedited certification of the vote in Salem so Sweeps sales could begin as planned.

Governor John King arrived shortly before 6 p.m. He was greeted by hundreds of spectators who were not there for horses, but were in for the action. Men in all fashion of hats and women in every kind of winter coat. Flashbulbs exploded as he followed the signs to "N.H. Sweepstakes." In the middle of the Rockingham Park betting floor was a sweepstakes information booth stocked with brochures about the lottery. The ticket counter had thirty-five machines, but six of them weren't working. Fifteen tellers worked the counter. As the ticket machines hummed with electricity, so did the onlookers.

Awaiting him at one of the machines was Lou Smith of Rockingham Park, and Ed Powers who would sell him the first ticket. King with deliberate motion waved the three dollars in the air before handing them to Powers. Before writing, he looked over the reporters who'd covered the sweepstakes story since the floor debate.

"I'm probably the first and only ticket buyer who hopes he doesn't win," he said. Everyone in earshot let out a laugh. "It would be too embarrassing." Asked what he *would* do with any prizes, he said he'd give the money to charity. "After taxes," he added to even more pleasant laughter.

King lifted the pen and, reminded of the ballot box, said, "I almost wrote 'Democratic.'" Then he played some more with Powers, asking whether he should use his temporary or permanent address. He signed his name and wrote "State House Concord N.H." He pressed the lever up, and the acknowledgment slid out. King examined the slip. It was number 0000001. He held out for the press to see it, then he raised the chance high over his head and the masses erupted with applause as if viewing a religious relic. Every which way he twisted, the paper pressed between his thumb and finger, blessing another group of people with its sight, the governor reveled in the triumph.

John King had just purchased the first legal lottery ticket in the United States in the modern era.

The second ticket was sold to Representative Larry Pickett. The evening was just as much his as it was King's. With a stage actor's strokes, he lifted the pen and announced his stage directions. He wrote ticket 0000002 out to The Grand Exalted Ruler of the Benevolent and Protective Order of Elks. In his old-fashioned elocution, he said, "I wouldn't dare buy a ticket for myself, because if I did and won a prize, that would be the end of the Sweeps."

The two men stepped aside for more photos, and the counter opened for general sales. There was no holding the surge back.

FOR THE NEXT FOUR HOURS, until they had to lock the door and turn the lights out, people came in wave after wave to buy their own legal lottery ticket. Everyone had dreams of extended vacations and paid-off mortgages.

There was some early trepidation. Men turned up their collars, hiding their faces. The clerks often had to reassure the buyers that what they were doing was perfectly legal, and they were not breaking federal law by taking the acknowledgments home. Massachusetts residents wanted to know if their home state would tax their winnings as income (answer: not if earned in New Hampshire).

"Where do I sign up for my kids' future?" one guy asked at the information booth before being pointed toward the counter. A little old lady wearing a Persian lamb coat, a racing form in her hand, purchased ten tickets for herself.

Mary Macy of Malden, Massachusetts, purchased nine tickets, one for herself and each of her eight friends. "I want a white convertible, a summer camp on the water, and a boat that sleeps three or four people," she said while leaving the window. "But, most of all, I want a heart operation for my son."

One woman asked if she could fill out a ticket for her dog. The clerk looked at her straight-faced and said "so long as he can identify himself when he claims his prize."

There was a bulk-purchase window for sales greater than ten tickets. The first volume sale was made to George Coffey. The fifty-one-year-old U.S. Department of Interior retiree had flown in from Silver Springs, Maryland, to play the Sweepstakes. He bought sixty-three tickets, fifty-two of which were for friends and neighbors back home. It took two hours to fill out all of the slips and double check the names. It cost him $189 to make his loved ones happy. Coffey said he'd been warned by a deputy sheriff in his county not to bring tickets home with him, but he said he'd take the chance.

Every machine was in perpetual use, with a line of four or five people waiting behind each one. Several of the machines got jammed when instead of pushing the lever *up,* some buyers yanked the handle *down* like on a slot machine. Adams Manufacturing had representatives on hand to make repairs on the spot, but the commission would find the ticket machines were highly susceptible to glitches from user error.

AS THE EVENING WORE ON, Governor John King wandered away from the crowd and stood by himself for a long while at the picture window, looking out at the racetrack below. What might have been going through his head?

King's father had died earlier that month. Bill Loeb had penned an eloquent eulogy on the front page of the *Union Leader* with a photograph of Michael

King. The publisher noted that the elder King's story could only have been written in America. An impoverished Irish immigrant could land on the shore of no other nation and watch his son grow up to be governor.

"Michael King has earned his well-deserved rest," wrote Loeb. "Let those of us who remain here firmly resolve this great nation of shall always be the land of opportunity."

It was a good legacy, was it not? A humble shoemaker who reared six children. It was a good thing to be remembered for.

King occasionally invoked his father when defending the sweepstakes. He could recall how his father was kind and nonjudgmental, having lashed out only once when one of his daughters was caught smoking. "A lady doesn't smoke," he'd snapped, and that was the end of the discussion. To the men of Michael King's time, it was scandalous . . . sinful . . . for a woman to smoke a cigarette. It had been a Puritanical time. But here in 1964, women smoked all the time without fear of social recrimination. Attitudes change. They were in a new age, and morals were trying to keep pace with the reality of modern life. Behind him in the reflection of that window, decent, hard-working men and women were gambling — out in the open, without fear of social recrimination.

It seems that moment overlooking the track would have been the proper time to contemplate his legacy. Why else wander away like a bride from her wedding just to smell the night air?

King was not a gambler — even though he had placed all his chips on this one initiative. A year after signing the sweepstakes bill, after becoming a national target of scorn and celebration, things had turned up aces for him. Still, it was not too late for the "noble experiment" to fail. There were booby traps awaiting — hidden in politics, in legal interpretations, and in plain consumer interest.

John King had no children of his own. What would be said in his eulogy? How would he be remembered? This act, starting this machine, this is what he will be remembered for. He had no children other than the school children who visited his office, the school children he hoped this lottery would benefit. Right here, right now. This was John King's legacy.

Ed Powers stood beside the governor and joined his stare into the inky blackness of the winter evening. They spoke softly and responded in delicate nods of agreement. What they said to one another can only be guessed. Powers likely felt it too, that even with the accomplishment of the Brink's case, he would be remembered most for what would become of the New Hampshire Sweepstakes.

It did not feel like a victory lap. Too much was still to be done. September would arrive soon, and it would still be another week to ten days before Sweeps tickets could be purchased anywhere else in the world but the Salem racetrack. Points of sale were limited to the hours the liquor stores were open and not on Sundays. They were going to have to sell one ticket every five minutes between this day and race day if they were going to make their goal of $4 million.

17

The Revolution Will Not Be Televised

BY MAY OF 1964 it seemed that everyone with three bucks and a tank of gas was contemplating a trip to New Hampshire to get sweepstakes tickets. For the first two to three weeks of sales, Salem was the only place to buy a chance, and the lines never got short. Demand was so great that Lou Smith opened the clubhouse early and stayed late, running the ticket counter from 9 a.m. to 9 p.m.

Reporters could not get enough of the characters that turned up at the Rock. A scribe for the *Concord Daily Monitor* asked people why they were buying Sweeps tickets.

"I'm sick. Very sick," said a short man in a green felt hat, chewing an unlit cigar. "Also I don't make too much money." The reporter from the anti-sweeps paper pressed further but the guy spat back, "Are you a cop or a nut? Get outta here. I do it because I'm *charitable.*"

A blonde who fell out of a Raymond Chandler novel stood behind them lighting her second cigarette. "Why shouldn't I?" she said. "I gamble when I cross the street."

The reporter worked his way to the back of the line and caught a chipper-looking fat man joining the queue. Again the silly question: Why do you buy Sweeps tickets?

"Well, you see it's this way, Doctor Kildare," he replied to the unwanted psychoanalysis. "I like to build schools . . . nice, big schools." Asked where he was from, the man proclaimed, "New Hampshire! You think I'd build *someone else's* schools?"

Having had enough of the journalist, an unidentified man in the line shouted back, "Buddy, why don't you be a good guy, shuddup, and buy a ticket?"

Meantime in Concord, the letters with cash kept coming in. By Memorial Day 1964, more than three thousand people got their money back, along with a form letter telling them tickets could only be purchased in New Hampshire at a track or liquor store. The challenge the Sweeps had now was keeping up with nationwide demand to get tickets without straying from the law.

THE FIRST FEDERAL ENTITY to weigh in on the now-operational New Hampshire Sweepstakes was the agency with the longest-standing opposition to the lottery: the U.S. Post Office Department. By cutting off the mails in 1890, the Post Office had fatally disrupted the Louisiana Lottery Company's stranglehold on the nation. Nearly three-quarters of a century later, the department wasn't willing to rethink its position.

Two weeks after Sweeps tickets went on sale, Washington attorneys for the Post Office and Justice Departments announced it was a violation of federal law to send acknowledgments through the mail. Whether or not the acknowledgments were real tickets, the postal regulation was open to the broadest interpretation. It prohibited anything to do with a "lottery," which the New Hampshire Sweepstakes unquestionably was.

Powers publicly yawned at the announcement. They'd never suggested it was legal or encouraged players to mail acknowledgments. The sweepstakes supervisors personally couriered the ticket strips, microfilm, and accounting receipts, so none of them ever went in the mail. Even the commission's paychecks were hand-delivered. To Powers, it was a non-issue.

The commission had yet to settle on a way to notify out-of-state winners that didn't involve a letter. Sending checks through the mail was also equivocally illegal.

Powers told reporters he saw nothing wrong with New Hampshire residents purchasing Sweeps chances for friends or business colleagues out of state "as a social favor." Nor would it be against postal regulations to mail a letter to those friends saying, "I have purchased a sweepstakes ticket in your name, number such-and-such . . ." He warned that anyone discovered purchasing tickets as a business or for profit however would be "in trouble."

Powers and Millimet, who were generally quick to respond to any legal remonstrance, were silent on whether they'd challenge this Post Office ruling in court. Having devised a system in which the tickets stayed in New Hampshire, they considered their strongest arguments were against the Justice Department's Wire and Paraphernalia Acts. Powers admitted using the mails was a "gray area" for the sweepstakes.

The *Concord Daily Monitor* took the mail question one step further. They obtained a copy of the form letter the Sweepstakes Commission sent to return unsolicited money from those mailing their office. The documents were addressed to "Person Interested in the N.H. Sweepstakes Program." It listed information about how the Sweeps worked and where tickets were available, and expressly said "no mail orders for tickets will be accepted."

The *Monitor* (perhaps too skittish to forward the document by mail themselves) forwarded the letter to the postmaster in Concord with instructions to send the document on to Washington. The General Counsel for the Post Office Department's Mailability Division sent an advisory opinion to the newspaper that the form letter "would appear" to violate federal code. The memorandum would be forwarded to the postal inspector in Manchester.

The latest plot twist landed on the front page of the *Monitor*. After Ed Powers talked to a *Union Leader* reporter he trusted, pointing out the origins of the story, Bill Loeb went on an editorial tear. His page-one response was to call the *Concord Daily Monitor* despicable for deliberately omitting from their report that they had instigated the investigation in order to manufacture the story.

The form letter debacle was a victory for the Committee of One Hundred and other opponents who had taken the position that *no* information about the Sweeps — regardless of the source or context — could go through the mail. Here was a true monkey wrench they could throw into the works.

A vexed Powers told the *Union Leader*, "[The form letter] is only sent out in answer to letters received in this office. It is not promotional material, but is merely used to inform people how to keep within the law."

WITHIN A WEEK of the form-letter crisis, the Post Office Department issued another statement saying the Sweepstakes Commission may have violated postal laws. The department pointed to press releases mailed from the commission to area newspapers and radio stations that gave updates on the latest weekly tally in ticket sales.

This time, it was the *Hanover Gazette* that initiated the probe. Editor David Hewitt, a founding member of the Committee of One Hundred, hand-delivered the envelope and its contents to the local postmaster. The material was accompanied by a two-page, single-spaced letter posing several questions about whether the "news release" (the words were surrounded by quotation marks each time it appeared) broke federal laws and what could be done to prevent further violations. The letter was signed, notarized, then countersigned by the Hanover postmaster and notarized affirming he received the request.

The Post Office's opinion was that mailing press releases — and any other correspondence — was also a likely infraction. Both memos had been advisory, but they would further consult with the Justice Department on the matter.

New Hampshire Attorney General William Maynard announced he was advising the Sweepstakes Commission to scrutinize current mailing policies. Powers told the press the commission would reexamine its procedures but did not think any of them violated the law.

Powers went so far as to say the postal regulations were antiquated. "I've got to be able to answer my own mail," he complained.

NEW HAMPSHIRE'S chief law-enforcement officer, Attorney General William Maynard, had remained largely silent on the issue of the sweepstakes. The post of attorney general was not a full-time position. Maynard maintained his private practice; the state of New Hampshire was more like his client. Maynard was a die-hard Republican, a political holdover with several years still on his five-year term, and an opponent of the lottery.

Maynard would visit the New Hampshire Department of Justice in the morning, but most of his lawyering in the afternoon was done from the back of any one of Concord's many bars. That's where clerks and assistant attorneys general would courier briefs and legal work, only to find Maynard drinking neat and arguing politics sloppily. No secret was made of Maynard's gubernatorial aspirations.

It was openly reported in local papers that Governor King and Maynard were not on speaking terms. Messengers went back and forth between their offices (and, presumably, the bars), but the pair had not spoken face to face in several months. Their animus was among the reasons King never asked his attorney general for an advisory opinion on the sweepstakes law and why he solicited Joseph Millimet to be the legal consultant on sweepstakes matters in the first place.

Questions about the Sweeps from state and local police outside of New

Hampshire were forwarded to Maynard. They wanted to know what were the regulations and case law regarding the lottery. They wanted to know how to spot counterfeit tickets. Of course, mail restrictions hampered Maynard's own ability to respond to all the inquiries.

When asked by reporters, Maynard confessed — with some embarrassment — that he did write letters to agencies regarding sweepstakes enforcement. He pointed out he was very "careful" about what he wrote and did not use the mail for "any information in furtherance of the sweepstakes program." Yet among the items mailed to law-enforcement agencies was a sample Sweeps ticket.

THE FEDS had another one-two punch for Ed Powers. The Post Office Department declared that any New Hampshire newspaper that mailed editions across state lines could not include any stories about the lottery. The law, 18 U.S. Code 336, read, "No newspaper . . . containing any advertisement of a lottery . . . shall be deposited in or carried by the mails of the United States." There were virtually no local papers that didn't use the mail to send some copies inside New Hampshire or out.

The airwaves, in the view of Congress, were in the public domain and broadcasting was a form of interstate commerce. Immediately after the Post Office announcement, the Federal Communications Commission issued its own ruling on broadcasting. The United Press International chief in New Hampshire requested guidelines on reporting results from the FCC on behalf of their member stations. Prohibitions against broadcasters conducting their own lotteries — defined by the FCC as making someone *pay* to have a *chance* at winning a contest — were already in place. By extension, the FCC said, radio stations risked stiff penalties if they carried results from the New Hampshire Sweepstakes "under the guise of a news story." The penalty for broadcasters was a $1,000 fine or one year imprisonment. The FCC advised stations to use "great care" in airing Sweeps results. "Only in unusual cases would lottery information be considered news," it said.

"How they can ignore the news about the Irish Sweepstake for all these years and now crack down on the New Hampshire Sweepstakes is beyond me," vented Powers to the AP. "It seems like a deliberate harassment of the New Hampshire Sweepstakes."

To have any chance at success, the Sweeps had to communicate with the public. These federal findings, which amounted to a media blackout, were the kind of uppercut that knocked a fighter to the mat. Powers dusted himself off and positioned the rulings as not anti-sweepstakes, but anti-press.

Powers accused the federal government of engaging in prior restraint, citing the landmark *Near v. Minnesota* censorship case. The press could not be prevented before the fact — even in cases of libel or scandal — from publishing its story. Powers said the feds were making determinations about what was and what wasn't legitimate news. He defended the First and Fourteenth Amendment rights of New Hampshire newspapers to print what they chose to print. In a not-so-subtle way Powers was calling out the state's media, challenging them to stand up for the constitutional rights they claimed to espouse.

With the mass media cut off, the commission made the only decision it could regarding announcing winners. It would post lists in each liquor store and racetrack — an imperfect solution, no doubt. The papers, mum on the professional dare thrown down by Powers, editorialized that thousands of people would jam the store parking lots to look for their names. They jeered the implication that people purchasing alcohol would have to stand in the presence of sinful gamblers. Hoping the overwhelming public demand would drive competition, Powers said, "We'll post the results at Rockingham Park and the state liquor stores, and the news media can make up their own minds."

Though not the final word on sweepstakes-related broadcasts, Powers got to thumb his nose at the FCC. The following week, he flew to New York City to be the guest on the CBS game show *To Tell the Truth*, with host Bud Collyer. Powers and two impostors tried to stump a panel of celebrity judges into guessing which one of them was the real executive director of the New Hampshire Sweepstakes. The prime time show had an estimated audience of 15 million viewers.

BY THE END OF THE FIRST TEN DAYS of sales, 29,741 tickets had been sold at Rockingham Park, the only location with working machines. That was $81,000 in proceeds. By March 23, liquor stores in the biggest cities and along the state borders had Sweeps ticket machines online. The *Daily Monitor* reported that Concord's liquor store had sold 110 tickets in the first day and a half. The first ticket was bought by all seven of the store's employees (each pitching in about forty-three cents to buy their dream). One man from Pennsylvania scooped up thirty-one tickets and spent a half hour writing out slips for friends and family back home.

Once all liquor stores had ticket machines, total store sales outpaced sales at the racetracks by two to one. The Sweeps were on pace for over a million dollars in sales before the summer tourist season would begin — the seasonal stretch during which the bulk of sales were projected. A rainy summer, one in which beach day-trippers and weekend lake sailors were discouraged from visiting, could kill sales.

THE SWEEPSTAKES HAD ADVOCATES in the nation's capitol. New York Congressman Paul Fino had long been pushing for a national lottery (with as much luck as Larry Pickett had previously had). He enthusiastically praised anything New Hampshire did, hoping it would raise his own political fortunes.

New Hampshire First District Representative Louis Wyman, a Republican, interceded on the state's behalf.[1] Wyman requested the general counsels from the Post Office Department and the Federal Communications Commission meet with Joseph Millimet and Attorney General William Maynard in his Washington office and clear up the gray areas these informal announcement were having on the sweepstakes. New Hampshire's other congressman, James Cleveland, would be there, as well as the top aide to Senator Thomas McIntyre. Underscoring how weighty was the gathering, FCC Commissioner Rosel Hyde made an appearance. For federal agencies and their appointees, a meeting request from a group of Congressmen was a command performance.

Wyman acted as a mediator between all the parties. The Post Office official, under the glare of the congressman, agreed the Sweepstakes Commission could receive and send mail for bona fide business, such as returning unsolicited money or answering questions about how the lottery worked. He stood firm on the position the commission could not mail notices to winners about their prizes or send lists of winners to third parties.

The attorney, conceding Power's point about prior restraint, said it would be legal for newspapers to print stories of a "non-promotional" nature about

1. A decade later, Wyman would serve as a U.S. Senator for three days in the closest election in Senate history. He appeared to have defeated Democrat John Durkin by 335 votes, but a recount had Wyman losing by 10. A second recount put Wyman ahead by 2 votes. Incumbent Norris Cotton resigned early and New Hampshire's Republican governor appointed Wyman, but three days later Durkin sought relief from the U.S. Senate (constitutionally, the arbiter in Senate elections). A Senate Rules Committee, after seven months' argument over whose seat it was, became hopelessly deadlocked. Finally, both candidates agreed to a new election, in which Durkin turned back Wyman by 27,717 votes.

the sweepstakes. Stories about sales numbers and people buying tickets were fair game. Information about the horse race, independent from the lottery, was fine too. Again, the line was drawn at printing the names of Sweeps winners.

FCC Commissioner Hyde and his general counsel capitulated to the same degree. Broadcasters could report legitimate, newsworthy stories about the sweepstakes' function and operation. Identifying winners over the airwaves was still verboten.

Basically, New Hampshire had won the right to publicize everything about the sweepstakes except the sweepstakes.

Millimet pushed back on the restrictions on disseminating Sweeps information. The sweepstakes was not an illegal gambling racket; it was a state-sanctioned enterprise with a charitable mission of raising money for education. He accused both agencies of hypocrisy, saying for decades they had allowed story after story about Irish Sweepstake winners in the country without a care. Neither had they attempted to do anything about the Mob's "handle" number, which appeared in daily papers from coast to coast.

Wyman proposed an outside-of-the-box solution. What if the names of the winners were printed in the *Congressional Journal*? Either he or Paul Fino could have the names of winners entered into the Congressional Record, then mailed out under their congressional frank. No federal law at the time prohibited the contents of franked mail. The Post Office counsel approved the workaround.

After the meeting, Senators McIntyre and Norris Cotton and Representatives Wyman and Cleveland drafted a bipartisan bill to exempt state-run lotteries from the 10 percent federal gambling excise tax, as well as the fifty-dollars-per-employee tax stamp. (New Hampshire was prepared to pay these taxes after the race, but only under protest). New York's Paul Fino signed on as an enthusiastic cosponsor. Although several states were watching New Hampshire, with ideas of their own lotteries percolating, not enough support existed for pro-sweepstakes legislation to gain traction in Washington.

Not yet.

THERE WAS, however, intense interest from ABC's *Wide World of Sports* to televise the race. Jim McKay's weekly ode to the human drama of athletic competition was a catchall of games of skill, feats of bravado, things that went fast, and things that crashed. From Acapulco cliff diving to Russian motorcycle ice racing, from billiards to bowling, *Wide World of Sports* was an almanac of athletics that was often exotic and frequently compelling.

ABC did not have the Kentucky Derby on its network. The Triple Crown had been carried by CBS for a decade and would be for another. There were no other horse races of interest on the calendar. James Spence, executive producer of *Wide World,* contacted Lou Smith to see if anyone had the television rights to the New Hampshire Sweepstakes. At a time when so many people were trying to purge the airwaves of the Sweeps, it was hard to fathom someone looking to put the race on national TV.

Millimet became liaison to ABC and secured an agreement to carry the race. NBC would have radio rights. The contracts represented millions of dollars of free advertising and mainstream affirmation that the lottery revolution was a national sensation.

Two weeks later, Spence called Millimet to say the FCC was giving the network trouble about running the sweepstakes. Having thought the matter had been settled, Millimet fired off an angry letter to the FCC general counsel, cc'ing the congressional delegation, the governor, and Spence at ABC. "After our conversations in Washington," he wrote, "I was under the impression that [you] share the opinions of Commissioner Hyde . . . You indicated that as long as the telecast was confined to dissemination of the usual information about a horse race, it could certainly be broadcast." Millimet demanded another meeting in Washington at the offices of the seven FCC commissioners. As a result, the general counsel immediately and emphatically wrote he would never contradict Commissioner Hyde and would remove any barrier ABC would have in conducting the broadcast.

That settled the matter. The revolution *would* be televised.

18

*This Is
a Test*

STATE AND FEDERAL law-enforcement agencies had by and large stayed
out of the sweepstakes before the public vote approving sales. The notable
exception had occurred at the top, when Attorney General Robert Kennedy in
the *New York Daily News* seemed to contradict what Deputy Attorney General
Nicholas Katzenbach told Joseph Millimet. That column, however, never
directly quoted RFK — and he never said anything publicly about the sweepstakes after that — so it remains possible the *Daily News* "scoop" had been little
more than printable hearsay of the standard Washington variety.

After the March vote, Katzenbach gave his first at-length interview about
the issue to the *Concord Daily Monitor.* He described their previous discussions
with New Hampshire as being informal and brief. Asked whether state and
federal law conflicted, Katzenbach said, "That depends on how it is administered. It is entirely up to the state of New Hampshire. The law as we see it is
not clearly in conflict with any federal statute."

Katzenbach said they continued to have concerns about racketeers, concerns they shared with the state. He also declined to speculate on whether
"acknowledgments" had the same legal value as lottery tickets. Katzenbach
said there were no plans for surveillance or other actions associated with the
sweepstakes, and the Justice Department would only investigate if it received
a criminal complaint.

The hands-off posture continued to pique journalists. Ted Rowse of the *Washington Post* wrote, "Federal authorities have not really faced up to the issues and are not likely to do so until they run up against some overt violation they can't duck. Then, and not until then, will the fur fly."

ROBERT KENNEDY and the Justice Department had pushed for the federal Wire Act and the Interstate Transportation of Wagering Paraphernalia Act because state laws on the subject were too weak. Now police in neighboring states, resigned to the fact they were going to see Sweeps tickets move through their cities and towns, wanted to know what they should do. Talking to police chiefs, state attorneys general, and U.S. attorneys, everyone seemed to have their own opinions.

The most likely route for tourists leaving New Hampshire went through Massachusetts. The Boston papers could not stop wagging fingers at the Granite State's flaunting of federal law. "Suppose," proffered the *Boston Record American*, "a Massachusetts resident, an old silver-haired grandmaw, or perky office Judy or an elderly school janitor" has their ticket picked for the race. Once the winners' names are publicized, "Will the federal snoops snatch the nice old lady, the lipstick Jill, or the old pappy-guy as criminals?" The scribe seemed to think so.

Massachusetts Attorney General Edward Brooke told a Boston radio show that he saw no issues with people bringing Sweeps tickets into the Bay State. "We've had border disputes since the beginning of time . . . but I think no serious problem we can't work out." Brooke disclosed that the two states had been meeting to share information, and he was satisfied with what he'd heard: "I understand it is not their intention to send tickets into Massachusetts for sale."

Brooke also said there were no plans to stop people at the border and search them for tickets. "They won't be able to say to you, 'Do you have a sweepstakes ticket in your possession?' I don't think we're going to have that sort of problem at all." He concluded, "I think people who fear this are just looking for problems . . . particularly in view of the Mapp case."

The reason cops would not stop motorists at the state line had nothing to do with courtesy. A recent Supreme Court case, *Mapp v. Ohio*, had placed a higher standard for search and seizure on state and local police. The Mapp case, like the Miranda case soon to follow, would be among a series of landmark decisions in the 1960s and 1970s that affected due process. Applying the Mapp case to the transportation of Sweeps tickets, Brooke correctly determined that officers could not simply question and detain people driving out of New Hampshire on the suspicion that they were carrying tickets — even if they believed the tickets were illegal. Officers would need a search warrant to nose around the cars of travelers if they wanted to get inside.[1]

Mapp only answered the question about police tactics. What remained open to interpretation was the lingering issue of whether or not acknowledgments could be transported across state lines. It wasn't long before the rest of New Hampshire's neighbors began to weigh in.

Maine's attorney general was the first to follow Massachusetts in declaring that bringing Sweeps tickets into the state was legal. In an advisory opinion solicited by the head of the Maine state police, Frank Hancock said that whether called an acknowledgment or receipt or ticket or counterfoil, possession did not constitute a breach of state law. Hancock determined that since the acknowledgment did not have to be retained in order to claim a prize, then the slip of paper had no value.

Attorney General Charles Gibson of Vermont came to the same conclusion two weeks later. Mere possession of an acknowledgment did not break state law. This meant New Hampshire's abutters to the east, west, and south were all on record as being hands-off. Gibson did warn citizens not to purchase sweepstakes chances from individuals scalping tickets in Vermont. Acting as a lottery broker, whether affiliated with a legal lottery or not, was still a punishable crime in the Green Mountain State.

In New Jersey, however, the deputy attorney general in charge of the Criminal Investigation Division said that residents found with a New Hampshire Sweepstakes ticket could be charged with a misdemeanor gambling charge, as well as being charged with being a "disorderly person." Penalties were fines up to $1,000 or a year in jail. The prosecutor in Camden County said people who bought more than one ticket or a group of tickets for friends or resale could face state charges for engaging in a lottery. He reported there were rumors of

---

1. Ironically, New Hampshire attorney general William Maynard's negligence in a high-profile homicide investigation in February 1964 led to a precedent further raising the burden for law enforcement. When cops wanted to search the car of Edward Coolidge, suspected of killing two teenage girls, Maynard signed the warrant himself. In 1971, the U.S. Supreme Court ruled the seizure was unconstitutional because the search warrant was not signed by a "neutral and detached magistrate." *Coolidge v. New Hampshire* became one of the most significant Fourth Amendment rulings of the twentieth century.

a man making weekly trips back and forth from New Hampshire, charging an extra fifty cents on each ticket he bought.

To prove its seriousness, New Jersey did something it hadn't done in anyone's memory. After a Union County man got his picture in the paper after winning a prize in the Irish Sweepstake, police issued him their own ticket (charge: being a disorderly person; fine: twenty-five dollars).

For its part, the New York state police announced they would attempt to arrest anyone for possessing an acknowledgment. A spokesman said selling tickets remained a punishable offense.

Connecticut state police had a devil of a time getting an opinion from the state's top prosecutors about whether officers could go after Sweeps players. After two letters to state Attorney General Harold Mulvey, the AG final replied that he had no idea and no jurisdiction over what he viewed to be a federal issue. Several county attorneys declined to speculate, saying what they did in their own county might not be followed in another.

While most of their state-level counterparts were brushing off the enforcement issue, federal U.S. attorneys for these regions were maintaining a hard line. Arthur Garrity Jr., the U.S. attorney in Boston, reminded reporters it was a federal offense to carry the receipt from New Hampshire to another state. The U.S. attorney for Connecticut stated his department would arrest anyone who resold or charged a fee to purchase tickets and bring receipts back to the state. New Hampshire's own U.S. attorney, Louis Janelle, saw no problem with sweepstakes operations.

With so many different points of view across the East Coast, the Justice Department in Washington issued an advisory memo to all U.S. attorneys. "There should be no particular difficulty in prosecuting anyone who travels to New Hampshire and brings back receipts for re-sale or who operates a 'service' offering for a fee to go to New Hampshire, purchase the tickets, and bring receipts back to a customer in another state," the memo read. "The difficult problem is the case of a tourist who carries receipts interstate either for himself or as a favor to friends."

Legally, there was no ambiguity for the DOJ. Crossing state lines with lottery tickets was illegal "whatever the motive." But the memo contained a warning for the U.S. attorneys: "It is recognized that prosecution of tourists will require the exercise of considerable discretion." The message from Washington seemed to be leave the nice old ladies, the lipstick Jills, and the old pappy-guys alone.

The press, still trying to untangle the web of contradictory positions, declared it would likely take the arrest of a ticket-holder and a judge to sort the whole thing out.

SIXTY-THREE-YEAR-OLD LOUIS HAMOD owned a small diner in Central Falls, Rhode Island. He had left a sign up near the cash register that read, "If you want New Hampshire Sweepstakes tickets, leave your name and address here." Many of his regular customers signed up, as Hamod said he would be driving up on Holy Thursday (the day before Good Friday).

A Central Falls police detective noticed the sign and reported it to his supervisors, who ordered him to keep the restaurant under surveillance. When Hamod left on March 26, 1964, he was followed to the border by the Rhode Island state police. From there, RISP Detective Edward Pare parked the car and waited for Hamod to return.

Five hours later, long after sunset, Pare spotted Hamod's car crossing back into Rhode Island on Interstate 95 and pulled him over. He yanked Hamod from the car and began searching it with his flashlight. He found what he was looking for: thirty-eight New Hampshire Sweepstakes acknowledgments. Each slip was made out to one of thirty-eight different people. The senior citizen was arrested and booked that night. At his arraignment on Good Friday, Hamod pleaded not guilty to possession of lottery tickets. He said he would appeal to Governor John King to have him pay for his defense.

Commissioner Howell Shepard came out swinging. He emphatically said Hamod was not arrested with lottery tickets, because the tickets he purchased were in the possession of the state of New Hampshire. Shepard said the slips were merely nontransferable acknowledgments and were "worthless scraps of paper."

Governor King all but disappeared over the Easter weekend, not even taking phone calls from the *Union Leader*. Attorney General Maynard could not be reached either; however, he was furiously trying to contact Rhode Island's attorney general, Joseph Nugent. The irony was that Maynard, the sweepstakes opponent, was doing all he could to get the charges dropped.

Attorney General Nugent told reporters that Rhode Island law appeared to forbid possession of New Hampshire Sweepstakes acknowledgments. Again, there was disagreement between the top state and federal prosecutors on the matter. They concurred that those acting as brokers, making money on the purchase or transportation of sweepstakes chances would be pursued, but U.S. Attorney Raymond Pettine declared the Justice Department would not seek charges against "reputable citizens" who had Sweeps tickets.

THE HAMOD ARREST put a chill on sales at Rockingham Park and other venues. Out-of-staters were responsible for 40 percent of New Hampshire liquor sales, and were expected to be an even larger segment of Sweeps customers.

Weekends at the Rock were always busy, yet the lines for Sweeps tickets were sluggish. Tourists, who normally filled out a slip and moved on within a minute, were spending more time quizzing the counter salesmen about what Hamod's arrest meant.

"The Rhode Island thing is being straightened out," one player was told. Another heard that Rhode Island was "confused." A seller erroneously told buyers he heard on the radio that the charges had been dropped. In the end, sales receipts for the holiday weekend were down from the previous week.

When eventually cornered by reporters, King declined to comment on the specifics of Hamod's case. He did remind the statehouse press corps of the other states that had determined possession of acknowledgments wasn't a crime and wondered aloud why Rhode Island had never arrested a single Irish Sweeps broker. The governor also said the state would not be providing counsel to Hamod — or anyone else who was arrested.

THE RHODE ISLAND ARREST worried no one more than Ed Powers (except perhaps Louis Hamod, whose liberty was at stake). This was the test case that everyone had been waiting for, and the state had determined it was going to sit on the sidelines. The commissioners concurred with the governor that they would not pay for Hamod's lawyer, meaning Powers could not put any of his operational money toward the fees. He decided he would do the next best thing.

Hamod's attorney, Deeb Sarkas, wrote to Powers and asked him to be a witness for the defense. Attorney General Nugent said they had no interest in asking Powers to testify for the state, as Powers wasn't "an expert on Rhode Island law." Powers went above and beyond Sarkas's request; he asked to sit second chair for the April 22 trial. It was a role he had played at the Brink's heist trial, so how could Sarkas say no?

Hamod was not charged with any federal violations. He wasn't accused of

breaking the Interstate Transportation of Wagering Paraphernalia Act. He was
to be tried in state district court for violating Rhode Island laws prohibiting
lotteries. The proceedings were over before lunch. UPI reported the two state
police officers described how they had followed Hamod to the border and
waited for him to return. Powers, the only defense witness, took the stand
explaining with much gusto how the New Hampshire Sweepstakes operated
and exactly why the thirty-eight acknowledgments Mr. Hamod was found
with were *not* actually lottery tickets.

After testimony, Sarkas asked Judge Guillaume Myette to quash the charge
for being vague. The complaint, he said, did not allege any conduct that violated
the state's anti-lottery laws.

The judge dismissed the charge — but not for those reasons. Myette said
he was concerned with "the method resorted to by our state police" and ruled
the search by Detective Pare was illegal. "I will not say we are confronted with
entrapment," he said, "but it was akin to obtaining evidence against our citizens
in such a way." The judge called it a "very unsavory way of enforcing the law."

Hamod was thrilled with the dismissal.[2] It was a victory for Ed Powers and
the sweepstakes too, but a lost opportunity as well. While the case was a public-relations win, sure to steady the nerves of out-of-state players purchasing
tickets, it didn't serve well to test the heart of the matter — the legality of the
acknowledgments. The can had been kicked down the road.

Before returning to New Hampshire, Powers met with Attorney General
Nugent. Try as he might, he could not convince the Nugent the slips from the
sweepstakes were kosher. Nugent told reporters he still believe possession of
New Hampshire Sweeps tickets was illegal under Rhode Island law and that
he would authorize the arrest and prosecution of anyone caught with them.

Three months later, police raided the home of a Providence man in search of
gambling paraphernalia. Vincent Scialo had been running numbers out of his
small cafe. Officers found a pile of betting slips for horse races and for numbers
pools. There were tally sheets and cash for payouts. Among the items seized
were two New Hampshire Sweepstakes acknowledgments, both made out to

---

2. It's worth noting that while the sweepstakes tickets had cost him just $114, Hamod's legal fees
totaled $5,000. Unable to get the state of New Hampshire to pay for his defense, a sympathetic Rhode
Island state representative filed a bill in 1965 to allow Hamod to sue the Ocean State for the $5,000. The
measure died in committee.

Scialo. While it was clear Scialo's bookmaking services covered several vices, there wasn't much evidence that he was trafficking large numbers of Sweeps tickets. In addition to all the other gambling offenses Scialo was charged with, the cops added on "possession of lottery slips" and "promoting a lottery." The lieutenant who headed the investigation said they wanted to throw the lottery charges in so they could have another swing at it.

In August, a Westerly man was arrested for having Sweeps acknowledgments in his home. Despite Rhode Island's zeal to get a sweepstakes conviction, each of the cases was thrown out due to illegal search concerns. Judging by the numbers, their efforts did little to sour Ocean Staters from going to New Hampshire for tickets.

Rhode Island would not play a role in the ultimate determination of the acknowledgments' legality. But New York eventually would.

19

The Sharpies' Loophole

DESPITE THE RHODE ISLAND DUST-UP, thousands of people were flocking to New Hampshire, and it wasn't even the summer tourist season. Governor King began fielding telephone calls from other governors and lawmakers seeking details on setting up their own lotteries. Among the first were the Canadians, Quebéc specifically, about the workings of New Hampshire's sweepstakes. Quebécers had been on record since 1934 as wanting a provincial lottery, but had yet to take any action. When King did not immediately respond, the barrister for the Royal Commission on Taxation wrote directly to Ed Powers. He even offered to come to Concord for a personal meeting if sending information by mail was prohibited.

There were several U.S. state nibbling around the edges of their own lottery proposals. They kept their power dry, looking to see how New Hampshire wiggled out of the federal knots — and just how much money the Sweeps would rake in. Rhode Island, ironically, was one of those keeping a close eye. Massachusetts advocates, still smarting from another New Hampshire first-in-the-nation claim, watched carefully. Vermont and New Jersey were also resurrecting their long-abandoned lottery projects. New York's lottery legislation was stalled, as were its attempts to start off-track betting, and would likely stay that way while Rockefeller remained governor. Kentucky planned on sending a delegation of state lawmakers to New Hampshire's first drawing to reconnoiter. California was the first state to make a move. Over the objections of the governor and the legislature, voters placed on the November 1964 ballot a referendum on starting a state-sanctioned, privately run lottery. The newly formed American Sweepstakes Corporation would be given a ten-year monopoly on its operation. The parallels between this proposal and the Louisiana Golden Octopus were startling.

Both Howell Shepard and Ed Powers had conceded to reporters at different times that other state lotteries would likely cut into New Hampshire's profit margin, especially if Massachusetts went into the sweepstake business. Neither was fatalistic about this. Shepard, Powers, and Governor King all believed that by the time any other state had implemented a lottery, the New Hampshire Sweepstakes would already be a national institution.

COMMISSIONER SHEPARD had some more bothersome news to report to Governor King. The bugs in the ticket machines that turned up on opening night at Rockingham Park were plaguing nearly all of the sales locations. Even given verbal instructions from the sales clerks, excited players still pulled down on the release handles instead of pushing up. It was a persistent user error that damaged the mechanical workings of the machine.

The more pervasive problem involved feeding the continuous roll of the tickets. Even without the mild abuse inflicted by the public, the paper often came dislodged from sprockets that advanced it, creating paper jams that had to be sorted out by attendants of various competency levels. Sometimes a small section of the roll would become hopelessly mangled, and the damaged tickets would have to be removed — no trivial act in a computerized accounting system that required every ticket to be filed in sequential order. The snafu with the machines caused one liquor store cashier in Hillsboro to hand out twenty actual tickets instead of the acknowledgments. Ten of the tickets were recovered by players in town, but New Hampshire state police had to track down the other ten from players in Massachusetts and Connecticut and drive them back home.

According to Shepard, the Adams Manufacturing Company in Chicago was not very helpful in diagnosing the cause of the paper jams or finding a solution.

King, his patience strained, asked what the commission was going to do about the kinks. Shepard brought in two new firms — one to improve the existing ticket machines, another to design a better one. He also revealed the state had yet to pay Adams its $40,000 for the machines it had delivered. King told Shepard not to pay the bill until the company was more responsive and he was satisfied with their work. The *Concord Daily Monitor* ran a four-column headline beneath the masthead, laying blame at the commission's doorstep. The *Union Leader's* story blamed the Chicago manufacturer.

IT'S UNCLEAR whether sixty-three year-old Rhode Islander Louis Hamod bought those thirty-eight tickets as a courtesy to his friends and customers, or whether he did so to make a profit. Thousands of people visited New Hampshire to get chances for themselves and others. A Sweeps ticket was the must-give souvenir of 1964, and the man who made it known he was vacationing in the White Mountains or on Lake Winnipesaukee was mightily harassed by cousin and co-worker.

No one ever accused Hamod of tacking a fee on or adding some other remuneration for his trouble, but there were those who were doing that.

The volume window at Rockingham Park saw lots of action. In the first couple of weeks, a Pennsylvania man passed the teller a list of more than one hundred names (the bulk purchases were now done by typewriter to accelerate the tedious process). A Washington, D.C., man casually told a national magazine that he charged each of his friends five dollars to make the trip on their behalf. The papers caught up with one New Jersey man (maybe the one Camden County resident cops had been hearing so much about) who said he spent his days off driving to New Hampshire to buy tickets for this "friends." He claimed by late July he had purchased twenty-seven hundred tickets. He declined to give the reporter his name.

In the hundreds of letters mailed to the commission, many were unsolicited offers to work as out-of-state brokers for the sweepstakes. Many people were familiar with the ins and outs of the Irish Sweep, and they never checked the fine print on New Hampshire's differences.

"I have sold Irish Sweepstake tickets for many years," one letter-writer boasted. "I can do a good job for you."

"I want a couple of books," said a patriotic businessman. "Rather this country than Erin."

"We handle other lotteries in this area to Asians and U.S. military personnel," wrote a syndicate from Japan. "We want exclusive rights in the Far East and Southeast Asia."

All of these would-be impresarios were politely turned down with Ed Powers's Post Office Department–blessed form letter: no tickets sold outside of New Hampshire; no tickets mailed outside of New Hampshire.

If the distribution of "acknowledgments" was Powers's loophole, the sharpies had finally found their own loophole. While the surrounding states had laws that prohibited private citizens from conducting or promoting lotteries, New Hampshire did not. Larry Pickett's bill, for all its safeguards, failed to address what legalizing the sweepstakes meant to nonstate employees looking for their own piece of the action.

It wasn't long after King bought his first ticket that agencies began to spring up around the state. For a fee — usually between fifty cents and a couple of dollars a ticket — buyers could call the agency located in New Hampshire and an agent would purchase slips on their behalf. Brokers placed classified ads in newspapers across the country. Altogether, the system wasn't dissimilar to the way theater ticket agencies obtained seats to Broadway shows.

The middlemen established their businesses with the secretary of state under such names as Lucky's Ticket Agency or Mr. & Mrs. New Hampshire Sweepstakes, but the office had no authority to shut them down. Neither did the Sweepstakes Commission, as enforcement power was not part of its legislative mandate. At one point, there were fifteen ticket agencies operating in the Granite State.

The Committee of One Hundred, still prowling, pointed to the ticket agencies as proof their predictions of racketeering would come to fruition. Now, said former Senate president Raymond Perkins, was the time to repeal the "insidious and evil" law before organized crime entrenched itself in New Hampshire.

Powers, whose FBI credentials were what had quelled the mafia hysteria in the first place, was now embarrassed by the unchecked nature of the ticket agencies. "I'm not in favor of these agencies, but we have no law enforcement power," he told the *Christian Science Monitor.* "We're not authorizing any such activity. And the men should consult their attorneys before taking any orders out of state because they might be doing something that is in violation of federal law." The executive director predicted the state legislature would either pass a law to make charging a premium on tickets illegal, or give the commission the power to license agencies and audit their books.

Concord Ticket Services owner Charles Cohan told the *Monitor* they were obtaining tickets on behalf of players from around the country, and business had been very good. They tacked fifty cents on to the price of each ticket and made players sign a contract giving the business 10 percent of any winnings. Concord Ticket Services claimed to have sold five thousand Sweeps chances between May and July.

"I don't mail any acknowledgments," Cohan insisted. "If people want them, I'll mail them after the race is over. They have to come to New Hampshire if they want to see the acknowledgment before the race."

To rub salt into the state's wound, the Internal Revenue Service said that the ticket agency was merely providing a service and not selling lottery tickets. That meant its employees did not have to obtain the fifty-dollar gambling tax stamp required from the state.

JOHN KING SUMMONED Shepard, Millimet, and Powers to his office to figure out how to deal with the IRS. In his first Washington meeting with IRS representatives, Millimet had received only an informal opinion that the state was liable for the 10 percent excise tax and the fifty-dollar gambling stamps. If that decision stood, it could suck up more than a half-million dollars of profit. The state had initially agreed to pay the tax under protest, preserving the right to challenge the decision in court.

The men were still confident about the strength of their argument that the Sweeps fell within the exception afforded nonprofit organizations raising money for charity. While not technically a nonprofit, the state was never taxed by the IRS as if it were a business. And if bingo games and raffles funded education, so surely too could the sweepstakes. Even the Justice Department had conceded the ticket machines could legally be shipped from Chicago because they were a "political subdivision." The governor ordered his team to seek a formal ruling from the IRS about the excise tax.

In May, Powers met with Charles Emlet, the Internal Revenue Service district director for New Hampshire. After three hours of heated discussion, Emlet said the state would not be exempted from the 10 percent excise tax. He was not swayed by Powers's argument that the feds had no right to tax a state program that raised money for educational purposes. Furthermore, the IRS would not waive the fifty-dollar stamp for each of the seventy-five sweepstakes clerks. Powers objected, pointing to the IRS's gambling stamp exemption for pari-mutuel wager clerks, which was what Sweeps clerks essential were.

Joseph Millimet flew to Washington for another high-stakes face-off. Senator McIntyre had summoned Assistant Secretary of the Treasury Stanley Surrey to his office (another command performance). Surrey listened to Millimet's rational, but didn't see any way around the issue due to the ambiguity of the exemption's wording. McIntyre was proposing Congress pass a tax exemption for state lotteries. As it was late in the legislative session, the measure could not get a speedy hearing without the support of the Treasury Department. Millimet urged Surrey to back the bill.

McIntyre's measure died in committee. King ordered any excise taxes collected to be put in escrow while the state prepared to take the IRS to court.

REPRESENTATIVE LARRY PICKETT, sitting in that leather chair at the Elks Lodge, felt New Hampshire was missing a golden opportunity to get sales from all parts of the country. If they could not meet the nationwide demand for Sweeps tickets, they would miss out on huge amounts of revenue. It seemed these rogue ticket agencies, taking calls from all corners, weren't hurting sales (who could argue the ticket services weren't actually increasing Sweeps sales), but the odor they left was unbearable.

Pickett publicly suggested Sweeps tickets should be sold at the World's Fair, but he had apparently forgotten that Commissioner Shepard had floated the same idea months earlier and had been crucified in the press for it.

Without the consultation of King or Powers, Pickett took a three-day trip to Washington, D.C., to brainstorm with legal minds. He met with a law professor at Catholic University — whom he did not identify to the *Sunday News* — who was said to have written many anti-gambling laws and was considered an expert in the field. When Pickett returned, he gave a speech in Keene saying he had found a way to legally supply tickets to anyone anywhere in the country.

Pickett's plan called for all civic and fraternal clubs and lodges in New Hampshire to buy tickets on behalf of members from outside of New Hampshire. Pickett said that everyone and their brother belonged to one of these fraternal organizations — the Elks, the Jaycees, Kiwanis, the Odd Fellows — or at least knew someone who did belong. Local chapters existed in every city in the world. Brother members from parts elsewhere could call the New Hampshire lodge and request tickets. The charge would be four dollars (fifty cents would go toward the club's charitable works, the other fifty cents to cover administrative handling). Pickett, who belonged to several fraternal organizations, offered to buy tickets himself for brothers anywhere in the world.

"There is absolutely nothing in the law books," his familiar voice intoned, "to prevent a person in New Hampshire from buying a sweepstakes ticket for a fraternal brother, whether he knows him personally or not."

Pickett said the Catholic University professor had thoroughly checked the theory and sanctified it. He offered to provide legal representation should any become necessary, arising from the plan. Pickett also told the crowd he felt it would be okay to send acknowledgments to fraternal brothers through the mail — although how he could assert that claim stretches the imagination.

"This is the solution," he declared with a smile. "It will make the sweepstakes the biggest thing ever to hit New Hampshire and the nation."

The Pickett plan didn't fuel much enthusiasm in Concord. There seemed to be little difference between what Pickett was proposing and what the ticket agencies were already doing. Despite his desire to act as a clearinghouse for fellow club members, the idea did not catch on.

THE CONCORD DAILY MONITOR displayed some solid enterprise journalism by doing what few in state government were doing: investigating the workings of the ticket agencies. When Charles Cohan registered the name Concord Ticket Services with the secretary of state, he listed his address as 683 Palmer Avenue in Teaneck, New Jersey. The *Monitor's* snooping revealed there was no 683 on Palmer Ave., as the house numbers jumped from 680 to 700. Cohan gave the landlord for the business's Concord storefront a different address: Lumber and Steel Salvage, P.O. Box 148, in Teaneck. A search of both the city directory and the telephone book failed to uncover any business named "Lumber and Steel Salvage."

Investigative reporter George Wilson found Cohan at an unlisted number (a curious rarity for those days) at 287 Vandalinda Street in Teaneck. Cohan sounded genuinely surprised that the *Monitor* had tracked him down.

Wilson asked how Cohan found his buyers. "I've done a lot of letter writing and mail stuff out to people. I've visited a lot of plants. I've sent out about 5,000 envelopes a week," he said. "It's expensive."

The reporter pressed Cohan about whether he thought he was breaking any laws by sending promotional information through the mail. "Oh, no," he replied. "I had my lawyers check into it. We submitted all mail stuff to the attorney general's offices in New Hampshire and Washington for them to okay it."

Attorney General Maynard said he never received any correspondence from Concord Ticket Service. He told the *Monitor* his office is prohibited from giving legal advice to private citizens. Even if he had received a letter from Cohan, his response would have been to go ask his lawyer.

The paper obtained one of the service's mailings. The envelope contained two documents. The first was a contract for a player to sign over 10 percent of any winnings to Cohan's operation. The second was a booklet called "Questions and Answers on Operation of New Hampshire Sweepstakes." It was taken word for word from a January Q&A article between Powers and the *Monitor* and was printed just small enough to be stuffed into first-class mail.

Though the *Concord Daily Monitor*'s sweepstakes stories been consistently dour and their editorials had been wolf cries, the ticket agency exposé had been explosive. The U.S. attorney for New Hampshire, Louis Janelle, had been a quiet ally and close friend to John King. Janelle was short, with a pompadour of platinum hair and thick glasses. He had been head of the state Democratic party during those years it was lost in the wilderness. When the Kennedy administration asked for a recommendation for the U.S. attorney's position in 1963, King had said Janelle would be the perfect appointment. Given all that the *Monitor* had turned up, Janelle was no longer able to ignore the tempest brewing. But like any crisis, this one also presented an opportunity.

The Post Office Department sprang into action by ordering the local post-master to seize mail to and from Concord Ticket Services. The department also said that all other ticket agencies using the mail to send advertising, contracts, or acknowledgments were in violation.

A federal judge found probable cause that Cohan had violated postal regula-tions. A postal inspector said he'd received several complaints against Concord Ticket Services from people who received their circulars. Cohan was released on $500 bail. He vowed to fight the conviction all the way to the U.S. Supreme Court and wouldn't close down his business until ordered to do so.

Two weeks later, an operation on the New Hampshire/Vermont border was raided and shut down. The two operators of the Twin State Ticket Agency of Walpole were arrested for mailing an acknowledgment to a woman in Bridgeport, Connecticut.

The dozen other ticket agencies still in business got stern warnings from state and federal officials. Smart owners stopped any use of the mail. As had happened in the case of the Louisiana Lottery Company, the postal crackdown severely weakened the agencies' ability to advertise, take bets, and distribute acknowledgments. They could still take phone sales, receive wire or bank transfers, and charge a service fee, but they had virtually no way of getting players to sign contracts assigning them shares to any winnings. It marked the slow decline of the rogue ticket agents. But choking off the agencies only made it harder for citizens from outside New England to get in the game. The ticket services claimed to be responsible for tens of thousands of ticket sales in 1964. The loss of the quasi-legal syndicates would be felt in 1965 and beyond.

"It almost seems that New Hampshire cannot lose its bet on fortune's wheel, unless self-respect is regarded as part of the state."

The *Reporter*, Jan. 2, 1964

Part Four

ALL OF KING'S HORSES

20

The Draw

THE FIRST DRAWING of names to be matched with potential racehorses was scheduled for July 16, 1964. As predicted, sales skyrocketed in June once the sunbathers rolled in. On the Friday after Memorial Day, daily Sweeps sales hit a record high of 14,863. Sales at liquor stores surpassed those at the racetracks by 2–1. The most lucrative venue was the store in Portsmouth, located on the interstate leading into Maine. Anecdotally, women purchased more tickets than men. Sweepstakes ticket sales jumped from an average of 34,000 a week in the spring to 150,000 a week in the summer. In the first three months of sales, players purchased $1 million in tickets, enough to prompt the first drawing.

Drawing Day for the Irish Sweep was like Mardi Gras in Dublin. The pageantry of the New Hampshire Sweeps was more like a bullion transfer at Fort Knox. On the day before the drawing the enumerated tickets were packed in large cardboard boxes and taken from the vault at Merchant's Bank and transferred to the back of an armored car. The car was escorted in a state police motorcade from Manchester to Salem. As the parade made its turn at the gates of Rockingham Park, dozens of print, television, and movie-reel photographers recorded the moment. There had been less security at Oswald's prison transfer in Dallas.

In a special holding room at the racetrack's concourse, dozens of cardboard boxes were lugged in front of the press and laid out at the six-foot-tall drum.

When all of the boxes were in place, Powers and James Kennedy opened them. These were the tickets sold from March 12 to May 29, each ticket having been mechanically separated from the roll. Altogether, 333,334 slips would be put in their giant fishbowl. It would take a total of two days to pull all 332 winners: 110 on Wednesday and 222 on Thursday.

The oblong boxes were too heavy and too awkward to dump directly into the window of the Plexiglas drum. Powers and Kennedy started grabbing handfuls of tickets and throwing them in bunches. A fistful of paper squares can be as slippery as soap, and stray tickets fluttered from their mitts if they squeezed too hard or moved too fast. Anything that landed on the floor was spotted by dozens of eyes — both natural and electric — and found its way into the wheel of fortune.

Once the tickets were in, Powers locked the draw window, smiled for more photos, then turned the post over to a pair of state police troopers. The armed guards watched the drum through the day and overnight. Race patrons at the Rock were able to look, but not touch.

THE GIANT SEE-THROUGH DRUM was only one-half of the sweepstakes equation. The other would be a variable for the life of the sweepstakes: the number of horses. The Sweeps prize schedule called for more than three hundred winners at different levels, but only about a dozen horses would run in the grand-prize race. Since every nominated horse represented a ticket winner, the question was how many *other* nominated horses would be in the smaller drum. The commission could expand or contract the size of the consolation prize pool based on the number of horses, and this flexibility ensured all promised prizes were awarded one way or another. But no one wanted to buy a Sweeps ticket in hopes of winning a consolation prize. The more runners — that is, the more chances that people would literally have a horse in the race — created excitement and anticipation. Yet if New Hampshire built it, there was no guarantee the thoroughbreds would come.

In January 1964, two months before the referendum, Lou Smith mailed nominating forms to stables across the country. The sweepstakes was open to three-year-olds who wanted to run the mile and three-sixteenths. The date of the race had not even been set but was listed as "to be run in early September of 1964," only nine months out.

In the world of professional racing, tens of thousands of foals are reared every year with the hope each one has the right stuff to be a champion. Sired from the distinguished and dandy, each colt or filly is groomed and evaluated on its future winning potential. Owners are in their own sort of lottery. Most of their horses will never race. Some are destined to run and come in last. Others will be competitive and will make money for the stable. Occasionally, someone gets a real winner.

It's hard to know whether you've got the next Man o' War at age one, but that's when it begins. Owners take the yearlings they think have a chance and nominate them for a slot in a future race when they come of age. Whether it's the Kentucky Derby or the Fort Erie Futurity, the owners reserve a spot for their colt two years out.

Nominating a horse requires payment of a moderate fee, a down payment on a future entry. Dozens, even hundreds, of horses get nominated for these events. Some of the bigger derbies require owners to renew their nomination with a sustaining fee six months out, allowing underperforming horses to drop out and milking more cash from those who still think they've got a chance. A portion of these fees get thrown into the purse for the upcoming race.

In the days before a race, the organizers (usually a track's jockey club) request a sizable entry fee, which keeps a horse in contention for a starting position. It's like a hand of poker when the card shark raises the bet: the players can either see the raise or fold. This play shaves off a majority of nominated thoroughbreds, but there will still be too many to run. Race officials will then determine what their final qualifier is — such as taking the horses with the highest earnings for the year or the number of lifetime wins. The size of the field is determined by the number of slots in the track's starting gate. The winningest horses might withdraw in favor of a race with a bigger purse, so weaker horses still entered have a chance of landing a spot in the ultimate field. Finally, owners of those horses selected to run have to pay a significant starting fee. The sum of these stakes are thrown in the pot for the winner to sweep up (hence the origin of the term "sweepstakes").

Smith set the fees for the nine-and-a-half-furlong sweepstakes at $10 to nominate, with an April 1 deadline. Horses would pay $500 to pass the entry box with an additional $1,000 to start. The purse for the New Hampshire Sweeps was estimated at $125,000, but could go as high at $150,000, putting it among the highest race payouts. The Kentucky Derby was at $158,000; the Belmont Stakes was only $110,000.

Before the March referendum, owners of 127 horses submitted subscriptions, with projections that there would be 150 signed up by April 1. When the deadline came, however, Smith announced that a record-breaking 332 nominees were in. This more than doubled the number of nominees for the Kentucky Derby (138), the Preakness (147), or the Belmont Stakes (146). Ninety horses had been nominated for all three legs of the Triple Crown; 71 of them wanted a slot in the New Hampshire Sweepstakes too.

The Sweeps, like the other classics, was for three-year-olds, so handicappers paid close attention to the stars among the two-year-olds. They included Golden Ruler, winner of the world's richest race: the $352,500 Arlington-Washington Futurity. Hurry to Market, winner of the $317,290 Garden State was among them. Roman Brother, Quadrangle, Bupers, and Mr. Brick were all $100,000+ winners in their sophomore years, and all were nominated for Rockingham Park. The undefeated Hill Rise was considered one of two likely favorites for the Kentucky Derby. The other favorite was Northern Dancer.

Northern Dancer's inclusion in the list generated buzz among sports reporters. The product of Windfields Farm, the bay stallion was the first serious Derby contender from Canada. Northern Dancer was small as a yearling and the farm had failed to find a buyer, so they ran the horse themselves. It was an investment that paid dividends for decades.[1]

At the Kentucky Derby, it was Mr. Brick who got off to the fast lead while Hill Rise and Northern Dancer stayed in the middle of the pack for the first ¾ mile. Bill Hartack, a future hall of fame jockey with three Kentucky Derby wins under his belt at that time, pushed the Canadian bay colt from sixth place to first at the one-mile mark. The legendary Willie Shoemaker, astride Hill Rise, drove the stallion hard and was gaining on Northern Dancer while blazing through the final stretch. Hill Rise was six inches taller and was making up the distance. Hartack, whipping the horse with his left hand, Hill Rise rubbing to his right, pushed Northern Dancer across the finish line by a neck. The horse that every buyer passed on won the Kentucky Derby in a track-record time of two minutes flat (a record only to be bested by Secretariat in 1973).

1. Long after his racing career, Northern Dancer was in high demand as a stud. While he earned $580,000 as a racer, he commanded $1 million stud fees, and his off-spring frequently sold in the seven-figure range. At his death in 1990, Northern Dancer was considered the greatest sire racing had ever seen. His heirs include 147 stake winners with a lifetime purse in the tens of millions of dollars.

Hartack and Northern Dancer won the Preakness, but failed to capture the elusive Triple Crown after showing at the Belmont, the longest race of the three. Quadrangle played spoiler.

It had turned into an unexpectedly exciting year for thoroughbred racing. Now a "Who's Who" of racehorses were setting their sights on the biggest sweepstakes New England had ever seen.

AT TEN O'CLOCK on the morning of July 16, 1964, the Plexiglas drum was moved to the outdoor grandstands at Rockingham Park. The gates were opened for spectators, and a good crowd was already in place when Ed Powers escorted a small group of dignitaries to an elevated stage. Powers introduced Governor King, whose remarks were kept brief lest the onlookers tear him to shreds in their impatience. After welcoming the sweepstakes commissioners, Powers introduced Miss New Hampshire, Elizabeth Emerson, as the person who would draw the lucky names from the wheel (another beauty queen, Wendy Farer, would select horse names from a smaller wheel). Powers then explained the procedure for the day. A horse would be drawn first, followed by the name of a ticket holder. The process would continue for all 332 nominated horses.

The microphone was turned over to Ralph "Babe" Rubenstein. He was called "the Voice of the New England Turf" and was the radio broadcaster who had been synonymous with regional thoroughbred racing for thirty years. Instead of the two-minute vocal sprint he was known for, Rubenstein would provide a spoken marathon of this-horse, that-person. All names called were winners, guaranteed $200 even if their horse never made the track.

Everyone took a place. A CPA, retained to certify the count, paced like a boxing referee. The beauty queens waited for their cues and Rubenstein asked that the first horse's name be drawn. It was Chanann, the great-great-grandson of Man o' War. Miss New Hampshire waited for the rotating wheel to come to a halt. The paper slips filled two-thirds of the drum, high enough to reach over her head. She stretched in and pulled out a white ticket and handed it to the announcer.

"Francis Gervais, 163 Kennard Road, Manchester, New Hampshire!"

A father of three daughters, an assistant sales manager at a uniform company was the first American to legally win a lottery prize in the twentieth century.

The crowd erupted. The wheel spun, and they did it all again.

The second ticket pulled paired Man of Freedom with Tony Altobell of

Rutland, Vermont. To the surprise of reporters who tracked him down, Tony was an eight-year-old boy. His mother told the papers she was "death on gambling," but had purchased eight tickets herself. The selection of a minor as the second Sweeps winner provoked sneers from the editorialists.

On the fourth draw, matched with Count Tario was the first female winner: Helen Casaletto of Malden, Massachusetts. A grandmother who still worked as an insurance premium collector, her husband, James, was a guard at the East Cambridge jail. "I'm a little shaky in the knees," she later told reporters. "I'm not going to spend the money until I see it."

Francis Seblone of Wethersfield, Connecticut, learned that luck cut both ways. On the twenty-eighth draw, he was paired with Mr. Moonlight — the seventh-place finisher at the Kentucky Derby and the first Derby horse to be pulled from the drum. The trouble was that Mr. Moonlight had died a month earlier.

Martin Zayacher of South Glens Falls, New York, got picked along with Golden Needles on the thirty-ninth draw. Then on the eighty-seventh draw, Zayacher's name came up again, this time paired to Gallant Leader. Journalists hunted down odds-makers at the track to calculate the likelihood of a double-drawing. They said the math was easy. The odds of being picked once were 333,333:1; the odds of being picked twice were 666,666:1.[2] Neither of the steeds was likely to run.

Ninety-six-year-old Milton Smith of Plaistow, New Hampshire, was a winner. He said if he won, he'd share his winnings with his thirteen grandchildren. Doris Jenkins of Lynn, Massachusetts, said if Steele's Run won the jackpot for her, she would "get some new teeth and get all dolled up."

"You must be pulling my leg," Doris Keenan told the *Record American* reporter who told her she'd been matched with Morning Mail. If she won, her plans were to "take a long trip."

Doctor William Taylor of Dedham, Massachusetts, had been in a car accident two months earlier and had been out of work. If Murad hit it big, Taylor said the cash would "pay off all my bills and get my creditors off my back."

---

2. While the bookies may have been good odds makers, they were poor odds calculators. We don't know how many tickets Zayacher purchased, but assume it's only two. The odds of having one of 334 tickets selected from 333,334 are roughly 1,000:1. The odds however of being pulled twice are actually 1,000,000:1!

There were several office pools. "N.E. Tel and Tel Co, Construction Department," "Furniture Shop Employees, Cornell University," and "Eve, Betty and Cecile, Mayberry's Shoes" were all selected. While the pools delighted reporters, they posed a headache for Powers and company, who needed to cut checks or bank slips to the names on the tickets. Pools raised the question, *Paid to the order of whom?* "Jule and Greet, Lucky Irish." "Resta, Benny & Angie" of Bristol, Connecticut. One ticket had no fewer than eleven names on it (as each person must have put twenty-eight cents toward the chance). The winner that gave them fits was Quick Quick's partner, "Old Man Sunshine," from Paulsboro, New Jersey.

Francis Ryan of Windham arrived ten minutes after the drawing began. He had a good feeling, and, seeking out Ed Powers himself, asked whether his name had already been called. Ryan took a seat in the stands with the rest of the dreamers, and he sat there for dozens and dozens of horses until Pennie Rice rolled out of the bowl. When Rubenstein called Ryan's name, the father of five leapt from this seat. Ryan bolted the stairs to the stage, his own "come on down" moment. When he got to the stage he found there was nothing for him. "I'm so excited," he said, "I don't even know what horse I got."

IN ADDITION to the famous thoroughbreds that got all the headlines, there were a plethora of lesser-known horses with names so vivid they enchanted the audience. They included He's a Gem, Watch It's Hot, Get Crackin,' Just Fancy That, and Quick Quick. Others included the literary (Ivanhoe, Peter Pumpkin), the lexical (Allegory, Rex de Plumbum), the literal (Needy, High Finance), the lascivious (Secret Desire, Cupid), and the liquory (Irish Whiskey, Gin). There was Golden Sunrise, Golden Ruler, Golden Needles, and Gold Frame. There was even a nod to students who stood to gain from the race: Three R's. Perhaps the best part of owning a racehorse was naming him.

There was one name spectators were waiting patiently to hear. Even those who knew nothing about horse racing knew the colt to beat. When Wendy Farer plucked Northern Dancer from her fish bowl, the spectators cheered like they hadn't before. Babe Rubenstein gave the call some extra oomph. All eyes shifted stage right as the giant wheel took another spin and came to rest. The thousands of paper scraps shuffled again, some stray leaves stuck to the walls of the Plexiglas by static.

Elizabeth Emerson reached in and dug down as deep into the piles as she could reach. Miss New Hampshire withdrew her bare arm and pulled out . . . *two* tickets.

There was an audible gasp from the audience. It was as if the earth stopped turning on its axis.

The magnitude of the blunder — with the entire world watching — was dawning on those on the dais. The commission huddled with the CPA about what to do. The biggest horse in the biggest draw in the biggest political experiment, this looked . . . *bad.* All of the public confidence in the process that Powers worked to build was in the balance. *Sports Illustrated* captured an epochal photo of Emerson, her "Miss New Hampshire" sash pinned across her figure, looking forlorn, her hand on her cheek and her mouth agape.

Their solution to the crisis was swift and simple: throw both tickets back and draw again. The mob applauded their approval, the only lasting harm being to two forever-unknown wagerers. The wheel tumbled some more times, giving the pot of gold a good stir. Emerson reached in as if retrieving honey from a six-foot-tall beehive. Withdrawing a single ticket, the smile returned to her face and spread among the crowd.

The new partner to Northern Dancer was fifty-three-year-old grandmother Freda Gardner from Seattle, Washington. "I've always been crazy about horse racing, but I've never won much. My husband and I like to play the long shots." Mrs. Garner worked as a statistics clerk for the phone company. Her co-worker, Margaret Rider, never won a nickel on the horses. They had each threw in $1.50 for a ticket and mailed the cash to a friend in New Hampshire who bought their chance. Hours after her name was pulled (and before it could be published in any newspaper), she received a telephone call from a man offering her $25,000 for her ticket. She declined.

JOHN KING could take great satisfaction in the public reaction to the drawings. Now that actual people were matched with actual horses, the sizzle only got louder. The national media reaction pivoted. While there were still the local holdouts who refused to be seduced, the national periodicals and newspapers in other parts of the country were doing stories about the many colorful would-be winners in their towns. The coverage was very similar to that of the Irish Sweepstake — happy profiles and human-interest stories, sugarplum dreams with nary a shadow of legal/political analysis.

Virtually none of the New Hampshire radio stations covered sweepstakes news; the state's only television station imposed a complete news blackout. The regional newspapers found their courage, however. Seeing the Post Office warning about non-newsworthy coverage for what it was — an empty threat — they forged ahead with many profiles about players and tickets sales. Several Boston papers, including the *Globe,* ran entire lists of drawing winners, seemingly in defiance of prohibitions on publicizing the lottery aspect of the sweepstakes. Market forces were clear: with hundreds of thousands in the running, winners lists sold *lots* of newspapers. In the build-up to the September race, the vast winners list covered three full pages of the *Boston Globe.* Even the *Nashua Telegraph,* an anti-Sweeps paper on the electrified border with Massachusetts, announced it would publish winner lists (but only to those in-state readers who subscribed for home delivery).

Powers's own solution to notifying winners was to avoid the mail and send telegrams. Instructions to Western Union explicitly said if the recipient could not be reached in person or by phone: "under no circumstances do not mail send." The telegrams would read "= CONGRATULATIONS YOUR NEW HAMPSHIRE SWEEPSTAKES TICKET DRAWN ON [date] AND ASSIGNED TO [horse's name] = = EDWARD J POWERS EXECUTIVE DIRECTOR NEW HAMPSHIRE SWEEPSTAKES." It's unclear how "Old Man Sunshine" was notified.

The geographic split among the first group of winners was stark. Eighty-six percent were from outside of New Hampshire. By day's end, when the first 110 contenders had been recorded, 33 were from Massachusetts and 16 were from New York. Only 15 lived in the Granite State. The balance of winners came from fourteen other states and two Canadian provinces. By post time in September, players drawn from the drum would represent thirty-eight states and four foreign countries.

If you could ask King what the sweetest moment the July 15 drawing was, it wouldn't be the boisterous congregation of the would-be wealthy. It wouldn't be the cheers he received as the lottery's conquering Aeneas. It would probably have to be the drawing of a horse named Alphabet.

Alphabet was a respectable horse, drawn forty-sixth from the drum. He was raised on Clairborne Farm, the Kentucky stable that would later produce Secretariat. In 1964, he had twenty-one starts and either won, placed, or showed in nearly three-quarters of them. The likelihood of him making the final cut were slim. It wasn't Alphabet's nomination that tickled King. It was whom he was paired with.

Miss New Hampshire passed the white ticket to Rubenstein who announced Alphabet's partner.

"Mrs. Elizabeth Perkins," he pronounced. "105 School Street, Concord, New Hampshire."

The commissioners began to buzz. *It couldn't be, could it?* Howell Shepard checked the ticket and the winner's address again. It was.

Elizabeth Perkins was the wife of former Senate President Raymond Perkins, a founding member of the Committee of One Hundred.

King never gloated, never addressed it in public. There was no need. The newspaper men savored the irony on his behalf.

The headline in one paper read, "THIS HOUSE DIVIDED." The article's opening line: "Things got into a fine fix Wednesday at 105 School St . . ."

21
The Final Stretch

A GROWING NUMBER of newspapers were running the weekly sales numbers, comparing the performance of various liquor stores as if it were the pennant race. The Salem racetrack was perpetually in the lead, selling well above four thousand tickets each week. Keene was often the number-one liquor store, averaging twenty-three hundred, but it was overtaken in the summer by the store on Nashua's Main Street (the city's second liquor store in the railroad square regularly sold another thousand). Portsmouth's store on the interstate was always in the top three, and its downtown location stayed in the top ten. The one thing these locations had in common: they were all border towns catering to gambling tourists whose vacation in New Hampshire lasted about ten minutes. By the end of July, a third million in sales was achieved, ensuring a third set of prizes and winners. This number broke the performance benchmark that upped the percentage in the winner payout pool from 35 percent to 40 percent of gross sales. With just over a month to go before the race, could the Sweeps reach the promised $4 million mark?

The second drawing was held two weeks after the first, on July 29 at Rockingham Park. It was an evening event, scheduled for two days. A thunderstorm sent the bystanders scrambling, but the job got done. Now every horse carried the dreams of two players, with the promise of more.

It's funny that the liquor store in Keene, Larry Pickett's hometown, would rank number one or two in sales. A popular destination for visitors from Connecticut and New York, the store started with one ticket machine and had to add four more to keep up with demand. What makes its success an anomaly is that on a map the closest venue to the state line was the Hinsdale racetrack, which primarily featured harness racing and didn't open until May — two months after Rockingham Park and most of the liquor stores had been selling the Sweeps. Hinsdale is in the very bottom southwest corner of New Hampshire, straddling Massachusetts and Vermont, but the track was accessible only by a series of winding back roads. It was easier to travel farther north on the interstate in Vermont and bang a right onto the secondary highway leading to Keene.

It was on one of these afternoons in late August when Anthony Fabrizio drove over New Hampshire Route 9 into Keene. In the parking lot of the liquor store, his yellow New York license plates blended in with those of every color: blue from Connecticut, green from Vermont, white from Massachusetts. Depending on the day, one could find license plates from Oregon and California.

Fabrizio was a fifty-eight-year-old printer at the *Elmira Star Gazette*. He made his purchases and drove back to Elmira, New York. When he returned, he was stopped by special agents of the FBI who had learned Fabrizio had been soliciting orders for Sweeps tickets. The man protested, saying he drove to New Hampshire for the scenery and some fresh air. "It was good for my health," he said.

Not convinced, the agents searched Fabrizio and found seventy-five sweepstakes acknowledgments, all made out to different people. The $225 he had spent on tickets would be worth more than $1,700 in today's dollars.

Having heeded the warnings of the Justice Department to avoid hassling tourists, the FBI had decided to look for someone who trafficked in a large quantity of tickets, someone who they could prove went to New Hampshire with the explicit intention of violating federal law. They thought they finally had their test case.

TICKET BUYERS weren't the only ones dreaming of fast money. The realization that a significant windfall for the state's cities and towns was on its way opened a new line of argument at the local level. Aldermen, city councilors, and selectmen all debated what to do with the cash that was going to appear in their budgets.

The chairman of the state board of education, however, had warned municipalities against including any Sweeps revenue in their budget projects. A per-town calculation was impossible to make, and it was unclear how soon after September 12 any money would be distributed. The chickens hadn't hatched, the thinking went, so don't start counting.

As the details filled, in and it was clear cash was on its way, local governments were faced with the enviable problem of figuring out what to do with it. The state said twenty-five dollars per pupil was the likely allocation, with payments by mid-December. Advocacy groups such as the New Hampshire Council for Better Schools argued the money should be used to increase existing education budgets to provide extras like books, building construction, or professional development.

But in the majority of New Hampshire municipalities, school boards and school districts lacked taxing authority, and their financial fate was determined by city or town governments. In many locations, the financial plan was to take the Sweeps check and put it into the town's bank account, rather than adding money to the education budget. The revenue would have the effect of lowering the property-tax burden.

This was one of the options Governor King had promised voters in the March sweepstakes referendum. A strict reading of Pickett's bill, however, seemed to nix this option. The bill said "such grants shall be used for educational purposes and no part of said special fund shall be diverted, by transfer or otherwise, to any other purpose whatsoever." But with no real guidance or enforcement authority from the state, town leaders had a free hand at putting the cash toward their own financial wish lists.

The *Nashua Telegraph* reported that in Merrimack — one of hundreds of New Hampshire towns where municipal and school budgets were approved by residents, not politicians, during the traditional Town Meeting — voters shot down a proposal to use $7,500 in Sweeps money to hire a physical education teacher, meaning their cash would go exclusively to property-tax relief. Bedford residents, on the other hand, allocated their $22,000 to create and stock a new library at their elementary school. Keene pledged to use its supplemental allocation to give all its teachers bonuses. A great number of municipalities simply kept sweepstakes revenue off their proposed budgets, meaning any cash coming in would automatically go into their coffers and reduce taxes by default.

On the state level, the financial impact of the sweepstakes was less ambiguous. House Speaker Stewart Lamprey said the Sweeps undoubtedly saved the state from a sales tax in 1963–1964, and would likely prevent any serious effort to enact one in the 1965–1966 session.

NEW HAMPSHIRE was just one of the more popular day trips in 1964. The New York World's Fair continued to draw tens of millions of people to Flushing Meadows, although attendance projections were lower than expected. All of the states that had invested in expensive exhibits complained that people liked to browse, but few were picking up their brochures or promotional materials. The New England pavilion turned out to be an impressive piece of architecture. Each day, thousands of visitors would stop in, view the exhibits from the five other states, then ask the New Hampshire staff what they knew about the sweepstakes.

The state's economic development director, Allen Evans, charged with running the World's Fair display, came up with a way to tie Sweeps interest with their tourism goals. Already Shepard and Pickett had been rebuked for their suggestions of selling actual tickets in New York, but Powers approached Evans to suggest giving away fake souvenir tickets, which they believed could be done without violating New York or federal laws.

The Granite State Machine company had fabricated a pair of low-tech souvenir machines called PADMAC ("patent pending"). The tickets were the same size as the real thing. It contained John King's signature and the state seal. On the front of these mock acknowledgments were answered most of the questions people were asking. They said the sweepstakes was legally enacted, the money went to education, public drawings were to be held throughout the summer, and the race would be on September 12. They also stated tickets could only be purchased in New Hampshire and buyers should not mail cash or money orders.

Installed at the end of August, the souvenir machines didn't have a telephone dial or a computerized accounting mechanism, but they did mimic the actual experience of purchasing a Sweeps ticket. Their metal window would open, and tourists would sign their name and address on the slip. When they punched a lever, their acknowledgment slid out. The back of the paper read, "You're sure a winner when you vacation in New Hampshire," and gave a list of great attractions around the state. The other half of the ticket stayed in the machine, the names and addresses collected to be added to the tourism department's mailing lists.

Their first day at the fair, a rumor circulated that actual New Hampshire Sweepstakes tickets were available at the New England pavilion. People shoved their way into the exhibition in search of tickets, only to be told the tickets there were just tokens. Considerably less attention was paid to Maine, Vermont, and the other New England states that day.

The two PADMAC souvenir machines displayed another feature of the actual ones: they were easily jammed. Overenthusiastic children tried to pull the tickets out of the slide window instead of the dispensary, pulling the two-sided paper roll off its feed track. This piqued the New Hampshire staff who had little training in how to re-spool or clear the jams. When word of the malfunction made it to the *Concord Daily Monitor,* the paper ran a front-page article declaring "Sweeps Machines at Fair Fail to Work," saying neither device was operational.

Nevertheless, upon his return from New York, Evans found a friendly ear at the *Union Leader,* who printed his claim the ticket gimmick was "an unqualified success" and his rejection of the stories of malfunctions: "There have been so many errors and distortions that I am sure some are deliberate. This is a definite lack of objectivity in reporting on the part of those who opposed the sweepstakes."

Evans said the machines had distributed more than a thousand tickets in the first three days and captured the names and addresses of future visitors. Even with the machines spitting out tourism information, the number of fairgoers asking for over-the-counter materials actually doubled. They had to add an extra worker just to keep up with demand. Evans also said each souvenir ticket cost one-and-a-half cents, while the brochures and catalogues were between fifty cents and $2.50 each.

THE ANIMUS between the federal government and the state of New Hampshire did not fade. The Internal Revenue Service had requested the state collect the federal gambling tax from prizewinners at the time of the sweepstakes. Governor King refused. They were already holding their excise tax burden in escrow. They weren't going to help Uncle Sam pick the pockets of their happy winners.

The IRS, on a revenue-collection level, was counting the ways it loved the sweepstakes. It expected to receive about $590,000 from the state of New Hampshire in excise taxes and gambling tax stamps. There was going to be a good bite on the winners too. Every individual's tax situation was different, but suppose their sweepstakes winnings represented their total yearly income for a person who filed jointly, took two exemptions, and claimed the standard deduction for 1964. Each $100,000 winner would pay between $45,000–$53,000 in taxes. The $50,000 winners would be bitten for $17,000–$21,000. And third-place winners kept only $18,000–$19,000 of their $25,000 payout. As the money would be earned in New Hampshire — where there was no income tax — they wouldn't have to take another hit, and they could write off the federal tax on their home state income tax burden. Yet if the state could sell $6 million in tickets, more than $1.3 million would go to the IRS.

Still perturbed by the harassment the Sweeps was getting, the governor and state's congressional delegation continued to needle the Department of Justice about its hypocrisy over targeting New Hampshire activities while never lifting a finger to crack down on the Irish Sweepstake in the United States. The feds had spent three decades grabbing sacks of cash and giving overnight accommodations in jail to ticket sellers, but never targeted the average guy who bought a ticket.

As if in response, the FBI finally made an arrest connected to the overseas lottery. Agents captured two Virginia men in Norfolk waiting to rendezvous with the *Irish Elm,* with money and counterfoils all destined for Dublin. The G-men made sure news of the arrests found their way into the papers. Part of the evidence was the names and addresses of hundreds and hundreds of American taxpayers who had bought the illegal tickets, but none of them were pursued.

The Post Office Department was not going to bend on its stance that winners' prize checks could not be sent through the mail. Although it seemed like the most obvious of the regulations obstructing the Sweeps, it was the last to be publicly addressed by Ed Powers. He had told reporters for months he thought using the mails to make payments was "a gray area," and he likely thought until the end there was wiggle room. But in the face of Post Office intransigence, Powers finally announced the Sweeps would wire prizes to winners by Western Union or deposit the money directly into winners' accounts via bank transfer.

With the exception of the excise tax, Ed Powers had checked off each of the major impediments facing the lottery at the time of its inception. He had managed to concoct a system to keep tickets in state, prevent scalping, notify and pay winners, and discourage underworld infiltration.

TICKET SALES continued to gain a furious momentum as August closed. The Sweepstakes earned another flurry of positive press surrounding the hundreds of would-be winners. A family of nine from Weymouth, Massachusetts, who got Bupers. A Quincy grandmother with Black Tyrone. A transit authority inspector from Boston paired with Trojan Mirage.

There was more than one tear-jerker in the group. When reporters called at the home of Stanley Lipiko of Brighton, Massachusetts, to get reaction on his pairing with Phantom Shot, the man's god-daughter said Lipiko had died less than a week earlier. He was a World War I veteran and had come to America from Lithuania. The woman, Sally Amshy, said the immigrant boarded with her parents when he first arrived. He worked as a window washer, never married, and had no children; Amshy was his beneficiary. She said Lipiko had purchased about thirty sweepstakes tickets "in the hope he could live comfortably."

The idea of living comfortably popped into the heads of more and more people. The last scheduled day of sales for tickets was Saturday, August 29. Officials figured they'd need two weeks to sort through the last-minute purchases and arrange another marathon draw. The sales trends were off the charts. They were giving up what was likely their biggest sales day yet: Labor Day, September 7, because including that day meant holding multiple draws four or five days before the race. Powers's men had projected that extending sales by those nine days — including the holiday — would bring them from the $3 million to the $5 million mark.

It was decided the final public drawings would be held in Concord. There were already a week's worth of Sweeps-related events at Rockingham. Also, the commission had purchased not one, but six of the mechanical ticket wheels at a total cost of $29,000. They could pull multiple names for each horse. It was settled: as every million in sales would come in, the staff would separate the tickets from their rolls and store them by dates of purchase.

Sales the last week of summer vacation were scorching. Beachgoers and mountain hikers who didn't get a ticket on their way in sure wanted one on their way out of New Hampshire. The liquor stores were only open on Saturday, but they did big business before shutting down for the holiday. Labor Day ended up being the largest one-day sale in the history of the sweepstakes; the Associated Press said $52,263 in Sweeps tickets was sold at Rockingham Park alone.

The final total of tickets sold in the first New Hampshire Sweepstakes: $5,730,093 — over 1,910,000 tickets sold in five-and-a-half months.

The August surge in ticket sales meant there would be an additional four drawings for the race — 1,248 names — so the fortunes of six people would ride with every horse (dead or alive). The multiple draw was held on the Wednesday after Labor Day and conducted at the Highway Hotel. On Thursday, entry fees and post positions would be announced for Saturday's event. It was fairly obvious at that close date which of the nominated horses were in the running, so players knew the handful of horses positioned for the big money. Even so, the suspense had not dissipated.

As post time approached, the owners of Northern Dancer decided their colt would not be running in the New Hampshire Sweepstakes. That meant it was now anybody's race to win.

22
They're Off at Rockingham

LOU SMITH looked down lovingly at his racetrack from the vast picture windows of the administration building dining room, the noon sun above. The racetrack publicist cracked the door. "They're here," he announced.

Smith turned and flashed a big smile at his guests — Governor John King, Ed Powers, and Commissioner Howell Shepard. They sat around a cloth-draped table as head waiter Jack McGuire placed lunch in front of them. The photographers were then allowed to come in and capture the moment of the four men smiling, all working together to create the New Hampshire Sweepstakes.

That was a year earlier, when the Sweepstakes seemed like a party so distant there was nothing to accomplish except plan. Now the moment was nearly upon them and Smith's team had more to do than a mad hare.

The publicist, Bill Stearns, said the New Hampshire Sweepstakes was literally giving him nightmares. Rockingham Park hosting a sweepstakes — the idea of which had been floating around Concord for more than a decade — seemed like an effortless boon to the racetrack, like winning the lottery itself. The Sweeps would match a middle-of-the-road, nondescript venue with a government-subsidized purse to make the track overnight into a premier destination — not just the biggest in New England — but on par with Churchill Downs itself.

In autumn 1963, Smith, Stearns, and New Hampshire Jockey Club treasurer "Mac" O'Dowd sat down with sports writers to discuss the barely hypothetical sweepstakes. They conceded the operation would largely be the state's; they were merely offering their plant to host the special event. The Sweeps Commission offered to start the purse at $100,000, and Smith thought Rockingham might be able to add between $25,000 and $50,000 to that amount.

All three men agreed the audience would be huge for such an event. Rockingham Park's capacity was thirty-five thousand in its grandstand, but the group estimated they'd draw sixty thousand people.

Where will you put them all? asked *Union Leader* sports editor Bob Hilliard. "The rest we will probably have to stand up in the infield," replied Smith. "Bill will have to work it out."

Bill Stearns turned to look at his boss, feeling like he'd been pushed from a plane with no chute. Unlike at the Kentucky Derby — where the infield became a boozy, brassy party spot for the sport's proletariat in the cheap seats — the infield at the Rock was not for spectators. Other than the electronic toteboard and some outbuildings, it wasn't used for anything. There wasn't even a way to get to the infield other than walking across the track.

"How will twenty-five thousand people get to the infield?" another reporter asked.

"Oh, probably by bridges placed at each end of the track," Smith said, as if that were as easy as moving a sofa.

Stearns piped in: "And what happens when we get them over there?" The PR man filled the silence by answering his own question: "They will need betting facilities, food and drink, comfort stations — and probably a hundred and one other things." His voice trailed off.

The track's parking lot could handle seventy-five hundred cars, but counting local schools and other facilities in Salem, they could come up with seventeen thousand spaces. Now they would need to get buses — lots of buses — to shuttle spectators to the track.

There would be perhaps four hundred writers and photographers looking to cover the race, and there wasn't enough room in the Rockingham Park press box to accommodate them all. Sterns speculated they might have to set up a media center at the high school. He was already getting requests for credentials from all over the world, which meant he'd spend days checking to see who was a legitimate reporter and who just wanted a free ticket.

The writers could see Sterns's face blanch as the magnitude of the operation seemed to crash down on him. He didn't have a good night's sleep for months.

IF LOU SMITH LOST SLEEP over the New Hampshire Sweepstakes, he never let on. He was in his late seventies, and the Sweeps had the potential to be the crowning achievement in his racetrack's unlikely existence.

Rockingham Park had been built in 1906 at a cost of $1 million and was hailed in the press as the finest racetrack in the world. Its proximity to the Salem train depot benefited the grounds, as travelers from Boston and other distant locations could take a train that stopped right at the clubhouse. The first horse races began on June 28, 1906, part of a twenty-one-day thoroughbred festival. There was no spectator betting; the only money to be made was among the racers. After three days of contests, constables shut the track down because they discovered bookmakers and coat-tuggers in the stands taking illegal bets. Horse racing would not return to the Rock for three decades.

Through the 1910s and 1920s, track owners planned innovative attractions such as aviation shows, county fairs, and car and motorcycle races. Around the loop they installed a wooden board track with banked turns like modern velodromes. This form of auto racing was extremely popular. Again the track operators were harassed by police when outside bookies were discovered making wagers in the stands. By the time the Great Depression began, the once-majestic track had fallen into disrepair.

Enter Lou Smith. Born in England, reared in New Jersey, Smith was one of six children of Jewish parents who had fled Russia to escape the czar. As a teen he ran away from home and literally joined the circus. His other odd jobs included raincoat salesman, boxing promoter, and silent-film distributor. Smith had investments in several tracks in the United States and Canada, but longed to own a venue himself.

Smith and his partners formed the New Hampshire Breeders Association and purchased the dormant track for $300,000 in early 1931. They invested $200,000 to rehabilitate Rockingham Park. They planned one full week of inaugural thoroughbred racing, but the sheriff shut down the track on day two because of underground betting among the spectators. It was clear to Smith that without legalized gambling there was no way to keep the Rock financially viable.

Smith set about educating uninitiated lawmakers on pari-mutuel betting.

Racketeers offered mutuel betting in which the odds and payouts were fixed. Players were collectively betting against the house. If the racketeers strategically set the odds, it was possible, after paying all the winners, that a large part of the pot would be left over as profit. Pari-mutuel betting, to oversimplify, allowed all the bettors instead to play against one another for shares of the entire pool — actual payouts determined by a complex algebraic formal. Legalizing pari-mutuel betting was appealing because it could be regulated and taxed by the state, and after the track took a reasonable commission, all the spoils went to the winners.

Lou Smith had an infectious charm. If he had lived in Kentucky, he'd have been "Colonel Smith," but in New Hampshire he was known as "Uncle Lou." His personality completely disarmed those he met. In 1933, he convinced legislators to pass pari-mutuel bill. Smith's strength, according to *Guys and Dolls* author and close friend Damon Runyon, was that his "methods were so open and above board they were almost bewildering." One might call Smith a "goodie-goodie" who never needed to grease palms in Concord. He was proud of the fact that getting his bill passed never cost him a red cent.

Horse racing and betting resumed at Rockingham Park in June 1933. The races featured thoroughbreds, standardbreds, harness racing, and steeplechases. Seabiscuit made the first of six appearances at Rockingham Park in 1935 and 1936 — unbelievably never winning a single race there. Lou Smith's reconstituted New Hampshire Jockey Club purchased Rockingham in 1936, and a new era began.

Smith's thirty-plus years at Rockingham were marked not only by how squeaky clean the operation was (especially compared to nearby Suffolk Downs), but by Smith's many philanthropic acts. He was among the first to start a retirement fund for horses, so they could live the remainder of their lives on farms (1 percent of every Rockingham purse was dedicated to the fund). Smith was the first to offer insurance and health benefits to jockeys. He even built a childcare center for use by spectators and employees during the races. A proud Jew, one of his closest friends was Cardinal Cushing of the Boston Archdiocese, and Smith donated millions to Catholic charities that benefited children with disabilities.

Already known as an incorruptible track, Rockingham Park developed a reputation as a glamorous destination. Smith entertained celebrity guests like Jimmy Durante, Judy Garland, Al Jolson, Charlie Chaplin, Mickey Rooney, Walter Winchell, Gloria Swanson, Frankie Avalon, and Bing Crosby. Its fame was such that submariners in World War II would shout as they launched their torpedoes, "They're off at Rockingham . . . !" In *The Sting*, Robert Redford is seen trying to place a bet at "The Rock."

Smith had an apartment built above the administration building so he could monitor operations around the clock. His wife of fifty-plus years, Lutza, was his constant companion. They had something in common with the Kings: they were not able of have children either. This likely fueled their great affection for and benefactions to sick and needy youngsters.

Most importantly, Rockingham Park was *the* cash cow for the state of New Hampshire. For a man with an angelic personal reputation, Smith was the king of the sin tax. Tax revenue from Rockingham Park provided 20 percent of state income.

Lou Smith drew a lot of water in New Hampshire.

TO RESEARCH the planned sweepstakes, Smith traveled to Ireland to meet with the Hospital Trust's Jack O'Sheehan, Joe McGrath's right-hand man, who had run logistics for the Irish Sweep for thirty years. Bill Stearns went to Kentucky to meet with Brownie Leach, the PR man at Churchill Downs, to get some idea of what to expect.

Both men returned from their junkets with a sober-eyed view of what needed to be done to capitalize on the race's national potential. While maintaining constant contact with Ed Powers, the Rockingham crew set about their own plans to make the day's event top-drawer and worthy of the classics. Stearns created a detailed dossier of how to promote the race throughout the 1964 season, not just in New Hampshire but across the country.

Throughout the spring and summer racing season, reminders of the big September finish were everywhere in Rockingham. There was great emphasis placed on words "first" and "first in the nation" — terms used synonymously for the state's role in the presidential primary. There were daily flashes on the message board, table-tent displays in the dining room. On the concourse sat three large blow-up photographs, each showing the finish of the Kentucky Derby, the Preakness, and the Belmont Stakes. There was a fourth blow-up, blank except for the words, "The Fourth Jewel. Who'll get it?" They placed banners across Salem streets announcing the Sweeps. The track's daily newspaper ads reserved the bottom quarter of the layout to push the upcoming sweepstakes (this was deemed permissible by all concerned parties because the ad promoted the race itself and not the lottery).

One week before the sweepstakes, Rockingham Park was to host a race called the Sweeps Prep. The purse was $25,000. The entrants were mostly Sweeps starters, giving them another reason to get to New Hampshire early and get comfortable with the track. They also gave local gamblers an additional chance to wager on the sport's best and gave handicappers one last opportunity to size up the field before the ultimate event.

Every week Stearns reached out to sports columnists across the country to promote the race. Staff compiled index files on all 332 nominated horses so information could be available at a moment's notice. Smith held a weekly press conference — "Uncle Lou holds court" — to maintain a constant level of interest. They reserved several hundred motel and hotel rooms for the weekend. Stearns ordered engineers to examine the weight load of the administration building roof to see if it would hold the number of television and moving picture cameras expected.

All of Rockingham would be decorated, bunting everywhere. The overflow crowd would be directed across an eighty-ton bridge to the infield. In addition to concessions, stands, and lavatories, preparations for placing bets in the infield had to be made. Ten thousand chairs were set up. There would be makeshift cashiers' windows, a counting room, a chalk odds board for the public, and closed-circuit TV. A first-aid facility with a fully staffed medical battalion and all needed supplies would be obtained. Maintenance barrels and fire extinguishers would be placed in strategic locations. A detention area for the unruly would be erected inside one of the garages.

Additional fencing around the infield would be required. The saddling area for the Sweeps horses was planned in a staked-out area of the infield, so spectators could see the preparations up close. Smith and Stearns envisioned a winner's circle of brick or peat moss, ringed by a horseshoe of potted mums. Electrical and audio cables would need to be run for a microphone and public-address system. A National Guard color unit would watch over the winner's circle, standing smartly at "order arms." Smith insisted there ought to be a bouquet of flowers for the wife of the winning horse's owner.

Lastly, they made plans for what kind of award would be presented to the owner, trainer, and victorious jockey in the winner's circle. Instead of a cup or trophy, Smith's preference was for a model of the emblematic Old Man of the Mountain, the shape of whose jagged profile was used in virtually everything "New Hampshire" — from state highway signs to the three-cent postage stamp. He sought to have such a trophy commissioned but failed to find a suitable craftsman. In the end, they would give a conventional silver cup to the owner; the jockey would get a nice set of sweepstakes cufflinks.

Orders were to save all programs and documents, transcribe all the speeches, and archive them for a future New Hampshire Sweepstakes museum. Smith believed profoundly that the Sweeps would continue in perpetuity as one of the premier American sporting events.

WITH POWERS and the Sweepstakes Commission holding the final drawings in Concord, the Salem track was free to operate normally during the last days leading up to the race. Governor King had declared a "Sweepstakes Week," a purely ceremonial decree.

For all the hubbub caused by the $100,000 lottery, the gambling regulars were ho-hum on the betting possibilities of the sweepstakes. One paper quoted a pony bettor saying the Sweeps was "nothing to spill coffee over." In every way, the horse odds and payouts were the same as other races,' and what was happening in the liquor stores didn't change anything on the turf. They weren't betting against Rockingham Park, nor betting against the New Hampshire Sweepstakes Commission. They were betting against the other bettors at the track for their share of the pari-mutuel pool. The purse and the publicity would draw better steeds — and triple the amount of bettors would pump up the handle on the pari-mutuel pool — but holding the ticket on one winning horse was not going to make any gambler rich.

The big money came from the exotic bets. They're the perfectas and tri-fectas, selecting the first two or three horses to cross the finish line. They're the Daily Doubles, picking the winners in back-to-back races. Rockingham Park was one of the few tracks that offered a Twin Double bet, which allowed bettors to pick the winners in four races. When interviewed by reporters, some gamblers pointed out the Twin Doubles that year had been as high as $15,000 — and the odds on hitting the Twin Double on a two-dollar wager were far better than winning the Sweeps on a three-dollar wager. All of the pony players, however, said they were going to buy sweepstakes tickets too.

While we can do no more than speculate why the Mob didn't aggressively target the sweepstakes for infiltration, as predicted by detractors, the same mechanical realities that made the Sweeps a poor investment for individuals held true for organized crime. Gangsters could fix a horse race (though no evidence of hanky-panky under Smith's reign at Rockingham has ever materialized), but to what end? Even if they could muscle the world's top jockeys riding the most prestigious thoroughbreds in racing with the intense scrutiny of state and federal law enforcement and the gaze of the national media upon them, what would changing the results accomplish? If the punters could play the toteboard right, lay a substantial bet on a long shot, they could get a sizable jackpot — but that was all chicken scratch compared to the side action: the lottery. They couldn't scalp or counterfeit tickets. They couldn't control who got picked or what horse matched whom. They couldn't skim. The best they could do was act as mules for groups of people who couldn't get to New Hampshire.

Fixing the sweepstakes so a specific horse won would only shift the $100,000 jackpot from one civilian to another. Corrupting the Sweeps, a once- or twice-a-year event, would be a high-risk effort with no vig. The underworld didn't need the sweepstakes. It had its daily numbers racket, and the state better leave their kitty all alone.

THERE WERE SEVERAL TIE-IN EVENTS scheduled before the race. On Thursday the tenth, Rockingham Park would put on a press buffet and reception. It was expected that the jockeys and other dignitaries would be made available for media interviews. On Friday night, the eve of the sweepstakes, there would be a formal governor's and Sweepstakes Committee's reception, a black-tie affair held at the swanky Wayfarer Inn in Bedford. Celebrities and other dignitaries would be invited.

The main attraction would be the Thursday 9 a.m. breakfast for the horse owners and trainers. The meeting would be open to the press. After eating in the track dining room, each of the owners would draw their post position by pulling a small silver horse from a bag. Each token would be numbered 1, 2, and so on, and the owners could keep the memento as a souvenir.

The park had planned for twelve racers, the maximum the starting gate could handle, but one of the teams pulled its horse at the last minute with no time to get another nominee to step in. The field of eleven was set, with nearly all the horses arriving for the Sweeps Prep race and taking daily practice runs around the track.

Starting in the number-one position would be Wil Rad, a bay colt of considerable pedigree that had finished a disappointing tenth place in the Kentucky Derby. First in the gate, he was the last to arrive in Salem, as his owners chose to wait until Wednesday to fly him from the West Coast — a questionable choice, said the sports writers.

Wil Rad had one appreciable advantage: his rider was Johnny Longden, the number-one jockey in the world. At age fifty-eight, he was also the oldest on the field, in a homecoming of sorts. The very first race of Longden's hall of fame career had been at Rockingham Park in 1935. He didn't finish in the money then, but at the time of the Sweeps, Longden had won 5,871 races for earnings of $23,650,467.

In the second position was St. Raphael. The horse was an up-and-comer, but had yet to perform as a contender. His owner seemed to think the colt was ready to jump to the next level and a strong showing in the sweepstakes would announce his arrival. The early line had St. Raphael at 20:1, but he too had a strong jockey in future hall of famer Sammy Boulmetis.

Purser was picked early on as an also-ran but turned things around at the Sweeps Prep. He swooped the field, took the win, and made it look easy. At 22:1, he paid off at $46.80. Now prognosticators said Purser was coming into his own and had a swell chance of finishing in the money. Local jockey Hank Wajda rode Purser in the Prep and would ride him in the Sweeps just as the horse was getting hot.[1]

Phantom Shot was worthier than his name. After winning only one start as a two-year old, the thoroughbred captured three major events over the summer of 1964. Odds-makers put Phantom Shot at 10:1. Jockey Phil Grimm had finished eleventh in the 1960 Kentucky Derby.

The fifth position was held by Gun Boat, a chestnut colt who finished in the money in all eleven of his 1964 starts. Gun Boat had a victory over one of the two favorites in the New Hampshire Sweepstakes, which made him an outside threat.

Ramant, like St. Raphael, was a horse with a promising future but no major achievements so far. He was a mudder who did best "off track." Rain expected on Friday could help his chances.

Rockingham Park was familiar ground for Old Stoney, the son of 1949 Kentucky Derby runner Old Rockport. Another dark horse, Old Stoney

---

1. Wajda held the Rockingham Park track record for the one mile sixty yards. He once stopped his horse in the middle of a race to give aid to an injured jockey. Wajda was killed at the Rock in 1973 when his foot got caught in the starting gate, and he was kicked in the chest while falling from the horse.

managed to impress at the Sweeps Prep by jumping to an early lead, only to tire and place to Purser. The second-place finish in the tough field made an impression.

Bupers, wearing number ten, was also written off until showing at the Prep. The dark bay colt, whose name was an anagram for "superb," was known more for sprinting, and might find the mile and three-sixteenths too tiring, but he had legs enough to give ticket holders hope. Bookmakers had Bupers starting the race at 8:1.

Prairie Schooner was also a sprinter given long odds because of the track length. He was the great-great-grandson of Man o' War. His trainers at the High Tide Stable felt Prairie Schooner was peaking, and the New Hampshire Sweepstakes was the venue at which to take a swing.

With Derby and Preakness winner Northern Dancer not running, and previously undefeated Hill Rise also on the sidelines, two thoroughbreds who skipped the Prep emerged as the favorites in the first New Hampshire Sweepstakes.

Knightly Manner had seven wins in 1964. Sports writers described him as "frisky." As a two-year-old, he was named Hill Rise's equal before the latter would have his championship year. Knightly Manner had nearly beat Quadrangle, the Belmont Stakes spoiler, at Saratoga two weeks earlier. Wearing number six on his silks, the bay colt would leave the gate at 2–1 odds.

The favorite in the field was coming out of the ninth position. Roman Brother, the "Mighty Mite," was the sentimental darling. This gelding was small, only 889 pounds and a shave over fifteen hands high. The horse suffered from anemia and was on a diet of liver and a regiment of iron injections. Roman Brother had finished fourth in the Kentucky Derby, fifth in the Preakness, then placed in the Belmont Stakes behind Quadrangle and in front of Northern Dancer. The writers thought Roman Brother would have won the Belmont had he not been shut off at the top of the stretch. He had three wins for the year by the time he got to Salem and was steadily accruing sizable earning for Harbor View Farms.

Fernando Alvarez would be holding Roman Brother's reins. A native of Chile, Alvarez had been astride the gelding for his Triple Crown runs and had an affinity for the horse. They had been in the top three with a mix of the best of the thoroughbreds, having finished ahead of Northern Dancer, Hill Rise, Mr. Brick, and Quadrangle at different times. Alvarez and Roman Brother were fresh off a victory at the American Derby and seemed to be cooking with gas. Odds were set on Roman Brother taking the Sweeps at 7–5.

For Rockingham Park, it was a dream lineup for a dream event. Publicist Bill Stearns was tossing and turning, but Lou Smith remained tranquil. On the eve of the sweepstakes however, it's hard to believe that even Uncle Lou didn't have trouble going to bed.

23

The Most Popular Thing Since the Revolution

AT THE GOVERNOR'S RECEPTION Friday night, September 11, the broad cast of characters in the tale of the New Hampshire Sweepstakes came together. King greeted the guests as a father of the bride would. There was his wife, Anna, who had packed countless lunches for him as he traveled the state. Larry Pickett, whose ten-year battle for the sweepstakes stood as a model of stick-to-itiveness, could be heard conversing in his distinctive locution. Howell Shepard and the rest of Sweepstakes Commission were there. Joseph Millimet, the legal mastermind who had guided the Sweeps through the federal pricker bushes that threatened to snag it, received congratulations. Even King's uneasy friend from Pride Crossing, Bill Loeb, with his wife, Nackey, was circulating among many of the important people he had vivisected in print. Lou and Lutza Smith were the ambassadors to the stable owners and others from the world of thoroughbred horse racing. Ed Powers, the man who had been King's "JFK" — charming the world while delivering on a world-class operation — was the second most popular person at the ball.

There had been a thousand people at King's inaugural ball two years earlier. This event seemed to bookend his term at governor. No Democrat had won a second term in New Hampshire, and though King remained popular, he could not assume he'd be the first. The Sweeps were going to continue whether he was governor or not.

More than a year earlier King had declared he was not a Solomon or a Caesar. And if during his two weeks of monastic seclusion, he could have seen the true path ahead of him, who knows what he would have decided? Did he know how he would have to fight the media? How he would fight the church? How he would fight the Committee of One Hundred? How he would fight the Justice Department? How he would fight the Post Office? How he would fight the FCC? How he would fight the IRS? How he would fight the "thieves, racketeers, and bums"? How he would fight all the naysayers, near and far, who said it couldn't be done? He had — so far — proven them wrong.

Outside, the world was changing. Johnson had just signed the Civil Rights Act, and Philadelphia was still smoldering from its first race riot. The Gulf of Tonkin incident had just altered the nation's level of involvement in Vietnam. The Masters and Johnson Institute had opened to study human sexuality. In Boston, the Beatles had arrived that weekend for their first concert in New England. On the upcoming Sunday, Bishop Primeau would say the first Catholic mass in English. The real sixties were underway. In New Hampshire, what had begun with a little old lady who couldn't pay her tax bill had blossomed into the first legal lottery. In less than twenty-four hours, six people would be $100,000 richer.

AFTER ATTENDING the late August Democratic convention in Atlantic City, John and Anna King had traveled by train to Holyoke, Massachusetts, to be feted by a local construction company. In his days practicing labor law, King had helped establish the union in 1949 and worked to get them a health and welfare fund and a pension — benefits that were hard for workers to come by. This trip was a reminder to King of how much he enjoyed practicing law.

There were two questions everyone wanted answered. The first was about the presidential race. King said the party was happy with the Johnson-Humphrey ticket. King admitted to being moved by the twenty-minute ovation given to Robert Kennedy when he presented a tribute film to his slain brother.[1]

---

1. King did all he could to mend fences with Johnson after supporting the RFK write-in campaign during the primary. Though LBJ let bygones be bygones, visiting New Hampshire and publicly praising the governor, King's relationship with the rest of the Johnson administration was never as warm as it had been with Kennedy's. At a formal gathering of the National Governors' Conference, King borrowed a waiter's outfit from the maître d' and served the table of representatives from the White House. King spilt their drinks, confused their orders, and spat insults. While the Johnson people did

Regarding the sweepstakes, to which many in attendance had purchased tickets, King said the Sweeps was "the most popular thing since the Revolution" and had exceeded their expectations. "There is nothing honky-tonkish about it. It does not stimulate gambling. It gives people a dream and a chance. People like it."

AS AUGUST ENDED, engines on the political campaigns began to purr. Former Governor Wesley Powell was again facing John Pillsbury for the Republican nomination. Powell was still on the outs with Bill Loeb, so the *Union Leader* beat him up pretty handily. Pillsbury was ignoring Powell and already punching at John King. The list of sins against the incumbent was long. Near the top: bringing the shame of the sweepstakes to New Hampshire.

On Labor Day weekend, when Sweeps sales broke all previous records, a riot broke out at family vacation destination Hampton Beach. Between five thousand and ten thousand high school and college students descended on the boardwalk Sunday night and started tearing up the place. Rioters told reporters the chaos had been planned, as weekend word-of-mouth forwarded the invitation to show up at Hampton for "something big." Local police were overwhelmed and asked for assistance from neighboring states. Governor King — who had been at a dinner party and turned up wearing a tuxedo — arrived at the beach around midnight to deputize members of the Massachusetts and Maine state police. A photo of King in black tie, seemingly inspecting the troops, was a source of ridicule seized by Pillsbury. He accused King of not acting decisively and jeopardizing public safety so he could rub elbows.

On primary election day, September 8, in a six-way Republican race for governor, Pillsbury beat Powell by nearly eleven thousand votes for the nomination. The third-place finisher in the Republican primary was Democrat John King, getting almost thirty-eight hundred write-in votes.

JOHN KING was hardly the only one seeking a victory as the horses ran free at Rockingham. There were sixty-six ticket holders on tenterhooks about the race.

A birthday gift got Margery Johnson into the running. Relatives from New

---

not recognize him, the other governors did. When the prank was revealed, the administration representatives had no choice but laugh along with the rest of room — though it's hard to imagine there weren't hard feelings lingering beneath the surface.

Hampshire had promised a ticket for her son, so she asked if they'd get her one too. A factory worker in Attleboro, Massachusetts, she was figuratively on the back of Knightly Manner — guaranteeing her at least $7,500 as a starting horse.

The parents of seven children aged 3–13 had been paired with Bupers, whose surprising show at the Sweeps Prep had ticket holders inspirited. Dave Powell of Weymouth, Massachusetts, worked for the Army Quartermaster Depot. Posing for a picture along with her litter of children, Jean Powell told the *Boston Globe,* "Maybe we can get a larger house."

Edna Marshall thought it was a joke when she got the telegram saying she'd been paired with St. Raphael. Mrs. Marshall didn't even buy a ticket; her husband had put her name on it without telling her, something he'd done whenever buying raffle tickets or other chances. Mr. Marshall had won $1,000 for his wife in the past. "I'm not making any plans to use the money until I get it," she firmly stated.

Walter Lewis of Salem, Massachusetts, had played the Irish Sweepstake for thirty years with the luck of a black cat. He had no idea he had made the final cut in New Hampshire until his neighbor raced over to meet him in the driveway after work. "Did you know your name was in the paper?" Lewis would be matched with Gun Boat. "I always had hope," he told a reporter, "but you never know how lucky you are until your ticket gets drawn."

Mrs. Ann Pernokas had thrown out her husband's acknowledgment along with a stack of paper slips and other domestic debris. "I thought that race was over," she said. "I don't know anything about horses." Fortunately, the actual ticket was still in New Hampshire, and Angelo Pernokas was twinned with Knightly Manner.

Another Knightly Manner cohort was Anne Brzezicki of Ipswich, Massachusetts. "Omigod," she said over and over again. "Omigod. Omigod." It was appropriate reaction; Anne was only nine years old.

Of the sixty-six people holding tickets on the starting field, only ten were from New Hampshire. The most mysterious was Erma Bartlett of Meredith, matched up with Old Stoney. She gave her address as being on RFD 2. The telegram alerting her to the match came back as undeliverable, and no one in town or at the post office knew her. Ed Powers said the check would be made out to Erma Bartlett — whomever she was.

A high school custodian in Berlin was allied with Bupers. His name was Henry Turcotte — the same name as one of the three Sweepstakes

Commissioners. The two men were not related, and either no one made the connection or thought it worthy of notice. For all of King and Pickett's joking about ruining the lottery if their own names were pulled, this was as close as you get. (One could argue having a spouse win was a finer fix; Mrs. Elizabeth Perkins was enjoying her $200 consolation prize for Alphabet — much to the chagrin of former Senator Raymond Perkins).

Fifty-two-year-old Frank Malkus of Carteret, New Jersey, was holding a ticket for Roman Brother. A barber for thirty-eight years, Malkus would close his one-man shop on Hudson Street every Wednesday and go to the track. He had played the ponies all his life and was a decent handicapper.

Malkus had never been to New Hampshire, hadn't even bought the Sweeps ticket. It was a gift from his brother-in-law, Stephen Babics, whose family vacation had brought them to the Granite State. Babics decided to get one ticket for each of his wife's six sisters. Eleanor Malkus's family was extremely close; she shared a duplex with another one of her sisters.

Finding out on Friday that they were matched with the 7–5 favorite, Malkus asked his wife if she wanted to go to New Hampshire for the sweepstakes. Apprehensive but exuberant, Eleanor had never been on an airplane. They hastily packed their bags, invited the Babics to join them, and dashed for the airport that night.

Before getting on the plane, Malkus stopped to buy a fresh box of cigars — just in case.

24

The Sport of King's

ON THE MORNING of Saturday, September 12, 1964, the doors at Rockingham Park racetrack opened before usual, with bands from high schools, CYOs, and veterans' groups playing to entertain the early birds. The planned post time for the sweepstakes was 1:30 p.m., but it was pushed back to about 5:30 to suit ABC's human drama of athletic competition. There would be a full undercard of nine other races, including a one mile and seventy yards, and a one and one-sixteenth of a mile.

Organizers had a complete parking survey of the town and placed color-coded signs to designated free parking lots (green) and paid lots (red). School janitors were asked to oversee cars parked on school grounds and point attendees toward shuttle buses in constant rotation throughout Salem. When people arrived at the racetrack, more bands were playing in the parking lot to greet them. Governor King, on behalf of Lou Smith, requested that one hundred National Guardsmen help control a crowd that could exceed sixty thousand — a suggestion loudly derided by leaders in Concord as going over the top.

Reporters were allowed to park on racetrack grounds. According to Bill Stearns's extensive logistics manual, a breakfast layout was prepared for the scribes who arrived in the morning. Hundreds of box lunches were passed out to reporters, staff, police, and anyone else on the clock.

Stairs had been built leading to the roof of the administration building for the media. There was a designated area for television and movie cameras, as they required the highest possible vantage point to see the far end of the track. Certain other reporters and cameras were allowed roof access; their press badges were printed in a different color. Every reporter got a press kit filled with stats of all eleven starters, track records, photos, and programs for the day. Armfuls of typewriters were borrowed from offices, and New England Telephone ran additional lines into the pressroom so reporters could file their late stories. A small platoon of messenger boys stood around waiting to be called on.

Stearns purchased two hundred plastic raincoats to distribute just in case the skies didn't cooperate. The morning had been clear and warm, but was getting cooler as the skies grayed. Conditions were right for a very fast track.

Rockingham hired extra staff just for the day. In addition to cashiers and ushers (who were given special light-green shirts or vests for the occasion), the plant had additional plumbers and electricians standing by. There were extra attendants in the jockey room to ensure all needs were met.

All of the hype over the race ultimately worked against it. The crowd of sixty thousand never materialized. According to the *Union Leader,* only an estimated eighteen thousand people — about the crowd for any other Saturday — showed up, with the lion's share of locals deciding to view the race on ABC instead. The ten thousand folding chairs in the infield remained mostly empty. Workers said many of the usual weekend faces were absent, likely hoping to avoid a mob scene. Even the VIPs seemed reluctant to brave the illusory crowd. "If I weren't a guest of the governor," one woman in an official box told the *New York Times,* "I would have stayed at home and watched on television."

INSIDE THE ADMINISTRATION BUILDING, Lou Smith and Larry Pickett were photographed together in Smith's private office. Each was on the telephone — although it's unclear whether both were actually barking last-minute instructions or just posing for the *Union Leader* photojournalist.

The twelfth of September was the only day of 1964 that reporters didn't seek out Ed Powers for comment. He was as much of a spectator as anyone else in the grandstands. His role was done. The books on the first year of the New Hampshire Sweepstakes were closed. They had made $5.7 million in $3 tickets. The cost for running the lottery, including prize payouts, federal taxes, salaries, equipment purchases, and the $100,000 they contributed to the racing purse, totaled $2,971,212. That left $2,768,089 to be distributed for education. While the gross exceeded expectation, the school's take fell short of the $4 million bar promised by Pickett when the sweepstakes bill passed.

Nonetheless, the commission's official position was that the Sweeps were an unqualified success. While people streamed in to see the results of the 1964 race, Rockingham Park was already selling tickets for the first of two sweepstakes runs in 1965.

INSTEAD OF GIVING the porch of the administration building to the press or the commission, the staff reserved the prime viewing spot for the Sweeps finalists who attended. A select group of journalists were allowed to watch with them. The *Union Leader* had three photographers shooting in three different film formats. One was dedicated to the porch just to get reaction shots from the lottery winners. The photographer equipped with the staff's only 35 mm camera — the newest and fastest the paper owned — was set trackside near the finish line.

A single row of lawn chairs of multicolor nylon webbing were set up for the Sweeps finalists. About a dozen of the sixty-six contenders made the trip, but each brought an entourage so the porch was crowded. Group members were social with one another despite the stark financial competition between them.

Frank and Eleanor Malkus, ticket holders on Roman Brother, sat in the back row to the right-hand side. He wore a nice fedora, stiff white shirt, and matching dark suit and necktie. A cigar chugged between his fingers. Mrs. Malkus sported a double string of pearls and proper white gloves, and wore a look of interminable disquiet. Before taking their place among the finalists, Malkus and his brother-in-law went to the pari-mutuel window and placed another ten-dollar bet on Roman Brother across the board (to win, place, or show). Maybe it was superstition. Maybe the lifelong pony player couldn't stand to have just a single wager on his horse — even if the potential payoff was 30,000:1.

The Malkuses were seated on the end with Carol Ann Lee of Worcester, Massachusetts. Like Eleanor Malkus, the twenty-one-year-old Lee had never been to a horse race before. Though shy and self-effacing, she was clearly the most radiant of the one-day celebrities. Lee was holding a ticket on Knightly Manner. A senior at St. Joseph's College in Maine, she was joined by her father and mother, her fourteen-year-old sister, and several girlfriends from school. The reporters could not stop waxing on about her beautiful hair, her herringbone wool skirt, her fine blue coat, and her pretty face. If their goal had been to find a star in the crowd, she was it.

Also rooting for Knightly Manner were Anne and Angelo Pernokas, the couple who had thrown out their acknowledgment. They had brought a pair of in-laws from Peabody to join them. Mrs. Pernokas was pessimistic about grabbing the jackpot. "If the Good Lord wants us to win, we win. And if not, we won't," she told the *Boston Globe*.

Seventy-nine-year-old widow Emma Chabot came from Norwich, Connecticut, to cheer for Phantom Shot. "I occasionally bet on the horses," she said with a wink. Asked what she'd do with the money if she won, Chabot said, "I'm going to *spend* the money, of course."

One of the players holding tickets on a favorite but not sitting in the VIP section was Paul Cordone of Gloversville, New York. He had been matched with Roman Brother. Traveling with his wife, Martha, his niece, and his sister-in-law, Cordone either didn't know about the private viewing area or chose to skip it. The family ran into a *Life* magazine crew that followed them to the edge of the chain-link fencing on the ground level of the track. His family was dressed smartly; he in a jacket and cross tie, the women in fur stoles. Cordone, a fifty-one-year-old beer distributor, had a thin ring of hair around his bald skull and a thinner line of mustache hair over his lip. Like Frank Malkus, Cordone had played the horses most of his life and came to Rockingham Park with a breast pocket filled with cigars.

Governor King made a brief appearance on the porch to wish all of the ticket holders luck before disappearing into Smith's private office. The handshakes were vigorous from the contestants well aware it was King's signature that had put the sweepstakes in motion. Post time was approaching.

From above, the finalists in the New Hampshire Sweepstakes watched as the eleven steeds were saddled in the infield, then trotted to the starting gate. They'd be shoved in according to the numbers on their silks: Wil Rad, first, all the way to Prairie Schooner, eleventh. Tiny prayers were said to God, Jesus, Yahweh, the Virgin Mary, Saint Fill-in-the-blank — anyone who could provide a divine hand. As a bugle called the racers to the track, Frank Malkus took out a fresh cigar, struck a match, then puffed and puffed until the rolled leaves came alive.

"Well," he said. "Here it goes."

AT 5:50 P.M., a time designated by Wide World of Sports, the stinging clang of the starting bell pealed, and the metal doors of the gate crashed open. They were off at Rockingham. Nine of the thoroughbreds got out cleanly. Purser and St. Raphael bumped each other. Jockey Hank Wajda moved Purser too fast, and the horse briefly went to his knees after clipping St. Raphael's heels. Wajda steadied the horse that'd won the Sweeps Prep and galloped on, finding himself ten lengths back as the pack went into the clubhouse turn.

Old Stoney, who had led nearly the whole way through the Prep before tiring, grabbed the early lead. He set the pace as the other horses stayed in a tight pack making the second turn on to the back stretch. As the straightaway opened up, Purser had made up the ground and galloped into tenth place, putting Roman Brother — the overwhelming favorite — in last.

High above the action, Carol Ann Lee peered in dismay as number 6, Knightly Manner, was stuck in the rear of the pack. Eleanor Malkus craned her neck and saw number 8, Roman Brother, bring up the rear. She placed a white-gloved hand on her husband's, patting it in consolation, though Frank Malkus paid it no mind. The longtime chalk player spotted what he wanted. With a snap of the crop, he could see Fernando Alvarez make his move on the back stretch. Roman Brother was climbing.

Purser, despite his late start, was still firing. At the halfway mark he was on Old Stoney's heels. At the three-eighths pole, Wajda moved Purser slightly from his path and seemed to cut off Phantom Shot who was about to make a move for first place. When they made the far turn, Old Stoney finally gave up the lead and Purser nosed ahead. Right next to him was Knightly Manner. Purser took the inside position, setting Knightly Manner up for the wider turn at the quarter pole. From the porch, Carol Ann Lee, white-knuckling her pair of binoculars, slid forward to the edge of her seat, as number 8 continued to steam forward.

Alvarez on Roman Brother, stuck in the logjam, exploited a hole that opened in the pack. Instead of taking the long way around, he could take the short way up the middle. He continued to pass the field. Sixth . . . fifth . . . fourth . . .

When riders made the final turn, for a brief moment *six* horses were neck and neck, running down the homestretch like a solid wall. One hundred thousand dollars riding on the winner, and for a flash it looked like all of them could win it. Alvarez took his horse on an even farther outside turn than Larry Adams riding Knightly Manner had, but Roman Brother stayed with both the leaders. Three horses were now breaking away. The sweepstakes was coming down to Purser, Roman Brother and Knightly Manner.

The rumble of the horses' hooves resonated like thunder as the trio streaked down the final stretch. At the mile-and-one-sixteenth mark, Roman Brother finally caught Purser and took the lead, but Knightly Manner was closing fast. Adams aboard Knightly Manner was swinging the crop hard with his right hand. Fernando Alvarez pulled Roman Brother's reins high, tugging the throat lash and urging him on for the last eighth of a mile. On the porch, Carol Ann Lee was now screaming, "Come on! Come on!" Eleanor Malkus's gloved hand that had rested compassionately on her husband's was now squeezing tightly. At track level, Paul Cordone pointed joyously with his cigar-clenched hand as the pack flew by left to right, his niece jumping up and down on the top bar of the fence.

The pace of the two horses for the last eighth of a mile was blistering. Knightly Manner, surging, had caught Roman Brother's tail. With each pounding step, the larger horse on the left pulling alongside the smaller one, their bodies undulating like ocean waves. Adams struck the hindquarters again and again. Knightly Manner's head was now even with Alvarez's saddle. The crowd made the noise of a hundred thousand people, demanding this breathtaking finish. The wire was right there . . .

By a half length, Roman Brother took the first New Hampshire Sweepstakes with a track-record time of 1:55.4 for a mile and three-sixteenths. Knightly Manner placed.

The drama didn't end when the race did. Purser, who would have pulled off the upset of the year had he not been knocked down coming out of the gate, finished third and Phantom Shot came in fourth. Phantom Shot's owners, however, claimed Purser had fouled the other horse at the three-eighths pole with a lane block, and demanded Purser's disqualification. The Sweepstakes Commission was ready to pay ticket holders of the third-place finisher $25,000 but had no policy that covered disqualifications. It took the judges a half hour to review film of the race, declare that no foul had taken place, and certify the results as official.

The rest of the field finished in this order: Old Stoney, Bupers, St. Raphael, Prairie Schooner, Ramant, and Gun Boat. Even though Johnny Longden, the winningest jockey alive, was at the reins, Wil Rad finished the Sweeps stone motherless last — just as he had done in the Kentucky Derby.

ON THE PORCH of the administration building, the lottery ticket holders exploded. Eleanor Malkus stood from her lawn chair, buried her face in her husband's shoulder, and wept. "I can't speak, I'm so excited." She unclutched one of her gloved hands, revealing a string of rosary beads she had been gripping.

Frank Malkus took off his hat and raised it over his head in victory, another six inches of cigar still smoldering between his smile. "When I seen him start to move on the backstretch, I knew I didn't have no worry." Some wag photographer handed the couple a prop cloth sack made to look like a money bag, and they posed with their pretend winnings.

What are you going to do with your fortune, the reporters asked. "Give it away," Malkus said in jest. *Are you going to close your barber shop?* "Are you kidding? I'm going to open another one!"

Malkus made even more money than his $100,000 grand prize. Roman Brother paid $3.80, $2.80, and $2.40 across the board.

Carol Ann Lee, who started the race watching demurely, leapt from her seat as Knightly Manner nipped Purser to finish second. She held her head in her hands and small tears appeared in her blue eyes. The college student flopped back down in her chair and began to cry, then laugh, then cry again. "I never thought about how much money I might win," she declared. "I never dared to think about it."

Surrounded by her friends, her parents, and her kid sister, Lee started to stumble away, a dazed look on her face. A swarm of writers refused to let her go. It was as if she won the big prize herself. *What will you do with your $50,000?*

"I'm going to spend some money on school," she answered. "I'll pay my sister's tuition too." Then she shrugged and said, "I guess I'll buy myself a car and I'll buy my sister a horse, then I don't know what else I'll do. There's just so much of it."

The penmen loved it. Her quotes were as rich as the jackpot she'd won.

"This is my first and last race," she said, "because no other one could be as exciting as this."

For Anne Pernokas, it seemed the good Lord made up his mind they should take home $50,000. It was a pretty good score for someone who'd only ever won a church bizarre. The family joy was not universal, however. When the parents called their daughter and son, they learned the seven- and eight-year-olds were disappointed they'd won money and not the actual horse.

Retired police captain Peitro Fiorentino had watched Old Stoney lead most of the way, only to finish with the also-rans. Nonetheless, he was thrilled with his $7,500 windfall. The Massachusetts resident said, "I'm going to Santa Anita [a racetrack in California] and leave it there."

Widow Emma Chabot was tickled by her $12,500 prize: "I've been widowed for twenty-nine years and have worked hard as a cook all that time until I retired. This is the first easy money I ever got."

Down on the track, Paul Cordone lifted his wife into the air and kissed her hard on the mouth. While still airborne, Martha lifted her calf like a silent-film heroine in their $100,000 ecstasy. This was the UPI photograph that ran in newspapers around the world, their version of the VJ Day kiss.

To celebrate the win, the *Life* lens man got permission to use the photo-finish camera. The magazine's story featured the official race photograph of Roman Brother and Knightly Manner and the finish line. Below it was an identical picture, except this one showed Cordone, alone on the track, running on foot toward the same finish line.

AROUND THE COUNTRY, other Sweepstakes winners watched the telecast in disbelief. James Goodrow, father of a three-week-old baby, won $7,500 on St. Raphael. Virginia Grund of Somerville, Massachusetts, suspiciously said, "I want to see how much Uncle Sam is going to take of my $25,000 before I start spending any of it." The unmarried secretary said, "I've never won anything before. I'm very unlucky, and it looked as though I'd be unlucky this time."

A pair of Boston-area fishermen hauled in $25,000 on Purser. The men, Lars Lunde and Joseph Jacobson, had been friends for forty years, and they celebrated their great catch by dining at a fancy restaurant that night. Lunde picked up the check because Jacobson had bought the $3 ticket. Lunde told reporters he wasn't excited about the win didn't want the publicity or people knowing he had come into a great sum of money.

Anne Brzezicki, all of nine years, was unruffled upon winning $50,000. *How do you feel about the news?* "Um, I don't know." *Why aren't you surprised by your big win?* "Well, people said it was a good horse." The girl said the money would stay in the bank until she went to college — in 1973.

IN THE WINNER'S CIRCLE, Governor John King presented the silver cup to Roman Brother's owners and trainers. The winners' take of the purse was $94,133, making Roman Brother one of the largest earning thoroughbreds in 1964. Jockey Fernando Alvarez received a ring from the National Jockey Guild and a pair of cufflinks from Lou Smith and Rockingham Park.

"I knew I had enough horse to win it at the half-mile pole," Alvarez said. Had he not found that brief opening in the pack, he wouldn't have been able to position Roman Brother for the last stretch.

Because they had been at track level, Paul and Martha Cordone made it across the infield bridge and into the winner's circle to congratulate and thank Alvarez. When the press learned these spectators were actually jackpot winners, they gathered the trio for a series of photos. With Alvarez between them, each of the Cordones planted a big kiss on the winning jockey's cheeks.

Realizing he was forever playing with house money, Cordone shouted out, "I'm even with the horses for life!"

Ed Powers told the newspapers the prize money would be transferred to bank accounts by Wednesday of that week. Later, King decided instead to invite all the winners to the governor's office to be presented their checks. The commission had been able to milk one last photo-op out of the 1964 Sweeps. Four of the six grand prize winners were able to attend and posed for a group picture with King, but the cameramen wanted a shot of Carol Ann Lee with the governor. She was the only sweepstakes winner who merited a solo photograph — and though one pic of the event would have sufficed, many papers ran both pictures.

The press corps gleefully noted that when Carol Ann Lee drove away from the statehouse, she was in a brand-new, red-leather upholstered, black-and-white convertible.

25
Unnoticed, Unmourned

JOHN KING WON REELECTION in 1964, making him the first New Hampshire Democrat to serve a second term as governor. King centered his campaign around John Pillsbury's past support of a sales tax and opposition to the sweepstakes. "Keep the Sweeps! Avoid a Sales Tax!" was his campaign slogan. He won by a record margin of ninety-six thousand votes.

In his second term, King finally won his battle against the tyranny of the tower. The square turret atop the state library that had blocked the view out his north window was torn down at his command. Library staff argued the tower was not an aesthetic flourish; it was an integral part of the Beaux-Arts building's structure. To this day, after repeated attempts to rehabilitate and reinforce the amputated wing, water leaks from that roof.

In 1966, the check presentation photo-op became a full-blown dinner reception. Bill Loeb, who in print never pulled a punch with "King John," wrote him a letter suggesting Ed Powers should give a brief biographical sketch of each winner. "There is some strong human interest and some quite heartwarming stories behind some of these winners," he penned, signing his name, "Bill."

King replied he wholeheartedly agreed, though his second term was nearly up. "If I am present at the 1967 dinner I shall certainly see to it that your suggestions are developed," he wrote. He signed his letter "John."

King was respected by both parties. He got along with the press. The old buckos still called him "John, me boy." He showed at wakes and weddings and at every country ball. The lawyer who didn't care to be governor continued to do a fine job.

In November 1966, John King — the sacrificial lamb — did something no Democrat or Republican had done in 150 years: won a third term as the governor of New Hampshire. On the same day, the biennial Sweeps sales referendum passed by a popular vote of 5 to 1.

COMING OFF their inaugural year, Ed Powers was certain the Sweeps would exceed — maybe double — its revenue in 1965. The operation had grossed nearly $6 million in 1964 but had been handcuffed by only six months of sales.

Representative Larry Pickett filed a bipartisan bill to allow sales of Sweeps tickets in facilities such as state parks, ski resorts, hotels, and local fairs. The commission would also get a "Sweepsmobile" to set up shop anywhere in the state. The highway commissioner blanched, learning tickets would be sold at tollbooths. "We have enough to do now just taking quarters," he lamented. "Where are we going to put all the cars?!"

The bill fell apart in the state Senate. Allies of the original 1963 bill — mostly Democrats — tabled expansion 13–8. The vote caught King flatfooted. North County senators said constituents were expressing concern about the propagation of legalized gambling in their communities — and why not see how the infant program performed before drastically changing it?

Blindsided by the defeat — the biggest of his tenure — King publicly denounced the state Senate in tones uncharacteristic for him. He said senators demonstrated an "utter lack of concern for our cities and town." The biggest hit on the state Senate came from Bill Loeb. Though both political parties had blood on their hands, Loeb's ire was directed at the Republican leadership he so often abused. He wrote the GOP "[stabbed] the Sweeps" and "[kicked] the electorate in the face."

The chance to expand Sweeps outlets was dead until 1967 at the earliest.

ACCORDING TO THE COMMISSION, early sales for the 1965 New Hampshire Sweepstakes were strong. Between 80 and 90 percent of 1964 Sweeps tickets had been purchased by out-of-staters, and by the end of October 1964 nearly 100,000 tickets had been sold for the first of the two 1965 races. The first running would be in July, the "Rockingham Park Special," while the September running would remain the "New Hampshire Sweepstakes Classic." The big difference would be that grand prizes were only $50,000 per race.

The hot pace of Sweeps sales cooled over the winter and didn't kick up again until summer vacation. The commission had missed the chance to increase points of sale, and the international news organizations that propelled Sweepstakes mania did not repeat their coverage in 1965. The Sweeps were no longer "news."

While the 1964 sweepstakes grossed $5.7 million, or, about $24 per pupil in New Hampshire, the 1965 sweepstakes brought in $4.5 million, $21 per pupil.

In truth, very little of the money earned by that first sweepstakes went toward education. Advocacy groups estimated that only 7 percent of the cash was added to local school budgets for extras. The rest was used by communities to offset property taxes. After putting itself through hell in its "noble experiment" to improve education, a paltry $194,000 was spent on schools. Factored statewide, that was approximately a buck and a half per student.

Some explanation might be found in the uncertainty about the exact amount of that first allocation and in the Department of Education's warning to towns about factoring that money into their budgets. Even in communities that were interested in supplementing their school budgets, it may have been thought fiscally irresponsible to spend money that might not appear. So when the cash finally arrived, too late to use in the fiscal year 1965 budget, the money gathered dust in the coffers and offset property taxes.

Though no hard numbers exist, the Sweepstakes Commission's financial records show a greater percentage of revenues were put toward schooling in subsequent years — but never close to 100 percent. Additionally, a growing problem for cities and towns was that Sweeps revenues were falling and payouts were shrinking.

For the 1966 Sweeps, legislators and the commission examined new ways to promote the program. They looked for ways to legally sell tickets through the mail or outside of the state (they couldn't find any). For the first time, they embarked on a newspaper and billboard advertising campaign. They added a $5,000 bonus drawing for losing tickets. Still, these gimmicks did not help revenues. Gross sales went down another 15 percent and the per-pupil award was $14.82.

More urgently, after a 3–2 statewide referendum, New York residents amended their constitution to allow a state-run lottery.

The bloom was coming off the rose.

IN OCTOBER 1965, the trial of Anthony Fabrizio began in a Rochester, New York, federal court. Fabrizio had been arrested by the FBI with seventy-five acknowledgments he'd bought in Keene. The Rhode Island case had been a critical test, but Louis Hamod had been tried by *state* authorities. In these proceedings, the federal judge made quick work of dismissing the government's charges — saying Congress did not intend for the Transportation of Paraphernalia Act to apply to legal gambling operations.

The ruling did not satisfy the Justice Department, which felt it had been true to its internal policy of leaving tourists alone but felt it had a true bookie in Fabrizio. Nicholas Katzenbach was now the U.S. attorney general. When he had met Joseph Millimet in 1963, he made clear his biggest concern was racketeers bringing tickets across state lines. His U.S. attorney in New York wanted to appeal the Fabrizio decision to the U.S. Supreme Court. Katzenbach gave the go-ahead to settle the issue of bringing sweepstakes acknowledgments across state lines once and for all.

On November 7, 1966, the Supreme Court heard oral arguments in *U.S. v. Fabrizio.* Speaking on behalf of the Solicitor General, attorney Jerome Chapman said a sweepstakes acknowledgment clearly fit the law's definition of a "record, paraphernalia, ticket, certificate, bills, slip, token, paper, writing, or other device" used in gambling. Also, nowhere did the law say it applied only to gangsters or illegal gambling. Chapman said that the federal government had the right to enact these prohibitions — not in its role as racketeering enforcer — but as a matter of interstate commerce.

Betty Freidlander, representing Anthony Fabrizio, argued the law did not apply in this case. Even if it were found that Fabrizio had transported the tickets to sell at a profit, doing so would not be running a wagering pool or bookmaking. If someone is carrying a ticket for a legal New Hampshire event, Freidlander said, then what he does with the ticket is legally irrelevant.

New Hampshire filed an amicus, and the court granted twenty-two minutes of argument to the state. Joseph Millimet explained the sweepstakes program had been drafted to stay within all applicable federal regulations. Millimet said that "paraphernalia" as defined was the means by which a wagering pool was conducted. Once purchased, the acknowledgments were no longer "paraphernalia" and had no value.

Chief Justice Earl Warren interjected: "Why do you give [the acknowledgments] if they have no value?"

The attorney stopped. Here was Millimet, arguing the biggest case of his career, and the nation's foremost jurist had asked him the most rudimentary question about the program he had spent years crafting. It was the fulcrum on which the entire New Hampshire Sweepstakes teetered, and he blanked.

"That," Millimet said after a pregnant pause, "is an excellent question, Mr. Chief Justice."

The entire courtroom burst into laughter, charmed by Millimet's schoolboy retort. "I thought it would be," Warren said, amiably playing along.

"I would say frankly to the Court that we give it to the people for" — another tiny pause — "psychological reasons. We give it to the people because it's a souvenir. It's a memento. It's *something*. It's a piece of paper they can look at after they pay their $3. It's the only reason we give it to them; it has no function whatsoever."

Justice William Brennan, also trying to decipher the importance of the acknowledgments, posed hypothetically that if he put six dollars in a New Hampshire ticket machine, he wouldn't want to leave without something to show he'd spent his money.

"The reason for that, Your Honor, is that you're a law-abiding citizen."

Brennan, in a tone that implied he'd never spend six dollars on a lottery ticket, said, "Oh, no it isn't." More laughter.

"That's why we give the ordinary tourist something to look at," concluded Millimet. "We don't think Congress intended to make the ordinary tourist a criminal."

ON DECEMBER 12, 1966, the U.S. Supreme Court ruled that taking New Hampshire Sweepstakes acknowledgments over state lines violated federal law. The decision was 7–2. Writing for the majority, Justice John Harlan wrote that Congress's intention was to thwart transportation of such material, no matter who carried it across state lines. The court ruled Anthony Fabrizio must stand trial and the lower-court judge must apply this new precedent. Justices Potter Stewart and Abe Fortas in dissension wrote Congress never "intended such an unanticipated result" as to make felons of the thousands of visitors to New Hampshire.

In Concord, Ed Powers could not play it cool. "How do you square this with the problems the nation faces today?" he shouted during a phone interview with the *Union Leader*. "They ruled in favor of pornography, but find something illegal about taking sweepstakes acknowledgments across state lines?"

Was this the sweepstakes' death knell? A *Nashua Telegraph* editorial said "the infinitesimal chance of being a winner in the lottery compared to the fine and possible jail sentence for violating a federal statute will hurt the lottery, let there be no doubt about it." The *Concord Daily Monitor* urged legislators to finally wake up and declared the "noble experiment" over. "Kill the turkey," they cried.

But it wasn't over. Sweepstakes ticket sales and races for 1967 continued. The Supreme Court had not ruled buying a Sweeps ticket was illegal; the justices simply said bringing one across state lines was. Some tourists realized they could tear up the acknowledgment; others worried little about the FBI chasing them for a ticket or two. (Among the winners in the 1967 Sweepstakes were three secretaries from the federal Department of Justice. They won $452 and were the only consolation-prize winners invited to the have their photographs taken with the governor.) King signed the expansion bill allowing ticket sales at 150 new locations, including grocery stores, banks, and hotels. People were forming "Sweepstakes Clubs" to pool ticket money and divide their winnings. Pickett proposed the Sweepstakes Commission could act as an in-state depository of acknowledgments for those who didn't want to travel with them. The state's congressional delegation filed bills carving out state lottery exemptions that received no support.

Ticket sales for 1967 were $2.5 million, a 33 percent decline from before the Supreme Court ruling and a 55 percent drop since the first Sweepstakes. The award per pupil for 1967 was $8.28.

DESPITE HIS OPPOSITION TO GAMBLING, New York Governor Nelson Rockefeller signed his state's sweepstakes bill in April 1967. Instead of twice a year, New York would hold drawings every month with a $100,000 grand prize. Rather than create a new racing event, the New York sweepstakes would match players with horses from races already run (so as to avoid any insinuation a race could be rigged to affect the lottery's outcome). Each ticket was $1. Instead of marketing to tourists and outsiders, New York officials believed nearly all of their tickets would be sold to in-state residents. They estimated annual earnings of $198 million, while New Hampshire was struggling to stay above the $2 million mark.

Republican Walter Peterson, the anti-sweeps lawmaker who had failed to stop Larry Pickett's nimble parliamentary maneuverings, became governor of New Hampshire in 1968. But as a chief executive crafting a state budget, Peterson got the religion. The governor's office would continue its support of the Sweepstakes Commission and the revenue it created.

By now, Lou Smith's support was dwindling. He decided Rockingham Park could not host two annual races for the sweepstakes. The notoriety the Rock had gained in 1964 did not grow with time. Owners of the top-tier horses wanted a slice of the Sweeps revenue in addition to the race purse. Fewer thoroughbreds of note were being nominated. It was clear the New Hampshire Sweepstakes was *not* going to be the fourth jewel in the Triple Crown. Smith said they'd dump the July Rockingham Park Special in 1968 and would host one main event in September. That year, thoroughbreds in the Sweeps Classic were replaced with harness racing.

Pickett proposed legislation that would allow the commission to base the July drawing on an out-of-state race, like the Irish Sweepstake, or even sell tickets up to ten days *after* the race. Instead Powers thought going back to one race with a $100,000 jackpot would reverse the sales slide. Nonetheless, the per-pupil award for 1968 was only $6.75.

HAVING BEEN REMANDED by the high court, the retrial of Anthony Fabrizio took place in Rochester Federal Court on October 31, 1968. The sixty-two-year-old looked wan as he entered the courtroom. The prosecution offered testimony from four Elmira, New York, residents who said they gave Fabrizio a list of names of people who wanted tickets. They also gave him three dollars for each chance and an extra dollar to cover his expenses. The sales clerk from the Keene liquor store said Fabrizio told him he'd bought more than seven hundred tickets that summer.

FBI agent Francis Jenkins described how a six-man team followed Fabrizio from Elmira to Keene, then back to New York. Under cross-examination, attorney Robert Napier got Agent Jenkins to admit that he too purchased three sweepstakes tickets while in Keene and drove back to New York with them. Flustered, Jenkins said the tickets were part of the evidence collected for the investigation. Then Napier asked who would get the $100,000 if he won the Sweeps. Even the judge laughed out loud and exclaimed, "That *would* be a problem!"

The strongest testimony for Fabrizio came from Ed Powers. Though called as a government witness, he eagerly explained to the defense that the acknowledgment was not a ticket, not necessary to retain, and had no value. The prosecution objected to the testimony of their own witness, but the judge allowed Napier to continue questioning Powers as his testimony was relevant to the question of "criminal intent."

It took the jury seventy minutes to find Anthony Fabrizio not guilty of illegally transporting lottery receipts. Upon hearing the verdict, he put his head on the table and wept. Outside, surrounded by reporters, he tearfully declared, "I will never buy another state lottery ticket again."

Reminded that he could now legally purchase sweepstakes tickets in his home state of New York, his tone changed. "I might think about it sometime," he said.

THE CROWNING MOMENT of the 1969 sweepstakes came when Governor Peterson presented each of the Apollo 11 astronauts with complimentary Sweeps tickets. Sales did not lift off, though. Nevertheless, when a two-month-old baby won $50,000 on Heat of Battle, the photos of the boy gumming the check were adorable.

The commission's annual audits showed that revenues had flatlined. Bringing in $2.05 million in 1968, the Sweeps raked in only $2.01 million during the summer of Woodstock. Less than $900,000 went to education that year. Even the New York lottery was underperforming. Instead of bringing in $30 million a month, the operation was averaging $5.2 million.

Though the Supreme Court refused to hear a 1970 case brought by New Hampshire and New York to settle the issue of bans on broadcast advertising, the FCC finally issued some clear guidelines removing the news blackout on lottery coverage. Regulators said it was permissible to air stories about winners, where they had purchased their tickets, and how many of them they had bought, among other information.

New Jersey in 1970 became the third state to implement a lottery, though it departed from the sweepstakes format. Pre-numbered tickets were sold to match a series of winning digits. Unlike New Hampshire and New York, players didn't have to spent time filling out names and addresses on counterfoils. The drawings were weekly, and the price point on these lottery tickets was fifty cents. Out of the gate, New Jersey grossed $6 million in weekly sales.

In July 1971, Ed Powers and the New Hampshire Sweepstakes Commission unveiled a new product. The 50/50 Sweeps ticket mirrored the New Jersey lottery, and the tickets were designed and printed by Mathematica, the same third-party lottery vendor used by New Jersey. Tickets were fifty cents, and drawings were held every Friday; weekly winners had a chance at a grand prize of $50,000. Numbers were picked by a rubber ball landing in a slot on a rotating wheel. Matching all five numbers in order nabbed the winner $15,000. Matching the last four digits yielded a win of $500, and matching the last three, $50.

The first winning 50/50 number was 34941. In trying to advertise the winning number, Powers found himself running into the same roadblocks he had run into in 1964. Most newspapers said they couldn't print the winning number because of the postal regulations. Broadcasters said the FCC's new rules did not allow them to say the number over the air. Powers was furious. For years the *New York Daily News* had been running the names of lottery winners in its out-of-state editions, as well as hundreds of stories about winners of the illegal Irish Sweepstake, but no one harassed *them*. It seemed all the stonewalling was reserved for New Hampshire. Powers resorted to flying airplanes towing banners with the winning numbers.

The commission was still running the $3 sweepstakes horse race, but the fifty-cent game was the boost the commission had been looking for. In the first three months of the program, 4.8 million tickets were purchased. At the end of 1971, total sales had rebounded to $4.2 million and the commission made a record $7.7 million in 1972.

The fourth state to get in on the action — Massachusetts — unveiled its own lottery that year. It was called "The Game" and was a near carbon copy of the 50/50 Sweep. At its first drawing in March, seven people won $50,000. In May, one winner took home $1 million.

New York and New Jersey had been far enough away, but the Massachusetts Game was the direct competition New Hampshire had always feared. Lotteries in Connecticut, Maine, Michigan, and Pennsylvania were nearly ready. After the Game's rollout, sales in the 50/50 Sweeps dropped 10.7 percent. More dramatically, $3 ticket sales for the sweepstakes race dove by 25 percent.

For Ed Powers, the handwriting was on the wall.

IN OCTOBER 1972, the Sweepstakes Commission voted unanimously to discontinue the New Hampshire Sweepstakes after the next race. With two weeks to go before the event, Powers estimated they would sell just 285,000 tickets — too few to fill a single drum. Instead, the staff would focus on revamping the 50/50 to increase the grand prize to $100,000. There were also plans to develop an entirely new kind of ticket. It would be called "Instant Sweeps," and players could scratch off a seal to see if they had won. (Massachusetts was about to be the first to unveil an instant game, and expectations were high.)

After selling 9 million tickets over eight years and netting $19 million for the purpose of supporting the state's public education system, it was over. Cancellation of the program got very few column inches in most papers. The *Concord Monitor* placed the story below the page-one masthead, but otherwise expressed no pleasure in its long-desired defeat to the Sweeps. The *Union Leader* downplayed the importance of the race, and Bill Loeb's editorial claimed the lottery had saved the state from a sales tax. The *Nashua Telegraph* literally gave more space to the World's Annual Chicken Pluckin' Championship than the final Sweeps race.

The *Portsmouth Herald* wrote the $3 Sweeps died "virtually unnoticed, unmourned." Lottery players obviously wanted more action than a twice-a-year race could provide, one that was legal only in New Hampshire. "We still think it's a precarious way to finance education," it concluded, "but then we're old-fashioned."

The final New Hampshire Sweepstakes was run on October 14, 1972, at Rockingham Park. The marquee event had been moved from the day's final harness race to the fourth in order to give reporters enough time to file their stories. Only the UL and the wire services were there.

Mr. and Mrs. George Panciera of Meriden, Connecticut, won $50,000 on Grocery List, inspiring copious puns about making bread and bringing home the bacon. Man in Black placed, providing $10,000 to Henry Peterson of East Hartford, Connecticut. Sea Yarn showed, winning $5,000 for Walt Kopp from Big Delta, Alaska. Smiling photos were taken with winners, jockeys, and horses alike.

The days were growing shorter and night covered the track early. The hands on the clock refused to stop. Executive Director Ed Powers looked on — the hair on his temples whiter than the day he left the FBI — with perhaps a bittersweet dash of nostalgia in his gaze. John King's "noble experiment" was over, but a new branch of the cultural sciences had begun.

The next horse race at the Rock started. Lottery players left to buy other tickets, dream other dreams.

Afterword

THE HORSE RACE that started it all—and the overwhelming opposition to it—have been swallowed by history. Scandal and sensation, savior and sin, when all of King's horses ran that thunderous mile and three-eighths, they surreptitiously changed the cultural direction of the nation.

Fearing a rash of litigation that would cripple state operations, Congress finally exempted state-run lotteries from federal anti-lottery laws in 1974. The measure, Public Law 93–583, was championed by U.S. Attorney General William Saxbe and finally got the Post Office, the IRS, the FCC, and the Justice Department out of the way.

As more states got into the game (twelve by 1981; thirty-three by 1991), lotteries revolved around scratch tickets. Then came numbers games: pick-them-yourself, daily drawings suspiciously similar to the rackets. In 1975, Massachusetts started selecting its numbers in a half-hour televised, game-show-inspired "Big Money Game." All that was missing was General Pierre Gustav Toutant Beauregard calling out the numbers himself.

Next came jackpot lotto games in which grand prizes could grow into the millions of dollars. Then multistate lottery games pushed jackpots into the tens, then hundreds of millions of dollars. Gargantuan payouts are so ubiquitous today that the public suffers from what the industry calls "jackpot fatigue" in which the casual player isn't motivated to buy a ticket unless the prize is greater than $300 million.

Though it got out of the horse-race business and now refers to itself as the New Hampshire Lottery, the official name of the agency remains the New Hampshire Sweepstakes Commission. When the "Instant Sweeps" scratch ticket was rolled out in 1975, revenues jumped from $5.5 million to $11 million. In 1977, the Pick 4 daily numbers began and sold two thousand tickets a day. A Pick 3 was introduced. Eventually New Hampshire added a daytime and an evening drawing for both the Pick 3 and Pick 4 (even Dutch Schultz's policy bank only used *one* number a day).

Long before Powerball or Mega Millions, New Hampshire joined with Vermont and Maine to start Tri-State Megabucks in 1985, the first multistate lottery. Income jumped from $15.2 million in 1985 to $94 million in 1990.

After initially being available in only 49 liquor stores, New Hampshire lottery products can now be purchased in 1,250 different locations. By 2013, annual sales grossed $280 million, netting $74.3 million for schools. Since the first sweepstakes race, more than $1.5 billion has been set aside for education.

In 1962, New Hampshire spent $2.4 million on state aid to education and ranked forty-fifth in the nation for educational spending. In 2012, New Hampshire spent $1.03 billion in state aid to education and ranked forty-sixth in the nation.

IN 1972, the New Hampshire state legislature repealed the biennial town-by-town referendum on the Sweeps. To ensure that money raised went to schools and not property-tax relief, New Hampshire voters in 1990 amended the state constitution to prohibit lottery proceeds from being used on any expenses except education.

THE 1950 BRINK'S HEIST took its place in the American conscience as one of the great crimes of the twentieth century. The subject of countless books and magazine articles, it inspired several films including *Blueprint for Robbery, Six Bridges to Cross,* and, loosely, the original 1960 *Ocean's 11* starring Frank Sinatra and the Rat Pack.

In June 1956, a Baltimore arcade operator flagged down a cop because some guy had passed a suspicious ten-dollar bill. The note was crumpled and fragile and smelled musty. Police grabbed the suspect in a bar with a roll of $860 in mildewed cash and another $3,720 in his hotel room. An FBI crosscheck of the serial numbers showed the money had come from the Brink's job.

The hood confessed that a guy named "Fat John" had asked him to launder the money outside of Boston. The bills came from a metal cooler hidden behind a partition in an office wall. The cash had been in $5,000 bunches wrapped in wet newspaper. Ed Powers's men in Boston hit Fat John's office, ripped apart the walls, and found an additional $51,906 in Brink's money wrapped in wet newspaper.

All of the dollar bills were in various states of decay, some falling to pieces when touched. They were filled with mold and insect remains. The wet newspapers the money had been wrapped in were from 1954, four years after the heist. Lab analysis showed the bills had been damaged before they were packaged in the newspaper, likely having been stored in a canvas bag buried in sand or ashes.

Of the $3 million in cash and checks taken from the biggest bank robbery in American history, only $56,486 was ever recovered.

AFTER LEAVING PRISON in 1960, Brink's stool pigeon Joseph "Specs" O'Keefe moved to California under the name Paul Williams (inspired by Red Sox legend Ted Williams). He worked odd jobs including—honest to God—chauffeur to actor Cary Grant. All the time, he stayed in touch with that all-American guy, Ed Powers.

O'Keefe hated hiding and using a pseudonym. "It's a bitch living under a false name. It would be like coming out of a cave," he said. Missing the autumns and winters, he returned to New England in 1973. For a time he moved in with Powers, who helped him find work as a house painter, a hospital security guard, a school janitor, and a bartender.

O'Keefe died in California under an assumed name in 1976. Powers declared O'Keefe "a perfect example of rehabilitation."

THE FALL of the Irish Hospitals' Sweepstake began when mastermind Joseph McGrath died in 1965, leaving operations to his son Paddy. The New Hampshire Sweeps had begun to cut into the Irish business, so Paddy McGrath approached the Irish government about starting a national lottery in 1966, but he was turned down.

The deed for each running of the Sweep needed to be signed by the minister of justice. In 1970, citing a shocking lack of detail in its operations, new minister Des O'Malley refused to sign the deed until he got answers. What he got were lots of threats from Paddy McGrath about workers getting laid off and political repercussions. Three years later, *Sunday Independent* investigative journalist Joe MacAnthony ran an exposé finally uncovering the Sweep's sordid doings. The backlash was so severe he went into exile in Canada. Likewise, a RTE television piece critical of the Sweep was produced but never aired. Nevertheless, the damage was done.

When Ireland did create a national lottery in 1986, the contract went to the Irish post office, not the Irish Hospital Trust. The last running of the Irish Sweepstake was in January 1986.

AFTER HIS COMMITMENT to the state mental hospital, anti-sweeps crusader Charles W. H. Witcomb returned to his family and led a normal but politically active, Christian life working as a financial planner for American Express. His views leaned far-right. He and his wife Frances donated to pro-life and abstinence education causes. In August 2002, while Frances was in hospice, Witcomb told his children he did not want to live life without his love. He stopped taking treatment for his own cancer. Bill and Frances Witcomb died within ten days of each other.

SWEEPS DETRACTOR Edward DeCourcy continued a long, respected career as editor of the *Argus-Champion,* winning more than 150 awards in his forty years behind his LC Smith typewriter. He won the International Golden Quill award for editorial writing in 1971 in a tie; he had written *both* winning pieces.

After twenty-one years at the paper, DeCourcy retired in 1982 and died in 2005 at the age of ninety-three.

IN AN EFFORT to gauge the federal government's true level of concern and scope of investigation into the New Hampshire Sweepstakes, this author filed a Freedom of Information Act request in 2012 with the Department of Justice for any documents related to the operation or surveillance of the New Hampshire Sweepstakes. No files could be located. One can infer either that the FBI did so little investigating of the state's sweepstakes and those associated with it that no case file was ever created—or that whatever materials collected at the time were not retained.

CHARLES COHAN, the Teaneck, New Jersey, man who ran the Concord Ticket Service, was found guilty in federal court in July 1965 of three counts of using the mails to distribute lottery information. He was fined $600. Cohan pled innocence and ignorance. The man who told reporters he vetted his out-of-state ticket agency with the attorneys general in New Hampshire and Washington claimed he didn't know sending lottery information through the mail was illegal.

THE *Union Leader* raised $1,200 to offset the legal expenses of Anthony Fabrizio. It is not known if he ever purchased a lottery ticket again.

AS THE POPULARITY of state lotteries has increased, so have criticisms. While the early New Hampshire warnings of Mob corruption and communism fell flat, legitimate concerns about the nature of lotteries and problem gambling remain.

It is undeniable that the odds on most jackpot games are incredibly long (hence the incredible payout). Players, critics say, do not take this into consideration—some even *expect* to win. They think the more scratch tickets they buy, the closer the odds move in their favor. While participation is relatively equal among income brackets, poor players spend a greater *percentage* of their income on the lottery, which amounts to a de facto regressive tax, affecting the poor more than the wealthy. Detractors say lotteries also use predatory advertising practices to target low-income players to entice further play.

Harvard Medical School researcher Ronald Kessler in studies funded by the National Institutes of Health says problem gamblers—across all forms of gambling—made up 2.3 percent of the population in 2008; several other peer-reviewed studies over the past forty years have the number floating between 2 and 5 percent. Fifty-plus years ago, a player took a risk by placing a bet with a shady bookie. State lotteries now bring the same action out of the shadows and into gas stations and convenience stores in virtually every community. One might say the problem gambler has just traded one supplier for another.

Economists say the disposable income dropped on lottery tickets would be better spent on consumer goods in the private sector—whether cups of coffee or new cars—stimulating job creation and economic growth. Also, there is the schadenfreude that comes from the plot lines and punch lines of those who squander their millions or find their lives ruined by winning the lottery.

While no one should be surprised that people with compulsive personalities act compulsively, or people who were bad with money *before* winning the lottery continue to be bad with money *after* winning the lottery, the negative impact of this "noble experiment" are legitimate and ubiquitous. The lure of the quick buck is addictive. In 2012, $65.5 billion in lottery tickets was sold, netting $16 billion for state coffers.

The argument can be made that if anyone is truly addicted to the lottery, it's the states that run them.

JOHN KING'S TICKET, 0000001, was sold at auction in June 2009 for $5,000. The heirloom was put on the block by an anonymous owner, presumed to be one of King's nieces or nephews. The high bidder for the ticket was . . . this author, purchasing by proxy for an advertising agency. The ticket was donated to New Hampshire Lottery.

LOU SMITH PASSED AWAY in 1969 after a brief illness. He and his wife gave away millions of dollars to philanthropic efforts, especially to Cardinal Cushing's Catholic Charities.

Racing revenues from Rockingham Park started to slide in the 1970s. A fire that destroyed the wooden grandstands in 1980 closed the track for four years. In the 1990s, as competing tracks started offering casino games and other attractions, Rockingham entered an inexorable downward spiral. Unable to keep pace with other tracks' purses, Rockingham attracted fewer quality horses, which meant the purses grew even less lucrative and the horses were of even lower quality. Live horse racing at the Rock ended in 2010 when the legislature defunded the regulatory functions of the state Racing Commission. Today, the track subsists on simulcast racing and charitable poker games.

LARRY PICKETT died in his apartment of a heart attack in 1967. He was eulogized for his three decades of service to Keene. As the laurel withers faster than the rose, Pickett did not live long enough to see his sweepstakes die. One generation remembered Pickett as the serious orator whose ten-year battle to enact the sweepstakes stands as a model of legislative doggedness. Others know him only as the source of the opening epigraph to Kevin Cash's polemic William Loeb biography: "Remember, son, whenever you get into a fight with a skunk you're apt to lose all your dignity because you're going to stink even when you win."

WILLIAM LOEB and the *Union Leader* remained the unquestioned power source in the state. Nationally Loeb's remembered for derailing the 1972 presidential campaign of then-frontrunner Edmund Muskie. Loeb had run a letter from a child who overheard Muskie comparing French-Canadians to Negros. Loeb had also implied Muskie's wife was an alcoholic. In an emotional defense outside the *Union Leader* building, Muskie appeared to weep (though supporters blamed the falling snow). The "Canuck" letter was later determined to be a fake and part of Nixon's dirty tricks operation.

Nackey Loeb was partially paralyzed in a car accident in 1977. Bill Loeb had been behind the wheel and never forgave himself. When he died of cancer in 1981, Nackey took over operation of the *Union Leader,* continued Bill's front-page editorials, and maintained the staunch banner of conservatism until her death in 2000. To this day, talk of sales and income taxes remain political poison in New Hampshire.

In 1985, when the New Hampshire Sweepstakes Commission proposed creating their multistate lottery with Maine and Vermont, a representative first made a secret visit to Mrs. Loeb to gauge her support.

JOSEPH MILLIMET'S PRIVATE PRACTICE—Devine, Millimet, & Branch—grew to be one of the state's largest and most prestigious law firms. The tiny man was a giant among jurists. His political work and efforts on behalf of First Amendment rights solidified his place in state judicial history. He urged all his attorneys to be involved in public service regardless of party, and he watched one of his Republican associates become governor in 1992.

Millimet made a fortune in the 1970s representing a local computer hardware firm in suing IBM for antitrust practices. The confidential settlement saved the company and earned Millimet a fee greater than any sweepstakes jackpot.

He practiced law into his eighties and passed away in 2006 at age ninety-two after suffering from Parkinson's Disease.

EDWARD POWERS retired from the New Hampshire Sweepstakes Commission in 1978, handing the reins to another former FBI agent, James Kennedy. With due respect to Larry Pickett and John King, Powers is recognized in the *Handbook of US Lottery Fundamentals* as "the father of US Lotteries." His example of running an honest, fair, and successful lottery with the highest degree of public integrity is the industry standard. Critics can say lotteries prey on the poor or the odds are for suckers. What they *cannot* say is the game is fixed and people don't actually win—or that such concerns have ever been legitimate. Powers's desire to give the player a fair shake still stands.

While in New Hampshire, Powers formed a coalition with the lottery directors in New York and New Jersey: the National Association of State Lotteries. As other states enacted lotteries, they joined the association and shared best practices. Powers testified before Congress on several occasions and was instrumental in winning the federal exemptions for state-run lotteries.

Upon retiring, he and Melva moved to Florida, and he became a paid consultant to states seeking to start lottery programs and to third-party vendors selling lottery products and services.

In 1989, the New Hampshire Lottery prepared to celebrate the twenty-fifth anniversary of the March 1964 referendum vote. Powers, who had undergone two bypass surgeries in the previous ten years, died on March 7, five days before the anniversary. As predicted, the news coverage of his passing focused more on his lottery legacy than his triumph in the Brink's case.

The day before he died, Powers wrote a long letter expressing his regrets for not attending the event. In his note, he reminisced about the rough road starting the sweepstakes and said what a thrill that referendum victory had been. He expressed his regret at not being there to meet Governor Judd Gregg, but remarked every governor since John King had supported the lottery and the power of the office was critical.

"The Sweeps is now out to sea with a full, clear wind behind it," he wrote, mentioning thirty other states had followed New Hampshire's example. "I am with you in spirit and take pride in the fact that I played a part in this pioneer venture."

BY 1968, Governor John King was a hawk on Vietnam and troubled by the left turn his Democratic Party was taking. He met several times with LBJ's reelection staff, to urge the president to actively campaign in the New Hampshire primary. King recognized the antiwar momentum of Senator Eugene McCarthy, but the Washington team did not take his advice, and King was left alone to represent the president in the Granite State. The governor punched hard, saying a vote for McCarthy would be "greeted with cheers in Hanoi."

Despite King's best efforts, Lyndon Johnson won the primary with only 49.6 percent of the vote. It was a moral victory for dark horse McCarthy who grabbed 42 percent of ballots by turning the primary into a referendum on the Vietnam War. Two weeks later, Johnson announced he would neither seek nor accept his party's nomination.

John King was contemplating a fourth term as governor in 1968 when a federal judgeship in New Hampshire opened up. King publicly said he wanted the position, but LBJ gave the post to a better political friend. King then heeded the call of Democrats to run for U.S. Senate against Republican Norris Cotton. Just as he had been swept into office on Jack Kennedy's coattails, King was swept out by Nixon's popularity in the state. He returned to private practice.

The following year, King was nominated by Governor Peterson to a seat on the state superior court. At age fifty, it was the fulfillment of his lifelong dream. In 1979, King was appointed to the New Hampshire Supreme Court and two years later became the chief justice. King had become the state's version of William Howard Taft: the only man to serve both as governor and chief justice. He held the position until the mandatory retirement age of seventy. Suffering from cardiac disease, John King died in a nursing home in 1996.

King, even as a lower-court judge, took seriously his role as a representative of the judiciary. He presided over a variety of criminal and civil cases, but he got the most joy from family court—specifically the days when he would approve adoptions.

An attorney recalled a divorce and custody case in which Judge King ordered all the parties to his chambers. "I want the attorneys and parents to stand over there," he ordered in the same direct style he had used to govern. "I don't want any of you to talk."

King asked the nine-year-old boy to sit upon his knee. He spoke softly to the child as he listened to the boy explain how sad he was that his mommy and daddy weren't going to live together. With his hand on the boy's shoulder, King looked grandfatherly in the great leather chair—the way he always looked when talking to a child. In the moment he seemed not to care about the law. All he cared about was helping the little boy crying in his lap. It was a poignant moment for the man whom everyone knew so wanted children of his own.

It was one boy, one day, in a long life of public service that fades into the past. Maybe he helped the boy, maybe he didn't. As naive as it sounds, King tried to help all the children he met. He hoped to improve their education with his "noble experiment." Modest, early century schools produced John King, Edward Powers, Joseph Millimet, and their like. Will our modern, lottery-flush education system produce more men and women of unquestioned probity, rare judgment, and courage?

Bibliography

Much of the source material for this book was uncovered in the archives of the New Hampshire Lottery, including news clippings from around the country saved between 1963 and 1973. Given the nature of this material and the way it has been preserved, it is not possible to accurately identify the source or date of every article, but I have reconstructed as many sources as possible in the lists below.

Excerpts and direct quotations from bills, laws, government documents, correspondence, legislative speeches, and other material in the public domain were taken from the official records, minutes, and archives of the New Hampshire General, the office of Governor King, and the listed archives.

ARCHIVE COLLECTIONS
Anna King Collection. New Hampshire Historical Society, Concord, NH.
Governor John King Sweepstakes Collection. New Hampshire Political Library, Concord, NH.
New Hampshire State Senate Archive. Concord, NH.
New Hampshire Sweepstakes Press Clipping Collection, vols. 1 and 2. New Hampshire Lottery, Concord, NH.
State of New Hampshire Archive, Concord, NH.
William Loeb III Papers. University of New Hampshire, Durham, NH.

PERIODICALS AND JOURNALS
The American Weekly. New York: 1949.
Argus-Champion. Newport, NH: 1963–1964.

Baily's Magazine of Sports and Pastimes. London: 1907.

Berkshire Eagle. Pittsfield, MA: 1963–1964.

Boston Globe. Boston: 1963–1964, 2014.

Boston Herald and *Boston Sunday Herald*. Boston: 1963–1964.

Boston Record American. Boston: 1963–1964.

Boston Traveler. Boston: 1963–1964.

Business Week. New York: 1965.

Chelsea Record. Chelsea, MA: 1963.

Chicago Sun-Times. Chicago: 1964.

Chicopee Herald. Chicopee, MA: 1963.

Christian Science Monitor. Boston: 1963–1964.

Claremont Eagle. Claremont, NH: 1963–1964.

Concord Daily Monitor and *New Hampshire Patriot*. Concord, NH: 1963–1973.

Connecticut Sunday Herald. Norwalk, CT: 1964.

Daily News. New York: 1963–1965.

Derry News. Derry, NH: 1963.

Los Angeles Times. Los Angeles: 1964.

Lawrence Eagle-Tribune. Lawrence, MA: 1963.

Lewiston Daily Sun. Lewiston, ME: 1965.

Life. New York: 1964.

Éire-Ireland: A Journal of Irish Studies. Vol. 29. Morristown, NJ: Irish American Cultural Institute, 1994.

Enfield Advocate. Enfield, NH: 1963–1964.

Family Weekly. New York: 1963.

Franklin Journal [transcript]. Franklin, NH: 1963–1965.

Foster's Daily Democrat. Dover, NH: 1963–1964.

Hanover Gazette. Hanover, NH: 1963–1964.

Harrisburg Patriot. Harrisburg, PA: 1964.

Haverhill Gazette. Haverhill, MA: 1964.

Irish Independent. Dublin: 2003.

Keene Sentinel. Keene, NH: 1963–1964.

Lewiston Sun. Lewiston, ME: 1963–1964.

Life. New York: 1963–1964.

Lisbon Courier. Lisbon, NH: 1963.

Look. Des Moines, IA: 1963.

Manchester Free Press. Manchester, NH: 1963–1964.

Manchester Union Leader and *New Hampshire Sunday News*. Manchester, NH: 1954–1973.

Milwaukee Journal. Milwaukee, WI: 1963–1964.

Nashua Telegraph. Nashua, NH: 1954–1973.

The New Englander. Boston: 1963.

New Haven Register. New Haven, CT: 1964.

Newark Star-Ledger. Newark, NJ: 1964.

New York. New York: February 2, 1976.

New York Journal-American. 1963.

New York Herald-Tribune. New York: 1963–1964.

New York Times. New York: 1963–1964.

NH Profiles. Concord, NH: 1963.

Parade. New York: 1963–1964.

Pasadena Star Ledger. Pasadena, CA: 1977.

Patriot Ledger. Quincy, MA: 1963.

Peterborough Transcript. Peterborough, NH: 1964.

Portland Press-Herald. Portland, ME: 1963–1964.

Portsmouth Herald. Portsmouth, NH: 1963–1964, 1973.

Post-Standard. Syracuse, NY: 1964.

The Princeton Alumni Weekly. Princeton, NJ: Jan 31, 1903.

The Reporter. New York: 1964.

Reader's Digest. Chappaqua, NY: 1963–1964.

Richmond News Leader. Richmond, VA: 1964.

Sarasota Herald-Tribune. Sarasota, FL: 1956.

The Saturday Evening Post. Indianapolis, IN: 1963–1964.

Somersworth Free Press. Somersworth, NH: 1963.

Sports Illustrated. Chicago: 1964.

State Conducted Lotteries: Hearing Before the Subcommittee on Claims and Governmental Relations of the Committee on the Judiciary, House of Representatives. Washington DC: 1974.

Sydney Morning Herald. Sydney, Australia: 1962.

This Week. New York: 1963.

Toledo Blade. Toledo, OH: 1956.

True. Breezy Point, MN: 1963.

Union and Rockingham County Gazette. Hampton, NH: 1963.

Wall Street Journal. New York: 1964.

Waukegan News-Sun. Waukegan, IL: 1963–1964.

Worcester Sunday Telegram. Worcester, MA: 1963.

BOOKS

Anderson, Leon. *To This Day.* Carlsbad, CA: Phoenix Publishing, 1981.

Anderson, Paul M., Ian S. Blackshaw, Robert C. R. Siekmann, and Janwilliem Soek. *Sports Betting: Law and Policy.* The Hague: T.M.C. Asser Press, 2012.

Bagley, Paul D. *Crosses in the Sky.* Durham, CT: Eloquent Books, 2010.

Behn, Noel. *Big Stick-up at Brink's!* New York: Putnam, 1977.

Belman, Felice, and Mike Pride. *The New Hampshire Century.* Hanover, NH: University Press of New England, 2001.

Bobbitt, William Randy. *Lottery Wars: Case Studies in Bible Belt Politics, 1986–2005.* Lanham, MD: Lexington Books, 2007.

Bradlee, Ben. *A Good Life.* New York: Simon and Schuster, 1995.

Broder, David S. *Behind the Front Page: A Candid Look at How the News Is Made.* New York: Simon and Schuster, 1987.

Byrne, James Patrick, Philip Coleman, and Jason Francis King. *Ireland and the Americas: Culture, Politics, and History.* Santa Barbara, CA: ABC-CLIO, 2008.

Caitlin, John. *The Lottery Book: The Truth behind the Numbers.* New York: Taylor Trade Publishing, 2003.

Capace, Nancy. *Encyclopedia of New Hampshire.* St. Clair Shores, MI: Somerset Publishers, 2000.

Cash, Kevin. *Who the Hell IS William Loeb?* Manchester, NH: Amoskeag Press, 1975.

Chew, Peter. *The Kentucky Derby: The First 100 Years.* Boston: Houghton Mifflin Company, 1974.

Clark Northrup, Cynthia. *The American Economy: A Historical Encyclopedia.* Santa Barbara, CA: ABC-CLIO, 2003.

Clifford, Mick, and Shane Coleman. *Scandal Nation.* Dublin: Hachette Books Ireland, 2010.

Clotfelter, Charles T., and Philip J. Cook. *Selling Hope: State Lotteries in America.* Cambridge, MA: Harvard University Press, 1989.

Coleman, Marie. *The Irish Sweep: A History of the Irish Hospitals Sweepstake, 1930–1987.* Dublin: University College Dublin Press, 2010.

Considine, Bob, and Joseph James O'Keefe. *The Crime That Nearly Paid: The Inside Story of One of the Most Famous Hold-ups in the History of Crime.* New York: Transworld Publishers, 1963.

Coogan, Tim Pat. *The IRA.* New York: Palgrave, 2002.

——— . *Michael Collins: The Man Who Made Ireland.* New York: Palgrave, 2002.

Cooney, John. *John Charles McQuaid: Ruler of Catholic Ireland.* Dublin: O'Brien Press, 1999.

Corless, Damian. *The Greatest Bleeding Hearts Racket in the World.* Dublin: Gill and MacMillan, 2010.

Curtin, Lawrence, and Karen Bernardo. *The History of Sweepstakes.* Key Biscayne, FL: Sweepstakes News, 1997.

Epstein, Richard A. *The Theory of Gambling and Statistical Logic.* Burlington, MA: Academic Press, 2013.

Ezell, John Samuel. *Fortune's Merry Wheel: The Lottery in America.* Boston: Harvard University Press, 1960.

Findlay, John. *People of Chance.* New York: Oxford University Press, 1986.

Fino, Paul. *My Life in Politics and Public Service.* Great Neck, NY: Todd and Honeywell, 1986.

Flynn, Kevin, and Rebecca Lavoie. *Our Little Secret: The True Story of a Teenager Killer and the Silence of a Small New England Town.* New York: Berkley Books, 2010.

Garavan, Thomas, Barra O Cinneide, Mary Garavan, Anna Cunningham, Ambrose Downey, Briga Hynes, and Trevor O'Regan. *Cases in Irish Business Strategy and Policy.* Dublin: Oak Tree Press, 1996.

Hall, Kermit. *The Rights of the Accused: The Justices and Criminal Justice.* New York: Routledge, 2000.

Harrison, Benjamin. *Public Papers and Addresses of Benjamin Harrison.* Washington DC: Government Printing Office, 1893.

Hutchinson, Robert J. *The Absolute Beginner's Guide to Gambling.* New York: Pocket Books, 1996.

Jesep, Paul Peter. *Rockingham Park, 1933–1969: A History of Power, Glamor, and Gambling.* Portsmouth, NH: Peter E. Randall Publishing, 1998.

Jones, Terry L. *The Louisiana Journey.* Layton, UT: Gibbs Smith, 2007.

Kelly, Robert J., Ko-lin Chin, and Rufus Schatzberg. *Handbook of Organized Crime in the United States.* Westport, CT: Greenwood Press, 1994.

Kendall, John Smith. *History of New Orleans.* Vol. 2. Chicago: Lewis Publishing Company, 1922.

Kirsch, George B., Othello Harris, and Claire Elaine Nolte. *Encyclopedia of Ethnicity and Sports in the United States.* Westport, CT: Greenwood Press, 2000.

McGowan, Richard. *The Gambling Debate.* Westport, CT: Greenwood Press, 2008.

———. *State Lotteries and Legalized Gambling: Painless Revenue or Painful Mirage.* Westport, CT: Quorum Books, 1994.

McMahon, Paul. *British Spies and Irish Rebels: British Intelligence and Ireland, 1916–1945.* Woodbridge, UK: Boydell Press, 2008.

Moehring, Eugene, and Michael Green. *Las Vegas: A Centennial History.* Reno, NV: University of Nevada Press, 2005.

Morton, Suzanne. *At Odds: Gambling and Canadians, 1919–1969.* Toronto: University of Toronto Press, 2003.

Musselwhite, F. W. *Earle P. Scarlett: A Study in Scarlett.* Toronto: Dundurn Press, 1991.

North, Mark. *Act of Treason: The Role of J. Edgar Hoover in the Assassination of President Kennedy.* New York: Skyhorse Publishing, 2011.

O'Brien, Timothy. *Bad Bet: The Inside Story of Glamour, Glitz, and Danger of America's Gambling Industry.* New York: Crown Business, 1998.

Pletcher, Larry. *It Happened in Massachusetts.* Guilford, CT: Morris Book Publishing, 2009.

Prendergast, Albert. *Not a Ship of Fools; The Incredible Voyage of the SS Independence.* Mustang, OK: Tate Publishing, 2009.

Ross, Shane. *The Bankers: How the Banks Ruined the Irish Economy.* Dublin: Penguin Ireland, 2009.

Savage, Robert J. *Irish Television: The Political and Social Origins.* Westport, CT: Praeger Publishers, 1996.

Scheper-Hughes, Nancy. *Saints, Scholars, and Schizophrenics: Mental Illness in Rural Ireland.* Berkeley, CA: University of California Press, 2001.

Schlesinger Jr., Arthur M. *Robert Kennedy and His Times.* New York: First Mariner Books, 2002.

Schorow, Stephanie. *The Crime of the Century: How the Brink's Robbers Stole Millions and the Hearts of Boston.* Beverly, MA: Commonwealth Editions, 2008.

Seed, Douglas W., and Katherine Khalife. *Salem, NH.* Vol. 11, *Trolleys, Canobie Lake, and Rockingham Park.* Mount Pleasant, SC: Arcadia Publishing, 1996.

Shelley, Ron. *The Lottery Encyclopedia.* Warner Robins, GA: Byron Publishing Services, 1989.

Siracusa, Joseph M. *Encyclopedia of the Kennedys: The People and Events that Shaped America.* Santa Barbara, CA: ABC-CLIO, 2012.

State, Paul F. *A Brief History of Ireland.* New York: Facts on File, 2009.

Sullivan, James. *Seven Dirty Words: The Life and Crimes of George Carlin.* Cambridge Center, MA: Da Capo Press, 2010.

Temple, Robert. *The Pilgrims Would Be Shocked: The History of Thoroughbred Racing in New England.* Bloomington, IN: Xiliris Corporation, 2009.

Thompson, William Norman. *Gambling in America: An Encyclopedia of History, Issues, and Society.* Santa Barbara, CA: ABC-CLIO, 2001.

US Census Bureau, *Public Education Finances: 2012.* Washington, DC: US Government Printing Office, 2014.

Williams, Thomas Harry. *P. G. T. Beauregard: Napoleon in Gray.* Baton Rouge: Louisiana State University Press, 1955.

Weir, William. *Written with Lead: America's Most Famous and Notorious Gunfights from the Revolutionary War to Today.* New York: Cooper Square Press, 2003.

Wintz, Cary D., and Paul Finkelman. *Encyclopedia of the Harlem Renaissance: K–Y.* New York: Routledge, 2004.

Zuckoff, Mitchell. *Ponzi's Scheme: The True Story of a Financial Legend.* New York: Random House, 2006.

WEBSITES

"American Lotteries." History of Lottery. http://historyoflottery.com/american _lotteries.html.

"Beginnings." History of Lottery. http://historyoflottery.com/beginnings.html.

"The Brink's Robbery." FBI. FBI, 28 July 2010. http://www.fbi.gov/about-us/history /famous-cases/brinks-robbery.

"Casino Expansion and Its Impact on Pathological and Problem Gambling Prevalence Rates." American Gaming Association. http://www.americangaming.org/industry -resources/research/fact-sheets/history-problem-gambling-prevalence-rates.

Cooper, Patrick. "Irish Sweepstakes Was a Scam Says New Book." http://www
.irishcentral.com/news/irish-sweepstakes-was-a-scam-says-new
-book-103917434-237718611.html.

De Szigethy, J. R. "At Long Last: The Conviction of Whitey Bulger." http://www
.americanmafia.com/Feature_Articles_521.html.

"Events: *29 May 1963, Luncheon (stag), Governors." John F. Kennedy Presidential
Library and Museum. http://www.jfklibrary.org/Asset-Viewer/Archives
/JFKWHSFSLF-023-008.aspx.

"Fifty Years of Winning." New Hampshire Lottery—Timeline. http://www.nhlottery
.com/Lucky/Timeline.aspx.

"History." Massachusetts State Lottery. http://www.masslottery.com/about/history.html.

"History." New Hampshire Lottery. http://www.nhlottery.com/About-Us/History
.aspx.

"The History of NASPL." NASPL History. http://www.naspl.org/index.
cfm?fuseaction=content&menuid=15&pageid=1021.

"Hon. John W. King Oral History: Sweepstakes." The New Hampshire Supreme Court
Society Hon. John W. King Oral Histories. http://www.nhsupremecourtsociety
.org/kingGallery.html.

"Inflation Calculator." DaveManuel.com. http://www.davemanuel.com/inflation
-calculator.php.

"In Memoriam: Joseph A. Millimet." NHBA—Bar News Issue. http://www.nhbar.org
/publications/display-news-issue.asp?id=3447.

"JFK in History." John F. Kennedy Presidential Library and Museum. http://www
.civilrights.jfklibrary.org/JFK/JFK-in-History.aspx.

"Lotteries in the Western World." History Of Lottery. http://historyoflottery.com
/lottery_in_the_westernworld.html.

"Modern Lotteries Around the World." History Of Lottery. http://historyoflottery
.com/modern_lotteries_around_world.html.

"NHAB Alumni: Tom Power." NH Association of Broadcasters. http://65.36.150.71
/alumni/power.html.

"Phalen v. Virginia 49 U.S. 163 (1850)." Justia Law. http://supreme.justia.com/cases
/federal/us/49/163/case.html.

"Stone v. Mississippi 101 U.S. 814 (, 25 L.Ed. 1079)." STONE v. MISSISSIPPI. http://
www.law.cornell.edu/supremecourt/text/101/814.

"United States, Appellant, v. Anthony L. Fabrizio. 385 U.S. 263 (87 S.Ct. 457, 17
L.Ed.2d 351)." US v. Fabrizio. http://www.law.cornell.edu/supremecourt
/text/385/263.

"United States v. Fabrizio." The Oyez Project at IIT Chicago-Kent College of Law.
http://www.oyez.org/cases/1960-1969/1966/1966_47.

Index